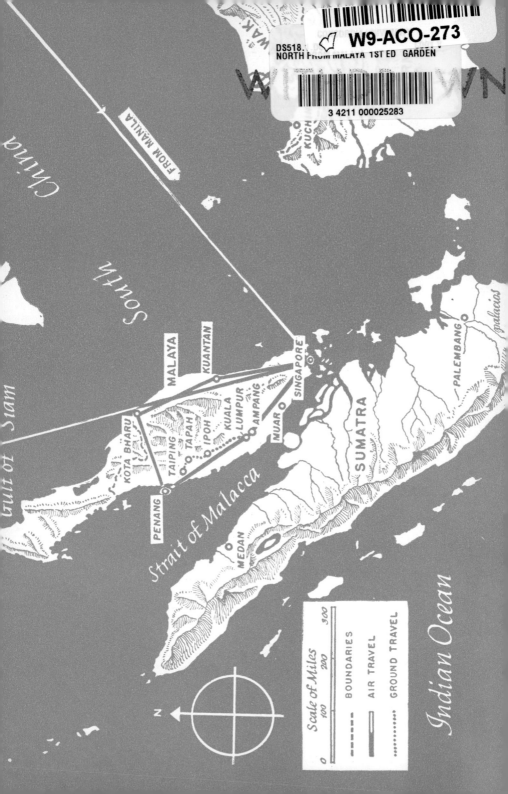

FROM MANILA

China

South

Gulf of Siam

MALAYA

KUANTAN

KOTA BHARU

TAIPING

PENANG

TAPAH

IPOH

KUALA
LUMPUR

AMPANG

MUAR

SINGAPORE

Strait of Malacca

MEDAN

SUMATRA

PALEMBANG

palacios

KUCH

Indian Ocean

Scale of Miles

0   100   200   300

————— BOUNDARIES

▬▬▬ AIR TRAVEL

••••••• GROUND TRAVEL

N

NORTH FROM MALAYA

BOOKS BY WILLIAM O. DOUGLAS

North from Malaya

Beyond the High Himalayas

Strange Lands and Friendly People

Of Men and Mountains

North
from
Malaya

ADVENTURE ON FIVE FRONTS

BY WILLIAM O. DOUGLAS

DOUBLEDAY & COMPANY, INC., GARDEN CITY, NEW YORK, 1953

Library of Congress Catalog Card Number 53–5614

To W. O. D. Jr.
who should have
been along.

ACKNOWLEDGMENTS

To Mercedes H. Davidson, who did the basic research on the book and prepared the maps; to Edith Allen, Helen Linde, and Gladys Giese, who managed the mechanics of the manuscript; to Elon Gilbert and Bob Sandberg, who made the jungle less oppressive, who took the photographs, and whose observations sharpened my understanding; to the To' Dalang of Kota Bharu, the players of the rebanna drums, the Malay villagers, the Burmese monks, the non-Communist, American-style revolutionaries of Vietnam, the men and women of our Point Four, ECA, and MSA—and others too numerous to mention —who helped me see the warm heart, the sensitive mind, the high character of Southeast Asia.

FOREWORD

Singapore is an island at the tip of the long, thin
Malayan Peninsula that stretches south five hundred
miles or more from the main Asian land mass. It lies hot and
humid about eighty miles from the equator. Below it are dozens
of islands, all licked by warm, wet winds and lush with vegetation.
Sumatra of the Indonesian group is a long dark hulk against the
southern sky, hardly twenty miles distant from Singapore. Small
islands, a few acres in area, dot the Strait of Malacca that runs
between. Most are uninhabited; some serve as quarantine centers
for incoming ships. Others conceal huge guns placed there by the
British years ago to guard the entrance of the Singapore harbor.

Those guns were fixed, facing the sea. Many people laughed
at the stupidity of the British. The Japanese landed up north in
December 1941 at Kota Bharu and Kuantan on the east coast of
Malaya and streaked down to Johore, on the mainland opposite
Singapore, over the black asphalt roads the British had built. The
guns at Singapore were pointed the wrong way to stop them. But
the Japanese would not have been halted anyway. As Grenfell,
in *Main Fleet to Singapore*, relates, the Japanese had command

7

Foreword

both of the sea and the air. Moreover, those who hold the mainland of Malaya have the power of life and death over Singapore. A huge water pipe, about six feet in diameter, reaches Singapore from Johore across a causeway. The Japanese Army cut the line and had Singapore at its mercy in a few days.

Singapore (a British colony) is a bustling modern city and the leading financial center and port in all of Southeast Asia. It has a multi-racial community that reflects most of the tensions of the area. Here the last of the rugged British capitalists still dream of empire. Here many Chinese live. They indeed constitute nearly 80 per cent of the population of Singapore and about 45 per cent of the population of Malaya. These Chinese command the wealth of the archipelago. Some are outstanding citizens like Tan Cheng Lock and C. C. Tan, who have a high standard of civic righteousness. Others are outlaws, working in the Communist cause. The Chinese community in Singapore and Malaya, as in all of Asia, is divided. Some look north to Formosa and Chiang Kai-shek for guidance. Others have shifted their loyalties to Peking and Mao Tse-tung. The Malays, who are native to the country, look with apprehension on the mounting power of the Chinese. And the Indians, a small minority and none too sure of their welcome, struggle to make Malaya their new home.

There is a conspiratorial atmosphere about Singapore. A Communist Politburo lives underground there, moving stealthily—laying carefully its plans for murder and terror. Every third member of a household staff is suspect. The lines of this Communist underground run in every direction out of Singapore, reaching to all the nations north and south. Singapore, like Hong Kong farther north, is a meeting of all the tides and currents in the schemes and affairs of men. One with long experience and a sensitive eye and ear could measure here the tensions that promise to tear this region to pieces.

But it is better to go north from Malaya to see for one's self the various people who inhabit the area, their conditions of life, their music and plays, the temples where they worship, the huts they

8

occupy, the paddies they work. Only in that way can their hopes and despair and, above all, their racial and ideological rivalries be fully appreciated. It is rich country—from Burma in the northwest to the Philippines in the northeast. There are tin, oil, iron, coal, and many precious minerals in the region. The land is rich in rubber, copra, fruits, and especially in rice.

Travel north from Singapore is hazardous, for the Communists are active. In Malaya and Vietnam especially there are land mines, ambushes, and hand grenades to avoid. This is hot and humid country, particularly in the summer. The jungle that chokes the land is more than inhospitable. It is an ugly ally of the enemy—the refuge of guerrillas who hide there by day and lay their nightly plans. This area is critically important in international affairs. It is a food-surplus area, long coveted by China, which borders it on the north. Today it boils with unrest, discontent, and revolution.

Part of the turbulence of the region is stirred by Red China. Part comes from racial tensions. Some of these racial tensions have their source in the imperialism of the white man. Some strike deeper and flow from the suspicions that one colored race has for another colored race. Part of the turbulence of the area is due to the feudalism that long held the masses in virtual servitude. Landlords and loan sharks made peons out of peasants. Political power was a monopoly of the select. Today that concentration of both economic and political power in the hands of a few is breaking up. Revolutions have arrived. And the Communists are doing all they can to capitalize on the discontent, insecurity, and uncertainty that follow in the wake of change.

There are five fighting fronts in this region—fronts which constantly erupt under Communist management. Four of them are in the heart of Southeast Asia. The fifth one—Korea and Formosa—overshadows the others. Trouble along this fifth front has repercussions throughout Southeast Asia. The friction between the West and China, the dissension between the Communists and the Kuomintang are felt in every community. The Chinese are

9

prominent in Southeast Asia. In Malaya they vie with the Malays for numerical superiority. Yet even where the Chinese are in the minority, they command wealth and power. "As China goes, so goes Southeast Asia" is an overstatement. But it emphasizes the importance of Korea and Formosa to every island, to every country in the area, as Purcell, in *The Chinese in Southeast Asia*, shows.

The five fronts have implications that are even more ominous. Their main threat is not Chinese. The guerrillas who haunt the jungles get their inspiration not so much from Peking as from the Kremlin. Their morale is maintained by the example of the Russians, by the press releases of the Kremlin. Their hopes for mortars, artillery, tanks, trucks, and planes are based on the strength of Russian industrial power. Their top command is the Politburo in Moscow.

Each front is, indeed, an overt act of a Communist conspiracy to expand the Russian Empire. Their whining lead is the signal of the Soviets' threat to the independence of nations. This is not a matter of surmise; nor does it require elaborate proof. The Russian flag I picked up near Kuantan on Malaya's east coast is evidence enough.

WILLIAM O. DOUGLAS
Washington, D.C., March 17, 1953

CONTENTS

11

Contents

Contents

PART V—FORMOSA, KOREA, AND THE FIFTH FRONT

ILLUSTRATIONS

PHOTOGRAPHS *by Bob Sandberg—LOOK, and Elon Gilbert*

15

Illustrations

16

PART 1

MALAYAN JUNGLE GUERRILLAS

CHAPTER 1

THE JUNGLE

We roared along a Malayan highway at eighty miles an hour in a tiny Austin. The driver was a thirty-year-old Indian by the name of Mohammed Eusoff. Elon Gilbert was up front; Bob Sandberg of *Look* magazine and I in the rear. The black asphalt pavement wound serpentine-fashion through the thick, lush jungle. The tires squealed on the turns, and when the fenders touched, they screeched. We were going so fast that on the straight stretches it seemed the car would leave the ground and take flight. We whirred under spreading rain trees, scraped jagged limestone cliffs, and roared across steel bridges. We raced through and around traffic, never using our brakes or our horn. A truck loomed up, heading toward us. A water buffalo ambled lazily in our lane. There was no space between the two that was big enough for an American car. All my driving instincts screamed for the brakes. But on we went. I think both Bob Sandberg and I ducked while the little Austin, at eighty miles an hour, whisked between the truck and the buffalo.

"Why this mad haste, Eusoff?" I asked.

"Bandits," he shouted. "This is very bad country. Many ambushes here."

"Eusoff, would you rather be killed by the Austin than by bandits?"

Eusoff relaxed enough to laugh, but in a few minutes we were back again at our mad pace.

This was bad guerrilla country. We had been with General Sir Gerald Templer, British High Commissioner of Malaya, on a four-day inspection trip. We had gone north from Kuala Lumpur to Ipoh and then on to Taiping. We had traveled the main highways and seen most of the twenty-five mile belt on either side of the route. Going north, we had been escorted by an armored convoy. Up front was a tank with machine-gun turrets. Next came General Templer and Lady Templer in a sedan. They were followed by larger tanks, by cars carrying the staff and various reporters, and then by trucks carrying soldiers. At the tail end was our Austin.

But now the inspection trip was over and we were on our own, headed two hundred miles or more through jungle land back to Kuala Lumpur. Eusoff was using the customary technique for driving the highways of Malaya. Civilians depend more on speed than on armor for protection against bandits when they travel by automobile. And highway accidents with their record of civilians killed are today in close competition with the guerrillas.

The places we passed were filled with memories of the hours I had spent with Templer. One spot—across a flimsy bridge heading into the jungle—carried memories that were especially vivid. Here Co. D of the Worcester Guards had been camped. I was with Templer when he inspected the troops and addressed them.

Templer, in his early fifties, is dark, slight of frame, and slightly stooped as a result of a back injury received in World War II. It seems he was in a car in Italy following a truck which was blown sky-high by a land mine. A piano in the truck came down on Templer, crushing him. But the bulldog determination which marks his jaw pulled him through, and today he is in excellent health.

We had gone a mile or more through an old rubber plantation to reach the military camp. The tall smooth trunks of the trees were all bent in the same direction, and the flat branches high above the ground let only spots of sunshine through. The camp was in a clearing between the plantation and the thick green wall of the jungle. Wooden buildings, raised on stakes, Malay-style, as a protection against dampness and snakes, served as the administrative headquarters. The troops were in tents whose sides were rolled up, showing freshly shined shoes, neatly rolled blankets, and trim cots. In one less disciplined canvas tent were eight Borneo head-hunters with *parang* knives and charms made of wild boar teeth at their waists. They were not much over five feet; their throats were tattooed; and they wore grins that stretched from ear to ear.

Templer stood before the troops, his hands on his hips, his jaw out, sweat rolling down his face.

"We are now killing or capturing, on the average, 150 guer-rillas a month. I want to step that up to 300 a month. Once we reach that figure, the end will be in sight, for the guerrillas can't stand those losses. There are only about 5,000 of them, you know. They will not come out and fight. We have to hunt them down like mad dogs in the jungle, one at a time.

"When you get contact, draw a fine bead. Get two guerrillas instead of one."

The General paused as he looked the soldiers up and down. Then he continued:

"Our problem is not only a military one. We have an enormous political job to do as well—public health, education, unionization of labor, raising the standard of living. We must also weld the various races of this country into a strong, unified nation. We can't do that job without law and order. But it's *that* job Britain must do. I want to get on with it. Give me two guerrillas where we've been getting one, and you and I both can go home soon."

Templer was appointed High Commissioner in February 1952. Churchill told him of his selection over a dinner table at Ottawa, adding these words: "Templer, you have absolute power. Use it sparingly. Power is a heady thing."

Templer is suited by temperament for what is probably the most difficult assignment any man could draw in this day and age. He is lighthearted and relaxed, though he lives in a harrowing environment. He has an energy that seems inexhaustible. He has a sense of humor, an understanding of people, and an instinct for troubles and tensions. A part of his perception and understanding traces to Lady Templer, who, like Eleanor Roosevelt, feels the pulse of a community and widens immeasurably the range of her husband's knowledge and influence.

Templer is well staffed. His deputy, Donald C. MacGillivray, is a broad-gauged man. So is Michael J. Hogan, the Attorney General. The Malayan Civil Service, on which Templer is heavily dependent, has stuffy, reactionary people in it who still dream of empire. But it also has a few imaginative men who see that the safety of the world lies in social revolutions that follow the democratic pattern. One of the best is T. W. T. Bangs of Kota Bharu, a tall, friendly Englishman turned Moslem, who works with the Malays as a brother and who is showing them how to develop home industries, increase rice production, and use other means to raise their standard of living by their own hands. And Malcolm MacDonald, Commissioner General for Southeast Asia, who makes his headquarters in Johore on the mainland opposite Singapore, throws his weight and influence on the side of an enlightened, liberal program for Malaya.

Some of the reform program which Templer has for Malaya must await the liquidation of the guerrillas. But much of it, as we shall see, is the key to the unrest that has churned Malaya and made the guerrillas strong.

There have never been more than 5,000 guerrillas in Malaya (perhaps as few as 3,000) since they started their campaign of terror in 1948. That small number has been pursued by 50,000

British troops (including British Regulars, Gurkhas, Fiji Island-ers, and Borneo head-hunters), 20,000 regular police, 55,000 Special Police, and about 250,000 Home Guard. Hundreds of guerrillas have been killed or captured. About an equal number of casualties has been suffered on the other side. Yet in 1952 there were about the same number of guerrillas as there had been in 1948, when the trouble broke out. When a guerrilla falls, there usually is a new recruit to take his place. No matter what their casualties, their strength has remained about the same.

At least 95 per cent of them are Chinese and close to a third of them women. Most of them are not Communists. Many are criminal outlaws; others have some cause to serve that links them with the guerrillas. But the top echelon—a good 20 per cent—are confirmed Communists; and they are in full control.

These guerrillas have two allies, the first and main one being the jungle.

The jungle comprises four fifths or more of Malaya. The culti-vated areas are largely the thin, winding strips of bottom land. The rest of the country is mostly rolling hills and jagged lime-stone ridges that in places rise nine thousand feet high. They are covered with trees, all strange in appearance to us of the West and, except for teak, strange in names too. The trees run one hundred feet or more high. Their boughs and leaves are so thick that few shafts of sunlight ever get through. Under them are thick stands of young trees and palms, lush parasitic vines hanging from branches, and bushes covered with thorns. There is no grass, no sudden stretch of meadows or open land. There are no flowers.

By day the jungle is deathly still. High in the treetops are monkeys, gaily colored birds, and brilliant butterflies. On top of the trees are orchids as lush, as vivid, as exotic as any in the world. They are purple, white, and pink, streaking across the treetops in brilliant flourishes. The orchids give an atmosphere of freshness and gaiety to the jungle when seen from above. But that impression is false and fleeting. Down below is a dungeon

23

filled with darkness, dampness, and the smell of death. Leeches race across leaves to get under one's clothing and onto one's legs. Mosquitoes and midges come up at night in a darkness that lasts twelve hours. The trees drip rain for hours after the daily storm has passed. The odor of decaying vegetation fills the nostrils. Visibility is never more than twenty-five yards and usually five or six.

Bees frequent the jungle. Malayan bees live on nectar; and since there is no winter, the honey accumulates in combs that hang from the trees like sacks, four feet or more long. There are tapirs, wild boar, leopards, and tigers in the jungle. In a few places there are rhinoceros and elephants and the most dangerous of all animals—the wild buffalo. High on the ridges where it's cool at night black bear prowl. Deep in the recesses are the tiniest deer in the world—the mouse deer (*plandok*), which is so small it can be roasted whole and put on one dinner plate. Deadly snakes haunt the jungle—cobras, vipers, and twenty-foot pythons. The pythons hang by their tails from trees, their bodies motionless against the trunks, waiting for their prey to pass underneath.

But the danger of the jungle does not come from the animals. They leave man alone. One danger comes from the melancholy of living there, from the absence of the sun. Subsistence in the jungle is also difficult. An occasional wild boar or monkey is about all one can expect. Food must come from the outside. But these days it is not melancholia or starvation that is the jungle's greatest threat. That danger is the guerrillas who haunt the place. They are a menace not only to those who travel the jungle; they are a threat to every motorist, every truck driver, every bus, every train. For these jungles come right down to the highways, railroads, and riverbanks. Ambushes are easy. A hundred men can lie concealed for hours or even days within a few feet of a paved highway, waiting for the car, the driver, or the passenger whom the high command has marked for destruction.

The jungle is almost impenetrable when the trees have once been cut and there is a second growth. Then it is a wild tangle of tall thick grass and brush that a man can only thrash or hack his way through.

The primeval jungle that is characteristic of most of Malaya has ancient runways known to the animals and to a few men. These trails lace the entire country together in a network. They are highways to the guerrillas, but unknown in large part even to the local police. A guerrilla, if pursued, can cover a wide territory with ease. If the pursuit is close, he can step off the trail a few feet and be completely swallowed up.

The hunt in the jungle is largely a matter of stalking. One waits like a tiger for the prey to move. The hunt is a cautious one—the movements stealthy, the pace slow, the nerves taut. The prey may be in range for hours and no contact made. The hunter may maneuver for days to get one shot. A whole platoon may be within call yet never in sight. The song of a bird or the screech of an animal may be a signal on either side. The game of stalking goes on quietly and endlessly. One rifleshot, quickly muffled in the dense undergrowth, may be the product of one week's silent work. It is man against man—rifles cocked, ears straining, eyes alert, bodies tense, all the instincts of self-preservation operating. The jungle is on both sides of the contest, as Chapman, in *The Jungle Is Neutral,* shows. It is friendly only to those who know its secrets and who can get on familiar terms with it. That is why Gurkhas, Borneo head-hunters, Fiji Islanders, who have the jungle as part of their immediate inheritance, are superlative when they have British training and British arms.

The habitat of the guerrillas may be known. It may in fact be common knowledge that a band of them operates out of the north slopes of a range overlooking a valley rich in tin mines. They may be somewhere in an area ten miles long and a few miles wide. Their camps are often on the edge of clearings which they have made to grow corn or tapioca. The clearings often can be spotted by aerial reconnaissance. It would seem easy, therefore, to send a force straight to the heart of their concentration and wipe them out.

But many natives would know when such an expedition was ready to strike; and the intelligence of the guerrillas is so well organized that they would be apt to learn of the raid long in advance. Moreover, their camps are always protected by electric alarm systems, by land mines, and by other protective devices that tell of the coming.

If a dozen modern armies pushed through the jungles of Malaya, working in a pattern that covered the whole Federation, they would meet no guerrillas. These guerrillas have standing orders from the Communist high command never to meet a superior force head on. Their orders are to give way and to let the jungle swallow them up. A guerrilla can easily cache his arms and turn up in a rice paddy as a peasant, in a rubber plantation as a tapper, in the bazaar as a merchant. And when the Army returns to its post, he resumes his guerrilla role.

The military program against the guerrillas is essentially a police action. That is why Colonel Arthur E. Young, a brilliant product of Scotland Yard, was brought in by Templer to organize the campaign. I talked with Young at Kuala Lumpur and instantly caught the enthusiasm of the man. He is tall, rangy, big-boned, and relaxed. He believes that even millions of soldiers could not stamp out the guerrillas. Man hunts are needed.

Dogs are of little use in the hunt. The leeches get into their noses to cause painful swellings and ruin the scent.

Trained police, using modern detective and intelligence methods, are needed—men who can trace guerrillas through the network of the villages, find their cohorts and their sources of supplies, track them to their lair, lay ambushes for them, or infiltrate the enemy's organization.

Malaya today is full of policemen—more than there are in all the rest of the United Kingdom. But they are largely untrained. They do not know the art of detection; they have no knowledge of counterespionage. They are merely men with guns who stand guard and go in pursuit when trouble breaks. Colonel Young's task is to set a training program for them. He hopes to train four thousand a month. They will start the biggest man hunt the world has seen. And because of the jungle, this man hunt will require all the skills of Scotland Yard and more. For the police are of a race different from the criminal. Only a third of the Malays, British, and Indians can speak Chinese. There is a racial alliance against law and order that has known few equals.

CHAPTER 2

THE CHINESE ACCOMPLICE

The guerrillas have more than the jungle as their ally; they have a substantial part of the Chinese community as well. Though the jungle is neutral, the Chinese villages frequently are not. Their influence has often been on the side of the guerrillas. But for the Chinese villages the guerrillas would have been liquidated long ago.

The Chinese guerrillas have a secret society of over 100,000 people, known as the Min Yuen. This society is their procurement, intelligence, and propaganda branch. The smiling and gracious Chinese behind the counter in the grocery store, the telephone operator, the bus driver may well be members of Min Yuen. Min Yuen collects food and distributes it to the guerrillas. Min Yuen sends word of every traveler, of every troop movement. Some villages and cities have been so co-operative that they offer practically a refuge and an arsenal for the bandits.

I visited one such—the town of Tanjong Malim in the state of Perak. It is a town of 20,000 people, fifty miles or so north of Kuala Lumpur, the capital of the Federation. It is one of the all-

Chinese towns on which Templer put a curfew for two weeks in the spring of 1952. No one could move out of his house for twenty-two hours a day. The order was strictly enforced by armed patrols. Templer did it not as punishment but in an effort to instill into this all-Chinese community some sense of civic responsibility.

Twelve Britishers, who were repairing a water pipe line, had been ambushed there. One was Richard Michael Clinton Codner, famous character in *The Wooden Horse*. There had been other murders; trains had been derailed; buses had been burned—all close to Tanjong Malim. When the investigators failed to get clues to the crimes, Templer went to Tanjong Malim and addressed the townsfolk, trying to get information. None of the 20,000 would talk. Twenty thousand people only sat and glowered at Templer. No leaders, no committee of citizens stepped forward to clean up the mess and restore law and order. That is why Templer imposed the severe curfew. He lifted the curfew only after the townsfolk had returned questionnaires with information leading to the arrest of twenty-eight men and women.

The guerrillas come to a village at night and use any threat or tactic to get food. Some villagers are active allies of the guerrillas, with sons, daughters, and other relatives on duty with them. Some are victims of the guerrilla system, without protection from the marauders and unable to withstand their pressure for fear of their lives. To protect them and at the same time to make the collection of food more difficult for the guerrillas, the British moved 510,000 people into 500 brand-new villages in less than two years. These were mostly Chinese squatters who had been thrown out of employment in tin or rubber during the Japanese occupation and had migrated from the towns to eke out an existence on the edge of the jungle. These isolated houses were easy of access to the guerrillas.

Scattered squatter families within a radius of a few miles were brought together into one village. Sometimes their old houses were moved. More often than not new ones were erected. A double barbed-wire stockade was put around the settlement and sentries placed in high towers to watch over it. The gates are closed at 6 P.M. and do not open again until 6 A.M.

I visited at least a dozen of these new settlements. They are without exception neat villages. The Chinese, unlike the Malays, always build their houses on the ground. In these Malayan re-settlements the houses sometimes have split bamboo sidings and thatched roofs; sometimes they are made of nondescript lumber with corrugated iron roofs. Each house has a garden plot and usually outbuildings for chickens, geese, and pigs. The normal Chinese village in Malaya is a disorderly-looking place with houses set in helter-skelter fashion without any apparent design. I talked with a kindly and elderly Chinese at the new village of Mambang Di-awan, located not far from Taiping and known in Malay as Spirit of the Clouds. It houses 4,000 people and has outlying garden tracts of 200 acres. This Chinese, wise in the superstitions of his people, told me of a problem that arose in the construction of the new villages. Malayan Chinese believe the evil spirits come from the north. Their houses, therefore, seldom have doors on that side. Moreover, the old Chinese villages are laid out with winding, zigzag streets to make it more difficult for the evil spirits to find their way.

The British, therefore, met with opposition when they made the streets straight and put the houses in neat rows. But there they stand today—most of them unpainted, many of them crudely constructed, but all of them trim and well kept.

In these new villages there are streets for shops, a community center, and a medical clinic or dispensary, usually run by the Red Cross. Each new village has a school designed to get away from the traditions of the Chinese vernacular or language schools that teach only Chinese culture and loyalty to China. Every child from six years up attends. There are playgrounds, ladders, teeter-totters, and tin-lined chutes. The older sister takes care of the younger child. The children romp and play after hours.

I sat on the school grounds at Ampang village (near Kuala Lumpur) late one afternoon. This is one of the new villages, with perhaps five thousand Chinese. The long, rambling schoolhouse, whose classrooms have two open sides, sits on a hill overlooking the village. The men of the village had returned from the nearby tin mines; the women went about on endless chores; the cries and shouts of the children carried far across the valley. I was to learn later that the coolie who came from China to work in the tin mines had sons who acquired the tin mine—grandsons who acquired many tin mines—and great-grandsons who are Communist guerrillas in the jungle. At Ampang I felt something of the bursting energy of the Chinese that causes them both to inherit the earth and to exploit it cruelly.

These Chinese are industrious people, making every clod of dirt useful to the human race. Their new villages throb with ceaseless energy. During every daylight hour there is some member of the family raking, hoeing, weeding, or in some other way manicuring the earth. In other parts of Asia I had seen people moving slowly and sullenly, as if they were about someone else's business— someone who was hated, not loved or admired. In Malaya the Chinese move as if they were about their own business.

Ampang this day seemed to be an anthill—an anthill that would destroy the easygoing Malay, an anthill that would leave no place even for the friendly Indian. In Malaya it is the Chinese who have the energy and brains not only to exploit the country but to operate the most dangerous underground Asia has known.

I visited Kuala Kurau with Templer. This is an old Chinese village of 5,000 people on the Kuala Kurau River, whose dirty mud banks this day were dotted with a host of white egrets. It's a fishermen's village, whose streets are lined with frames for the drying of nets. It seemed to be the dirtiest village I had ever seen. Elon vowed that the only way to clean it up would be to submerge it under five feet of water. One does not need to see the fish to know they are there. The odor is carried hundreds of yards on the softest breeze. A formidable fishing fleet goes out each morning, the sampans returning at irregular times during the day. The nets bring in fish as large as our salmon and as small as our smelt. They are cured in warehouses; they are smoked over a hardwood fire; they are laid out for drying on platforms of coarse screens several feet off the ground and raked with bamboo brooms every few hours so that each side of the fish catches the sun. The houses are packed close together, each with a garden, each with a family of ducks and geese raised on the offal of the fish. Pigs—the ugliest I have seen—run everywhere. Hundreds of small sampans are tied up in a dirty, sluggish canal running to the river. Houses are on one side, warehouses and bazaars on the other. In the middle of the town is a nondescript temple.

The bazaar has restaurants with electric refrigerators (filled with cold Danish beer) and shops where almost any household utensil or article of food may be obtained, even to apples from Australia. Men, women, children flocked to doors and windows to look at us; dozens of bicycles pulled up as the riders joined the onlookers.

The villages of Malaya I had visited were relaxed, friendly places, where people gathered around with curiosity but with smiles. Not so the Chinese. These Chinese glowered at us. There was not a smile on any face. Nor was there fear. The expression was a sullen one that gave no sign of welcome, no show of hospitality. The atmosphere was tense. All was quiet. The hucksters were silent. No shouts filled the streets or market places. The geese hissed, a few babies cried. There were hundreds of people staring, but not a word of greeting or recognition.

I had loitered behind Templer and his party, taking movies with a three-turreted camera. When I caught up with him he was talking through an interpreter, trying to fathom some of the deep secrets of the operations of a Chinese fishermen's guild that seemed to dominate Kuala Kurau.

When he finished he turned to me and asked:

"Tell me, what do you think of this Malayan situation?"

There was a twinkle in Templer's eyes as he stood facing me, his hands on his hips, his hat on the back of his head.

"What do I think of Malaya? I feel very lonesome here, General."

But it is better to go
north from Malaya
to see for oneself
the various people
who inhabit the region
and the paddies they work.

We stood in the shade
of Gaal Kampon
and quenched our thirst
on the milk
of these young coconuts.

The Sakai have a flute
that is distinctive
in only one respect
—it is played
not by the lips
but the nose.

The dresses of the Malay women
are gay and bright
with reds, yellows, and blues.

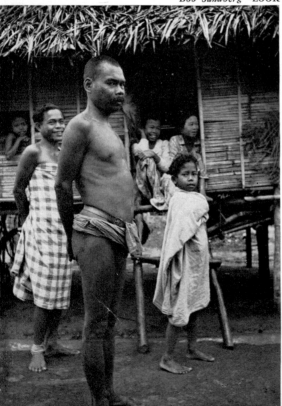

The Sakai men wear only
clouts of cloth or bark.

"Why should you feel lonesome?"

"Because I am apparently the only one in the country who doesn't have a gun."

The General threw back his head and roared. Then, mimicking severity, he pointed to my movie camera with its turret of three lenses and said, "You are a fine one to complain. With that confounded machine you have every one of us on edge. Looks worse than a Sten gun."

Templer was interested in finding a middleman who dealt in the fish brought in by the fleet. One Chinese was produced who walked half a mile to reach us. He quickly told Templer that although he did not deal in fish he would be happy to find us a dealer. So we walked with him a half mile to a shop where this Chinese smilingly said there was a dealer in fish. But this man was bathing in the dirty canal that passes through the town; and he refused to come out of the canal, even to greet the General.

Templer and I turned into a side street, where Sir Gerald thought he surely could find a middleman. We found a warehouse where fish were being cured. One man was working there who politely said in broken Malay that he could not speak to us because he did not speak Malay. An interpreter was provided; and through the interpreter this man told us he was not a middleman but a fish curer who bought his fish from the fishermen and sold them to a middleman.

The General did not give up. We entered another warehouse filled with fresh fish. The man in charge disclaimed any knowledge whatsoever of middlemen, but said that if the General was interested in a man who sold ice, he would be happy to find him one. Forthwith he pointed to the first Chinese who had been brought to Templer as a middleman in fish. "This is where the little play started," Templer grinned. "Let's call it a day."

As we walked back to the caravan waiting at the entrance to the village, Templer said:

"Some town, this Kuala Kurau. It's run, you know, by a Chinese secret society. In all the years we have been here, this place has never been under our civil administration. The secret society has its own police, its own tax collectors, its own courts."

A major on Templer's staff joined us.

"How is the town after dark?" I asked.

"The unhealthiest place in Malaya," the officer replied. And pointing to the expressionless faces of the men and women who watched us pass, he added, "If we could know half as much about the guerrillas as these Chinese villagers, we'd have the problem licked shortly."

Templer spoke up. "Remember that old coot I was talking with in the fishermen's warehouse? I wager he's in command of a good piece of underground."

There were no overt acts, no unfriendly gestures during our hour's visit. But the atmosphere was thick with hate. And my thoughts were about the same as those of one of the young British troopers, who shouted to me in a Cockney accent as the caravan started up: "Not a healthy place for a Britisher or American after dark."

At Tangog Lumpur on the east coast of Malaya I got new insight into the organization of the Chinese community against the government. I went to the east coast to get to know the ancient Malay culture. I will describe my experiences in a later chapter. Suffice it here to say that I saw the native Malay villages, the women who weave silk cloth by hand, skilled silversmiths, Malay dances, and the famous shadow plays. I recorded the rousing rebanna drums of the jungle on my portable machine; I ate in Malay homes and stayed long enough to feel the placid quality of the life of these gentle people and to catch some of the spirit of Malaya that Katherine Sim put into word pictures in *Malayan Landscape*.

I had been told that the east coast was a quiet, restful place, unmolested by guerrillas. I went by air to Kuantan, the town made famous at the beginning of the Japanese invasion of Malaya on December 8, 1941. For it was off Kuantan that the *Repulse* and the *Prince of Wales* were sunk. It was at Kuantan that the Japanese made one of their landings. Donald F. Thompson, an able New Zealander in the Malayan Civil Service, met me at the airport, which is about nine miles from town. He apologized for the condition of the road and the roundabout way it led, explaining that he chose this road because the other two were badly infested by guerrillas.

This was August 14, 1952. A company of Gurkhas had been in the jungles around Kuantan for two months, furtively stalking guerrillas. In that two months' period they had killed thirty-eight. But they had left the night of August 12, 1952, with as much secrecy as possible. The guerrillas had such good intelligence, however, that they knew at once of the withdrawal and the very next day had started to draw tight their noose around Kuantan.

These Kuantan guerrillas are organized into the Seventh Regiment. Their Tenth Regiment, headed by a Malay, Wan Ali, had also operated in this neighborhood. Wan Ali had gone to a native wise man (*pawang*), who had pronounced incantations over him and slipped a silver ring on one of his fingers. At the end of the ceremony the *pawang* had pronounced Wan Ali invulnerable to everything but a silver bullet. But Wan Ali—one of the few Malays turned guerrilla—was killed by a lead bullet. By the summer of 1952 most of the Tenth Regiment had been wiped out.

In 1952 the all-Chinese Seventh Regiment still was strong. It was the one that had survived the stealthy hunt of the Gurkhas and was once more closing in on Kuantan. We knew through confidential sources that they were close at hand, planning ambushes and arranging for the laying of land mines. Word of their presence traveled quickly through a network of informers who are paid $2,500 (Malay) for delivery of a live guerrilla, $1,250 for a dead one, and $50 to $100 for information concerning their movements and operations. One of the headquarters of the guerrillas was Tangog Lumpur, not far from Kuantan, and we went there for a visit.

Kuantan is about a mile or so from where the Kuantan River

(a favorite haunt of crocodiles) meets the South China Sea. Across the river from Kuantan is a headland that leads back into the deep, dark jungle. At the outermost point of the headland sits Tangog Lumpur, a village of 2,000 people.

We crossed the Kuantan River in a rented sampan. The sampan, about sixteen feet long, looked and felt like a heavy canoe such as one finds in northern Maine waters. It sat, however, a bit lower in the water and carried a mast in the center. The Malay boatman paddled us over against the wind with long, powerful strokes. And we returned prettily on whitecaps under a singing sail.

Tangog Lumpur, like Kuantan, is predominantly Malay, only 10 per cent of the people being Chinese. Tangog Lumpur (which means Dirty Village) sits on a spit of white sand decorated with a thick stand of tall coconut palm trees. Naked boys were playing on the beach and screaming as they splashed in the ocean. Malay girls in gay dresses of orange and red watched over fish drying on tall wooden platforms. The village well was the busiest place in town. Women were there with five-gallon earthen jugs. Men were filling kerosene tins to carry home on a long pole that stretched between them. Grinning Malay men, wearing only loincloths, dipped cool water from the well and poured bucket after bucket over themselves. Beautiful Malay women, bright with colors, stood pleasantly in the shade, watching.

Tangog Lumpur is a fishing village. Every morning at dawn the fleet of sampans, with their nets, goes to the ocean. I saw them return late one afternoon, their white sails full, their sterns low, whitecaps rolling along their gunwales.

The fishermen are Malays; they take the perils of the sea in these handmade craft. When they reach Tangog Lumpur, the Chinese take the catch. Perhaps the Chinaman owns the sampan and pays the Malay a wage; perhaps Chinese and Malays are partners in the fishing venture. More often than not the Malay sells his catch to the Chinese merchant, who dries the fish and ships them out to city markets. Whatever the precise arrangement, it is the Chinese who grows rich in the enterprise, the Malay who barely makes a living.

A Chinese merchant at Tangog Lumpur has a daughter who married Loo Hien, one of the top command in the Seventh Regiment of the guerrillas. Loo Hien has been hiding in the jungle with his regiment for four years. During that time his wife, an attractive Chinese woman about thirty years old, has had two babies. On each occasion there was much talk and gossip about it. Who was the father? Had Loo Hien slipped into the village unnoticed? One day a British official, a friend of mine, went to Tangog Lumpur for clues as to the whereabouts of Loo Hien. He interviewed Mrs. Loo Hien and confronted her with the gossip.

"Surely your husband must be around here," he said accusingly.

"No, no," she replied.

"Then who is the father of your children?"

"Oh," she said blushingly, "a traveling salesman."

"Same traveling salesman for the two children?"

"No," she snapped. "Two different ones."

A few days later the Gurkhas closed in on a guerrilla camp not far from Tangog Lumpur. The enemy had been warned of their coming and left. But their evacuation had been so fast they had left many records behind. One of these records told of the visit of the British official to Mrs. Loo Hien, of the questions he asked and the answers she gave.

The Gurkhas did not kill or capture Loo Hien. But his wife knows the jungle where he sleeps. And in Tangog Lumpur the Malay natives say that if her house is in danger of becoming a trap *she* will choose a dark night to go to *him*.

CHAPTER 3

GUERRILLA TACTICS

The guerrillas of Malaya date back to the occupation of Malaya by the Japanese from 1941–45. At
that time the British, Malays, and Indians joined hands in the
underground with Chinese Communists. The guerrillas then were
a unifying influence. Their popular name was Tiga Bintang,
meaning Three Stars, one each for the Chinese, Malays, and
Indians. The Allies dropped food, guns, grenades, and ammunition. The guerrillas flourished; the jungles became home to them.
Some of their exploits against the Japanese were heroic. But they
preyed more heavily on the civilian population than on the
Japanese; and they took punitive action against Malays and
Chinese who in any way collaborated or co-operated with the
occupation army. In this period the Chinese guerrillas laid the
basis for much of the bitterness that exists today between the
Malays and the Chinese.

When the Japs surrendered and the British returned, the
guerrillas were treated as heroes. Chen Ping, the Communist
who presently directs the guerrillas from his secret hide-out and

who has a price of $250,000 (Malay) on his head, was indeed decorated by the British at the end of World War II for his exploits as leader of the famous Force 136 during the Japanese occupation. For two years after the war there was apparent peace in Malaya. Then in June 1948 the guerrillas returned to the jungle and started the Red insurrection that is now in its fifth year.

One can get in Malaya numerous explanations for the commencement of terroristic practices. I was told by Chinese that the fault was with the British. They claimed that at the end of the war the British were niggardly in their treatment of the guerrillas; that they paid them only nominal amounts for their heroic underground work and even arrested some of those who came out of the jungle and turned in their arms. According to these Chinese, the guerrillas renewed their warfare only after satisfying themselves that they were not going to be fairly treated by the British Government.

The attitude of the British on that score may have influenced some to rebel. But it did not influence the Communist high command. The 1948 Communist Conference in Calcutta directed the resumption of jungle warfare by the fall of that year; but the guerrillas' timetable was unexpectedly advanced as a result of the labor policy of the British.

After the war the Communists dominated the labor movement in Malaya. They promoted trade unionism and placed their men in key positions of each union. Meanwhile, the British, to counteract this, promoted other trade unions that were free from Communist taint. It was the breaking of the Communist unions and the outlawing of the Communist Party, as I will relate in a subsequent chapter, that caused the Chinese Communists to take to the jungle. That was in June 1948.

The Chinese Communists then started their insurrection to "liberate" outlying areas of Malaya. The aim was to hold one "liberated" area and extend their control to other "liberated" areas, gradually forcing the British out. Their tactics failed, owing to dogged British determination. But irrespective of what the official British pronouncements may be, the Communists came perilously close to paralyzing the whole country. They had (and still have) bountiful supplies of guns, ammunition, money, and food. They had (and still have) excellent intelligence.

In Malaya one must figure that every third member of his household staff works for the guerrillas. A government official, a police or Army officer, a labor leader, a businessman, a plantation owner, or any other prominent person dares tell no one in his family (except his wife) and no one in his office (except those in whom he has complete confidence) where he is going tomorrow. Sir Henry Gurney, Templer's predecessor, made that mistake. He had an aide send word to the Chinese servants in charge of his cottage on Fraser's Hill (near Kuala Lumpur) to get the place in readiness for him and his wife the following week end. A servant told the guerrillas, and 60 of them lay in wait for several days in order to ambush Sir Henry. They opened fire on the convoy that escorted him. Sir Henry spent his last moments gallantly. Though mortally wounded, he opened the door of the car, got out, and ran up the road. He was of course riddled with bullets. But his ruse succeeded. He drew the fire from the guerrillas, saving the life of his wife in the car behind.

Late one afternoon I was with Templer in his office in King's House—the massive, villa-like residence of the High Commissioner that sits majestically on a high hill overlooking Kuala Lumpur. He had just finished recording on my tape recorder a talk which he had especially prepared for the American public. We were to join Lady Templer on the veranda for tea. But the General would not leave this office in his own home until a British officer took over his desk. Sir Gerald, one-time Director of British Military Intelligence, whispered, "When one has forty servants, he must assume that some of them are spies, no matter how carefully they are screened."

I talked with Norman Cleaveland about the security problem. He is an American who has kept Pacific Tin Consolidated Corporation in operation every day of the insurrection. This tin mine is in the Ampang Valley, only a few miles from Kuala Lumpur. It is a dredge operation, employing about thirty men. The office is about a mile from the dredge. The jungle lies on two sides of the mine. The dirt road from the office winds through fields of tall grass. Cleaveland would not let me go to the dredge in broad daylight without an armed escort. For over four years Cleaveland has taken his men to and from the dredge in armored cars. Four years ago an armed band of forty guerrillas operating within a mile of the dredge started to ambush the employees and officials. If they killed Cleaveland, it would be potent propaganda. They would by that act demonstrate their ability to murder on a selective basis. They would impress on every official, on every important personage that he too was vulnerable. They would show the "proletariat" that they were out only to kill the "imperialists."

I asked Cleaveland how he managed, with forty men dedicated to kill him, to move safely in this small valley for four years. His problem, he said, was to guard against regularity of movement. If he went to the dredge every morning at eight or every afternoon at three, an ambush would soon be laid. Even an ambush of an armored car is often successful. The side plates stop bullets, but grenades and land mines often wreak destruction from below and kill the occupants. Land mines in Malaya have indeed blown armored cars 100 feet off the road. Cleaveland goes to the dredge frequently, but his trips are often days apart and always unscheduled.

The wisdom of Cleaveland's example was brought sharply home in Taiping, a predominantly Chinese town in western Malaya about 250 miles north of Kuala Lumpur. Lieutenant Hunt was a young British Intelligence officer who married in the spring of 1952 and looked for a house in Taiping. There was none available. Maxwell Hill, 5,100 feet high, is a heavily wooded ridge overlooking Taiping, where the British have a radio station. There are cottages there, and the place is refreshingly cool after the humidity of Taiping. Tweed clothes and a roaring fire are indeed welcome at night. To solve their housing problem Lieutenant Hunt and his bride took one of those cottages. The guerrillas quickly learned through Chinese servants that he left Maxwell Hill every morning at eight and returned every evening at six. The road is a winding, tortuous one, even for a jeep. One morning about seven-thirty Hunt kissed his bride good-by, took his brief case, which contained highly secret material, got in his jeep, and started for Taiping. As he rounded a sharp corner he found a tree across the road. A band of guerrillas opened fire, wounding and disabling his bodyguard. Then they came up to Hunt, shot him dead, and went off with his brief case. But before they left they administered first aid to the wounded, indicating once more that they killed only on a selective basis.

They make a specialty out of placing road blocks to intercept buses. They frisk the passengers and usually turn them loose. Then they run the bus into a ditch and set it afire. They sometimes employ this tactic in setting up an elaborate ambush. Not far from Ipoh, during my visit, the guerrillas intercepted a truck that was going into a rubber plantation, turned the driver loose, and set fire to the truck. The driver reported the episode immediately. A police squad, armed to the teeth, crept cautiously up the road on the alert against an ambush. There was no sign of the guerrillas. The police searched the vicinity for clues and then, resigned to the fact that the bandits had escaped, started down the road to the main highway. They were now relaxed, off guard, and easy victims for the ambush that had been laid. They had gone hardly a quarter mile when the bandits opened fire. Of the fourteen police who made the trip, only four escaped to tell the story.

The guerrillas destroy property as they destroy people—on a selective basis. They seldom molest a dredge in a tin mine, even though its replacement would cost well over a million dollars; they seldom interfere with a power plant or a sub-station. They frequently cut lines and chop down poles that carry power. But they leave the business intact. They figure that if it were destroyed, the tin mine would be out of operation for months on end. Then the employees might blame the guerrillas for their unemployment. Moreover, if the employees are kept on the job, they will have funds against which the guerrillas can levy tribute.

The guerrillas engage in big business. They bring untold millions into the Communist treasury each year. In 1952 the guerrillas received about 10 per cent of the crude rubber produced in Malaya. In 1952 they got millions of dollars of protective money from the rubber, tin, fishing, and lumber industries.

This is the way it works. Last year a Chinese capitalist wanted to put up a lumber mill on the east coast near Kuantan. His logging operations would take him to the jungle and expose his loggers and his truckers to the guerrillas. He made a deal with the bandits. For the payment of so much a month his operations would be immune. To insure the safety of his equipment, the guerrillas made one requirement—that he paint his trucks yellow with a distinctive red bar so that they would be readily identified. He did that. At Kuantan I saw his mill and his operations. He is doing a thriving business in guerrilla land with no interruptions whatsoever.

Hundreds of tin miners, thousands of rubber planters, many fishermen pay like tribute. The Kinta Valley, which has 400 mines and produces 60 per cent of Malaya's tin, has one of the worst nests of guerrillas in all Malaya. They draw heavily on the industry, especially from the Chinese. The Chinese also own many rubber plantations in Malaya. They too pay tribute to the guerrillas, often in crude rubber.

A tin mine that does not pay may be destroyed. Moe Pak Kion had an open gravel pump mine near Kuala Lumpur. The price of protection was $100 ($33 U.S.) per month per sluice from the owner and $2.00 (Malay) per month from each employee. Moe Pak Kion refused to pay. On April 10, 1949, his pump houses and other buildings were burned. His workmen were held as prisoners for an hour and released unharmed. *They* had paid.

If a rubber plantation will not pay protection money and does not have the means for providing military security, it may suffer a heavy penalty. An owner or manager who refuses to pay tribute may be ambushed; his rubber tappers may be tied to trees and mutilated; his rubber trees may be slashed. Hundreds of owners and managers have been murdered; dozens of tappers have been cruelly tortured; hundreds of thousands of trees have been slashed. During 1952 the guerrillas were slashing from 10,000 to 20,000 trees a week. One gash from a knife will make the tree bleed copiously. A slashed tree, though not killed, will be out of production for at least nine months.

With their huge financial resources, the guerrillas keep themselves well fed and well cared for.

The new Chinese village (though it now has two barbed-wire fences around it) is still a source of food for the bandits. In any Chinese community a guerrilla seems able to find a willing seller. In every bazaar there is a member of Min Yuen; in every Chinese settlement there is someone who will get supplies to the bandits. But the reports from the underground are that the resettlement of the Chinese in the new villages has made it increasingly difficult for the guerrillas to get food, medical supplies, and funds. They are living more and more on tapioca and wild bananas. Wei Keiong, a member of the Communist high command who surrendered late in 1952, reported that this shortage of food was having a profound effect on the morale of the Communists.

The Malays were never as co-operative with the guerrillas as the Chinese. On August 16, 1952, I was with T. W. T. (Bill) Bangs on a trip to various Malay settlements out of Kota Bharu, the east coast city where the Japanese landed on December 8, 1941. Bangs is head of the Rural and Industrial Development Authority, an agency with a program somewhat like our Point Four and our ECA, which I will describe later. I traveled with Bangs as he inspected his numerous projects. At the end of one afternoon we stopped at Gaal Kampon, a Malay village perhaps fifty miles southwest of Kota Bharu, ten miles off the highway, and deep in the jungle. We reached it by the narrow jeep road built by RIDA. Gaal Kampon has perhaps a dozen thatched houses set on stakes about five feet high. The villagers dropped what they were doing and gathered around for a visit. They were friendly, gracious, and smiling. A village notable had a young man climb a high palm tree and drop down some green coconuts. Another villager cut the top off them with a heavy machete as sharp as a razor. It had been a blistering hot day and the perspiration had soaked our clothes through. We stood in the shade of Gaal Kampon and quenched our thirst on the milk of these young coconuts. Then the villagers told us what had happened at Gaal Kampon the night before.

Kota Bharu and the surrounding country were reputed to be free of guerrillas. We learned differently. Several guerrillas (all Chinese) had visited Gaal Kampon shortly after dark the previous evening. They came asking for food. The current price of rice was two dollars a gallon. The guerrillas, lush with funds, offered to pay twenty dollars a gallon. Clever to the smallest detail, they said, "All rice will bring twenty dollars a gallon when we take over. Rice is low in price now because of the British—they are depressing the price, taking the profit for themselves." These Malays—passionately nationalistic, anti-guerrilla, and suspicious of the Chinese—refused to sell the bandits food on any terms. Corruption among the Malay police is not unknown. They sometimes succumb to the Communist offers of high prices for food and arms. But by and large the Malay villager is an exception.

The British are another. When I visited Kuantan I talked with a Britisher who owns a rubber plantation ten miles or so out of town. It has been idle since 1948. The guerrillas have sent emissaries, promising full protection on payment of a few hundred Malay dollars a month. The Britisher has refused; and the plantation still stands idle. Few Britishers have paid protection money, for they know too well the stakes involved.

The reason why many of the Chinese are not so scrupulous is complicated. There is first the tradition of the Chinese village.

When the Chinese coolies first came to Malaya, they mixed with the other people, for they had left their own women behind. But when the Chinese women arrived in Malaya, the aloofness of the Chinese community increased. Since they had come on a temporary basis, they decided to live apart. Moreover, the Chinese brought with them the secret society and the bandit. Long before the Communist guerrillas appeared on the scene, Chinese shopkeepers paid protection money to lawless Chinese elements. The aloofness of the Chinese community, its secret societies, its tradition of tolerance for bandits—these helped create a state within a state. This was made to order for the Communist guerrillas.

Another reason involves the attitude of the Chinese toward the British. They are not sure whether the British will be in Malaya another year. The Japs ran the British out; and Red China, if relieved from pressure in Korea, may turn south for more adventures. In that case the British (they think) may once more leave Malaya. Overseas Chinese have always taken pride in a strong national regime in China. Malayan Chinese are no exception. Not many are Communists. But many who are not either respect the achievements of Mao Tse-tung or take a hedge against the day when he may rule Malaya. They therefore feel they must cultivate friends with the guerrillas, come the day the Communists are in power.

The cruel fact is that the Chinese community, if it so desired, could rid Malaya of the guerrillas in a few short weeks. They know their camps, their trails, their headquarters, their high command. And knowing all this, they stand mute. That is true of the Chinese coolies, the Chinese merchants, and even of many Chinese millionaires.

It is also a cruel fact that the Chinese community pays a heavy annual toll in blood and tears to the guerrillas. In the year 1952 the guerrillas killed 342 *civilians*. Most of these were Chinese—those who refused requests for food, those who declined to cooperate, those who gave information to the military. Indeed, of all the civilians who have been killed by the guerrillas since 1948, approximately three quarters have been Chinese. In the beginning the Chinese schoolteachers were the main targets. Those who did not espouse the guerrilla cause to the youngsters but worked against it were liquidated. The guerrilla terroristic methods held the Chinese teachers in line. That goes far to explain why the number of new recruits for the guerrilla ranks has held up in spite of the heavy casualties.

The guerrillas still wax strong. Their camps are well built. Some have schools in which the Marxist doctrine is taught. One guerrilla camp in the Ampang Valley was a village of rather modern houses that could accommodate 100 families. It was so laid out that no other house could be seen from any other one. The houses were spick and span, the gardens neat, and the latrines had bamboo seats.

Life in the jungle is hard in any case. It is wearying on the hunted as well as on the hunters. The guerrillas take account of the factor of fatigue. They have two rest camps for their forces—camps deep in the jungle of southern Thailand, not far from the Malayan border but many tortuous miles from Bangkok.

The guerrilla command is smart and resourceful. For no matter how many guerrillas are killed, the number on active duty remains about the same. They call their forces the Malayan Racial Liberation Army. They promise to liberate all of the colored races from the British. They sell young Chinese recruits with talk like this:

"Come with us and you'll soon run the country. The big Red Army of China will liberate all of us."

The high inspiration for it all—if not the high command—traces back to the Kremlin. At Kuantan I saw a Soviet flag picked up in a guerrilla village just captured by the Gurkhas. It had the hammer and the sickle, the star, and the blazing red of Russia. That flag is the symbol of the evil conspiracy which the Chinese, aided by the jungle, have laid upon Malaya.

CHAPTER 4

JUDAS ISCARIOT

There are aborigines in Malaya—the proto-Malays, the Pygmies, and the Sakai. I did not see the first two, but I visited three camps or settlements of the Sakai. The Sakai—who number over 16,000—are short in stature and slight in build. Their heads are long and narrow. Their skin is light yellow, their noses low and broad, their eyes dark and deep-set, their lips thick, their hair black, coarse, and wavy.

Centuries ago they gave way before the Malays as the North American Indians gave way before us. As I have said, the Malays settled largely along the rivers and developed a simple fishing and agricultural economy. The Sakai remained at the heads of the valleys and in the jungles, living largely on monkeys, wild pigs, roots, and fish. They make clearings and plant rice, sweet potatoes, bananas, and tapioca. But they seldom settle in any place for long. Even when they make a clearing, they stay only a few seasons.

The reason is that in Malaya the clearings become unproductive and sterile very fast. There is a quick leaching of the soil owing to rains and the constant high temperatures. (The rainfall is about 100 inches a year, the daytime relative humidity 75 per cent or more, the daytime temperature between 80° and 90° the year round.) The sandy elements and the humus in the soil are soon washed out. There is little of value left for plants, except in areas where the runoff is negligible. The jungles get more nourishment from their decaying leaves than from the clays on which they stand. Once the jungle is removed, the top soil disappears in a few months, leaving only the sterile clays. That is why the Sakai have constantly to make new clearings. That is why the rubber plantations must have legumes or secondary forests growing between the rows.

The Sakai are animists; they live in a spirit world, timid, frightened, alert. The evil spirits come in wind, lightning, thunder. They come in water. They descend from trees. They may cast a plague on the whole village, cause one death, strike hard at a single family, or destroy a crop. When that happens the Sakai will flee the place. They have their shaman or medicine man; and when the shaman dies they tie the body high in a tree so that a tiger may rend his body and release his spirit.

A hundred years ago none of them was literate. Today all are still illiterate. I talked with Britishers who have worked among them and know them well, and they all said the Sakai I.Q. was so low that they never could master much book learning. One said that he had trained Sakai to count up to three. I commented that one who could get to three could with perseverance get to ten. But this teacher doubted it. They are indeed childlike in their attitudes and conduct. They can be made docile and subservient by kindness. They can be frightened to panic by ominous gestures. They are terrified at the sight of human blood. Only a few are terrorists. Ah Sin—hanged at Taiping on October 1, 1952—was one.

The Sakai have a language of their own. They usually make fire with flint and steel and the pandanus leaf. Some have a small cylinder of buffalo horn with a tight-fitting piston, and with these

49

they make fire in the manner of the Diesel engine. Their huts are simple affairs made of bamboo sides and palm-leaf (*atap*) roofs. Like the Malays' huts, they stand on stakes high off the ground. The interiors are conspicuous for dirt, filth, and disorder. In the jungle they throw all refuse under the house. They do the same when they are resettled in more modern villages.

Major P. D. R. Williams-Hunt—adviser on aborigines—married a beautiful Sakai girl and brought a group of her people to Batu Caves, a small settlement near Kuala Lumpur. The day I visited it the Major was having a quarrel with an old, old Sakai lady whose kinky hair had turned snow-white and hung unkempt over her shoulders. She had shoveled the refuse of her establishment under her house. The Major protested, saying it should be buried. "If we put it under the house in the jungle, we can put it under the house here," she screamed. And under the house it went.

A Sakai seldom wears clothes above the waist. The women wear a sarong type of skirt made of cotton or of the *tapa* cloth which they make by beating the inner bark of the *artocarpus* tree. The men wear only clouts of cloth or bark. Women often wear necklaces of seeds or beads. Both men and women wear quills in the nose. And they are especially fond of fresh flowers and sweet herbs, which they wear in the hair.

The Sakai have no art of any consequence. Their musical instruments, whose music I recorded, are primitive. Their drums are fair, but their skill in playing them is not notable. Their stringed instruments are crude affairs with little range. They have a flute that is distinctive in only one respect—it is played not by the lips but by the nose. Their orchestras produce music that has little fervor, for the Sakai play rather mechanically, as most small children do.

The greatest accomplishment of the Sakai is probably their blowpipe, which I saw them use in one of their villages near Telok Anson in Perak. When we arrived at this Sakai village, the women and children peered at us through cracks in the walls of the houses with fright in their eyes. Most of the men stood at a distance, watching. A few were persuaded to come near; and finally Templer, with gentle persuasion, induced four of them to get their blowpipes.

The pipes, which are about nine feet long, are made of bamboo especially selected and carefully bored and polished within so that the tube is uniform in size and smooth. The pipes have a rounded mouthpiece. The arrow or darts (about nine inches long) are thin round strips made from the leaf ribs of palms. The point is notched half through so that it will break off in the flesh of the game. The other end of the arrow rests on a small slug of pith which fits the tube so tightly and yet moves so smoothly that it gathers the air behind it, propelling the arrow with force. The point of the arrow is coated with poison. This poison is usually made from the latex of the *upas* tree. The *upas* poison is an alkaloid that paralyzes the heart. Another poison is the *legup*, made from a vine. It has a strychnos base and is the more powerful of the two. The Sakai say that it takes only minutes to kill a monkey with a poisoned arrow and not much longer to kill a pig or a tiger.

We put a target about the size of the head of a kerosene tin in a tree about fifty feet distant, and the Sakai took aim. The blowpipe is doubtless a dangerous instrument. But the Sakai caused me to lose some of my faith. One after another they puffed their cheeks out until they were taut, and then blew. There was a soft swish as the arrow left the pipe and sailed toward the target. But no Sakai came closer to the target than three feet. Each explained to Templer, through the interpreter, that this was his bad day, that the big storm that had just passed made the arrow heavy, that the target was too far away.

There is one thing in which the Sakai are superlatively expert. They know the jungle as well as the leopard and the deer know it. They know the ancient runways, the short cuts, the way around a dismal swamp; they know the limestone caves where man is protected against all weather. The Sakai were aligned against the

Japanese during the occupation as they have been against every invader. They worked closely with the Malays, the Indians, the British, and the Chinese during the occupation. They were treated kindly by the underground and, so far as I could learn, they never betrayed those friends. The stories of their exploits are legend. They knew before anyone else that the Japanese were going to strike at a particular point in the jungle. Sometimes they would tell the insurgents of the coming of the Japs four days in advance, giving the underground ample opportunity to prepare an ambush. When the insurgents were able to take the initiative against the Japs, it was often due to intelligence borne on the fast feet of the Sakai.

Since 1948 they have been tools of the Communist guerrillas. The guerrillas exploit these simple people, making real slaves out of them. They herd them into remote sections of the jungle, force them to make clearings, and then, by threats of violence, make them grow crops for the guerrilla army. Hundreds of Sakai work in regular peonage for the bandits, getting no more return than slaves would get. The Sakai are also used by the Communists as guides in the jungle and as an intelligence unit in their organization.

Templer wants to break up that alliance. He has endeavored to resettle many of them in new villages. The government cleared the land for the sites, supplied materials for the new houses, and supervised their construction. They put the Sakai who settled there on food rations so they would be independent of guerrilla pressures. But even this did not give these new Sakai villages immunity. The one near Telok Anson that I visited with Templer was nervous with apprehension. These men and women had been slaves of the guerrillas and were fearful of what punishment might be meted out to them for co-operating with the government. Their fears rose to panic proportions a few days after Templer and I were there. The guerrillas appeared at night, demanding food. The whole village was stricken with stark fear. Men, women, and children immediately evacuated their new houses, left their crops behind, and rushed like children to the police, demanding protection.

Templer's task of breaking the alliance between the guerrillas and the Sakai and of enlisting these aborigines on his side of the struggle is a difficult one. The Sakai now have a long habit of working with the guerrillas. The ties between the Sakai and the guerrillas have become close. Moreover, the Sakai are so simple, so childlike, that no argument based on principle, no explanation of the nature of the Communist conspiracy would make any impression. They are children who must be won by simple methods. They must also be wooed cautiously. They have no discretion. If a confidence were entrusted to them, would they hurry to tell the guerrillas? Certainly they could be frightened into divulging any secret. And the guerrillas have been so intimate with the Sakai over the years that perhaps their natural childish impulse would be to warn the guerrillas of an ambush which they were helping the British prepare. The Sakai know the jungle better than anyone else. But can they be trusted?

I made no contribution to the problem that is perplexing to Templer. But I supplied an incident that highlights it. On the inspection trip I left Templer at Tapah, Perak, and went with Lady Templer to visit a Sakai settlement a few miles out of town. This was a small village of perhaps twenty families on the edge of the jungle. It was a nondescript place with meager huts high on stilts. There were no chickens, geese, or pigs in the yards, only miserable-looking dogs. (Cole, in *The Peoples of Malaysia*, reports that the Sakai never eat any animal they raise but for eating purposes will exchange their pets for another's.) The Red Cross had set up in this Sakai village a dispensary that was octagon-shaped and made of galvanized iron. An attractive British girl—Ceila Compton—ran it. Since the Sakai have mostly malaria, skin diseases, and pneumonia, it was for those ailments that Miss Compton was primarily prepared. She showed us about the village and introduced us to its characters. One old man, who seemed to have an obsession about sharp knives, followed us

53

around like a leopard. Another old man with a mat of white hair sat on a log, staring at us as if he were behind bars. One young couple proudly showed us a gibbon they had captured in the jungle and had made a member of their home. Another young Sakai couple held up their son, about two years old. Miss Compton explained that most of the Sakai had no religion but that a few had been converted. The people with the gibbon were Moslems; the ones with the young son were Christians.

"He even has a Christian name," Miss Compton said. "An unusual one."

"Obadiah, Nehemiah?" I asked.

"Certainly not," she said with a chuckle. "His name is Judas Iscariot."

Templer laughed when I told him the story and then added with a twinkle in his eyes, "Do you mean to suggest that every blooming person in this country is against us?"

CHAPTER 5

BRITISH JUSTICE

There was a Chinese woman in jail at Ipoh when I was there. I did not see her, but I judged from her pictures that she was in her late twenties. One picture showed her with a pistol on her hip and hand grenades in her belt. When captured she wore khaki trousers and a brown shirt open at the throat. Her name was Lee Ten Tai, alias Lee Meng.

The authorities had to change jailers on account of Lee Ten Tai. By hook or by crook, by guile or by sweetness, she planned to get the jailer to sleep with her. The hours of her blandishments were after 2 A.M. And she put much ingenuity into the project. I inquired about it, seeking to learn her motive.

"Her motive?" one of the attorneys snorted. "She's charged with a capital offense and will probably be hanged. But she's smart enough to know that British justice would never permit a pregnant woman to be executed."

A lady jailer was substituted for the male guard during the long night hours. Lee Ten Tai took her revenge. She spat and cursed at the woman when she passed her. She taught the inmates of her block the *Internationale,* and they sang it at all hours of the night, cursing the British in the interludes. And at one stage she led a hunger strike in the Ipoh Police Station. She is the one whose death sentence was commuted and whom the Russians proposed to exchange for the Britisher, Edgar Sanders.

The criminal law of Malaya has been written to fit the state of siege. The High Commissioner has promulgated Emergency Regulations defining crimes, fixing the penalties, and describing the powers of the police and local authorities.

Possession of a gun, pistol, hand grenade, or other lethal instrument without a permit carries the death penalty.

Demanding, collecting, or receiving supplies for the guerrillas carries the death penalty.

A person who is found "consorting" with one who is in illegal possession of firearms or explosives may be sentenced to death or life imprisonment.

One who knows that another has committed an offense against the regulations and who fails to report it may be sentenced up to ten years.

Possession of guerrilla literature (defined as "terrorist documents") carries up to ten years' imprisonment.

Measures may be taken against a community that aids and abets the guerrillas. Fines may be levied collectively on all or a part of the inhabitants, or the shops in the area may be closed or allowed to be open only at specified hours.

Provision is made to control the articles of food and medicine and all printing supplies in any area for the purpose of preventing their movement into guerrilla channels. Violation of these controls entails fine and imprisonment. Arrests without warrants are liberally allowed. Searches and seizures without warrants are also freely permitted. Where a business is being run to aid the guerrillas, it can be made subject to a sort of receivership or wound up and dissolved.

Persons (not citizens) who in the opinion of the High Commissioner have aided and abetted or consorted with persons who they knew or had reasonable cause to believe were acting "in a manner prejudicial to public safety or the maintenance of public order" can be deported or detained. They are deported or detained without trial. Detention is for a period not exceeding two years, though it may be extended for another two years.

Habeas corpus is suspended. After eighteen months, however, a person detained can get a review of his case by a civil authority. But the detention remains largely a discretionary matter. As a practical matter detention is used to confine people against whom a criminal case cannot be made out. One tried and acquitted often is sent to a detention camp if he is deemed dangerous to the nation.

These are large departures from the Anglo-American standards of criminal justice. But they are defended on the grounds that the crisis threatening the nation demands severe measures. It truly does; and the use of protective custody, if ever warranted, is necessary for the dire circumstances confronting Malaya. Whether it is abused is a much-mooted question in the country.

Mohammed Ysoff, head of the Government Workers Union, whom I met in Penang, thinks the detention law is sometimes used unfairly. He pointed to the case of the Battery Workers Union that was headed by three Chinese. This union struck against the layoff of 200 men. This was in the spring of 1952. The union officials were arrested and put in protective custody on a charge that they were either Communists or Communist sympathizers. In August 1952 the union officials were still in jail. I do not know more about the merits of the episode than what union men and a few American observers told me. But it is clear that the detention law is viewed in the ranks of labor with fear and suspicion. There is no doubt that some managers have used it as an instrument of terror against trade unionists. It has in fact sobered the activities of labor leaders and, as one British observer noted, made workers hesitate to strike even to remedy justifiable grievances.

In August 1952 Templer hustled one whole Chinese village

(Permatting Tinggi), consisting of sixty-odd people, off to a detention camp. The hands of the guerrillas were deep in this village, where a government official (a Chinese) had been murdered. No one would talk. Templer went there and addressed the villagers, seeking information. None would speak publicly; none would speak privately; none would fill out a questionnaire Templer left with them.

But these episodes, oppressive as they are, do not make Malaya a police state. Malaya is subject to an armed conspiracy of terror, the like of which few countries have known. Extreme measures are needed to save the country from complete demoralization and destruction. If the long-term objectives were repressive, the detention camps would be vicious instruments. But the program the British have for Malaya is largely an enlightened one, as I will relate. And the protective custody is used mostly to make sure that that program will have an opportunity to develop and not be destroyed under a Communist rule of terror.

In the courtrooms there is a flowering of British justice. Every guerrilla charged with a crime has a lawyer assigned to defend him. At Ipoh, Perak, there are thirty-five members of the Bar. The Registrar of the court assigns these lawyers in rotation. The assignments are heavy, for the court at Ipoh tries dozens of these guerrilla cases a year. The members of the Bar therefore serve over and again, giving much of their time to this public service. The defenses tendered are not *pro forma;* they are real and earnest.

There is no mob atmosphere about the courthouse. Photographers are prohibited. A lawyer is in contempt who, prior to the trial, talks to the press about a case or releases evidence for publication. Even a picture of an accused held in jail cannot be taken unless he gives his consent.

In a land where terror and violence burst repeatedly on the people, where deaths from Communist violence are common, where armed conspirators stalk every important person, the accused are treated more tenderly than in American trials. At Ipoh

the courtroom presided over by Mr. Justice E. O. Pretheroe
(Gray's Inn) and Mr. Justice J. B. Thomson (Middle Temple) is
a place of quiet dignity. Matthew G. Neal, an able New Zealander, is the prosecutor. The prisoner is in the dock, guarded by
a soldier. The prosecutor is distant from him, unable to shake his
fist under his nose or to storm and rant. The proceedings are calm
and deliberate. Confessions made by the accused to the police
are more freely admitted in Ipoh than in London. But in Malaya
the courts are as strict in invalidating confessions as are American courts. They are scrutinized with care for the use of force,
fear, or other such inducement; and if they are shown to be
involuntary, they are excluded from evidence.

The accused does not have the benefit of a jury trial. The Judge
sits with two Assessors who act in an advisory role. Members
of the Chinese community often serve as Assessors. But they
fear to do so because of possible retaliation. One Chinese Asses-
sor, who lives and works out of Ipoh far from police protection,
was shivering so hard when it came time to announce his decision
that he could not speak but had to write it out. Another looked
as though his eyes were going to fall out from fright. The Chinese,
when asked to serve as Assessors, often produce sick certificates
or frankly state they are afraid to sit in a particular case. For conviction the Judge and the Assessors must be satisfied of guilt beyond a reasonable doubt. It is not a system whereby defendants
are railroaded to conviction. There is careful weighing of evidence. The Judge charges the Assessors as a jury is charged,
stating the law and often commenting on the evidence. Many of
those accused are acquitted.

At Ipoh, See May was convicted and sentenced to death. Telling
evidence against her had been given by other surrendered or
captured bandits. Like every defendant, she was given the choice
of three alternatives—to give evidence on oath and submit to
cross-examination, to make a statement from the dock without
any such liability, or to remain silent. She elected to make a
statement from the dock.

"I am also called Lean Thai. I have been living in Ipoh all the time. Just after the Japanese surrender I was in Ipoh and always have been. I used to visit associations and clubs. Hence I know many people. There are many who are good to me and there are some who are bad to me. At the beginning of 1948 I had an elder sister who was married to someone in Singapore. I followed her to Singapore. There I lived until 1950 and then I returned to Ipoh. My intention was to spend a few months here and then return to Singapore. Meanwhile my sister died. In Ipoh I stayed with an old woman by name Chow Yin. This woman was arrested the same time I was. As I had been living with her, she knew all about me and I would have called her as my witness, as she was a good family woman. I asked my counsel to get her as my witness, but I was told by him that she had committed suicide. She knew everything about me. Now I cannot call her.

"Now this group of surrendered devils—I don't know them at all and I don't know why they say they know me. They are a group of 'rotten things.' They have harmed many people and now they want to harm me as well. This group of rotten devils say I was in possession of a hand grenade, but I never was. When I was arrested there was no hand grenade with me. That proves that I had no grenade. They say that I have lived in the jungle, but as I have said, I have been in Singapore and Ipoh. I have never taken any photographs in the jungle, and those produced are not mine. That is all."

Other statements are not as calm and reasoned. When I was at Ipoh a trial of two Chinese girls was ending. These girls were charged with a non-capital offense. They both elected to give evidence on oath.

When the first one was sworn, she turned to Mr. Justice Thomson and snarled, "If we win, you die; if you win, we die." His Lordship asked her whether she had anything to say on the merits of the case. She replied in the negative, and Mr. Neal did not cross-examine. His Lordship said, "Thank you, madame," and had her returned to the dock.

The second one was sworn, and she too whirled on His Lordship, screaming, "If we win, you die; if you win, we die."

Then each of them was asked whether she had any witnesses. Each answered in the negative. His Lordship thereupon said, "I find you both guilty as charged and convict you accordingly. Have you anything to say before I pass sentence upon you?" Each answered "No."

Then His Lordship addressed the following remarks to them: "I am sending you to a place where you will meet quite a few of your friends. I hope I am able to send a lot more of your friends to join you. Five years rigorous imprisonment."

British judges are seldom ruffled even at the violent views of the accused. They go about their work in a calm, dispassionate way. They create in a community a tradition of tolerance, fairness, and decency. And yet they are as firm as the oak.

I spoke of these things at a dinner in Ipoh. The dinner, held at the Station Hotel, was tendered Mr. P. Sankey, an Indian who had long been Assistant Registrar of the court and who, pursuant to the regulations of the Malayan Civil Service, was retiring at the age of fifty-six. The dinner was attended by about fifty people, including the Bar of Ipoh and the court attachés. Mr. Justice Pretheroe presided.

In my extemporaneous remarks I referred to the great tradition of the Bar that gave every defendant in a criminal case the right to be represented by counsel. I mentioned the policy underlying it as expressed in one of our leading American cases (*Powell* v. *Alabama,* 287 U.S. 45, 68):

"The right to be heard would be, in many cases, of little avail if it did not comprehend the right to be heard by counsel. Even the intelligent and educated layman has small and sometimes no skill in the science of law. If charged with crime, he is incapable, generally, of determining for himself whether the indictment is good or bad. He is unfamiliar with the rules of evidence. Left without the aid of counsel, he may be put on trial without a proper charge, and convicted upon incompetent evidence, or evidence irrelevant to the issue or otherwise inadmissible. He lacks both the skill and knowledge adequately to prepare his defense, even though he have a perfect one. He requires the guiding hand of counsel at every step in the proceedings against him. Without it, though he be not guilty, he faces the danger of conviction because he does not know how to establish his innocence. If that be true of men of intelligence, how much more true is it of the ignorant and illiterate, or those of feeble intellect."

I referred to the resolution of the Maryland State Bar Association, unanimously adopted in June 1952, respecting the representation of an accused by counsel:

"In the opinion of this Committee, it would be preferable to follow the precedent of the New York Bar Association in the case of the Socialist members of the New York legislature. In that matter, Charles Evans Hughes and the other lawyers with him defended the Socialists as representatives of the organized bar. The public realized that the action was taken by the bar not because of any sympathy with the philosophy of the persons involved, but because the bar, as a body entrusted with carrying on the great traditions of our system of justice, realized that the more serious the charge the more essential it is that the accused be represented by reputable and able counsel.

"We recommend that on the request of any person charged with being a Communist or subversive person in criminal or in disbarment or in other proceedings, this Association shall appoint one or more lawyers to represent such a person and that such appointment and the reason therefor be made public. Any such appointment would be subject to the condition that the lawyer be free to defend the case in such manner as to him seems proper as an officer of the court."

I spoke of Thomas Erskine, who was the great defender of civil liberties in England when intolerance ruled late in the eighteenth century. Erskine's defense of Hardy, Tooke, Thelwall, and Thomas Paine brought new prestige to the British Bar. He stood before an aroused public to defend purveyors of the unpopular ideas of that age. In the midst of those trials he stated, "From the moment that any advocate can be permitted to say that he will or will not stand between the Crown and the subject arraigned in the court where he daily sits to practice, from that moment the liberties of England are at an end." Great pressure was put on Erskine not to defend Paine, charged with seditious libel for his book *The Rights of Man.* Lord Loughborough stopped Erskine in the street one night and said, "Erskine, you must not take Paine's brief."

Erskine, looking him full-face, answered, "But I have been retained, and I *will* take it, by God."

I ended my talk at Ipoh with a reference to England's record in Asia. England may be cursed, abused, and justly indicted for many imperialistic practices. But wherever she has been—India, Pakistan, Ceylon, Burma—she has left behind concepts of due process of law that recognize the worth and dignity of even the most miserable person and his right to the equal protection of the law. Due process of law is indeed the embodiment of all the civil liberties that we of the West hold dear and that the Bar in beleaguered Ipoh was defending with courage and devotion. The tradition of due process of law gives spiritual strength to the forces opposing Communism in Asia. In fact, it sums up the basic conflict between the free world and Communism.

CHAPTER 6

LABOR BRINGS THE REVOLUTION

"Why, it's getting so that these women can now afford Kotex." The speaker was a bluff Englishman who manages a rubber plantation near Kuala Lumpur. He had a pistol on his belt and a pith helmet on his head. His sleeveless shirt was open at the throat. He wore shorts and knee-length stockings. He stood facing me as he talked, the sweat running down his face.

We had been on a tour of the rubber plantation, riding jeeps and escorted by a half dozen armed men who followed in an armored car. We had seen the rubber trees and the men and women who worked them. Some were keeping the rows free from high undergrowth, others were tapping the trees, some were collecting the white latex from the little cup at the bottom of each cut and pouring it into a bucket.

These people were Tamil Indians, once cruelly exploited. They have constituted for years the bulk of the labor force of the rubber plantations. Prior to 1910 they were indentured labor, brought over from India and placed in the most miserable labor lines man

Kuala Kurau
is an old Chinese village
of 5,000 people
on the banks
of the Kuala Kurau River.

Elon Gilbert

Moe Pak Kion had
an open gravel-pump mine
near Kuala Lumpur.

Bob Sandberg—LOOK

Elon Gilbert

The magnitude
of the educational program
in Malaya
is indicated by the fact
that is has to be
conducted in four languages
—English, Malay,
Chinese, and Tamil.

NOTICE
DO NOT SPIT ON THE FLOOR—

*The prevailing wage
for rubber tappers
in Malaya
is ninety cents a day.*

Bob Sandberg—LOOK

*There was a twinkle
in Templer's eyes
as he stood facing me*

has known. They were indeed ignorant, terrorized, half-starved slaves. British and Chinese capital grew lush out of their work. The history of the reforms, many of them inspired from abroad by men like Nehru, is too long to relate here. But in spite of the vast improvements, the tapper's wage in 1938 was 50 cents a day for males, 40 cents a day for females. By 1941 those wages had risen to 60 cents and 50 cents respectively. And in August 1952 the prevailing wage was $2.80 (Malay) a day for men and (as traditional) four fifths of that amount, or $2.25, for women.

The prevalence of the employment of women is indicated in the following tables, containing a breakdown of employees on rubber estates (both European and Asian) over 100 acres in the Federation of Malaya for 1952.

Rubber tappers working at the piece rate:

Chinese
- Males 20,600
- Females 21,400

Indian
- Males 22,000
- Females 20,000

Rubber tappers working for a daily wage:

Chinese
- Males 3,003
- Females 3,008

Indian
- Males 17,005
- Females 17,250

Malay
- Males 4,000
- Females 4,000

Field Workers:

Chinese
- Males 4,600
- Females 6,500

Field Workers:—Cont'd
    Indian
        Males 9,008
        Females 14,004
    Malay
        Males 4,007
        Females 4,003

These figures show that male and female workers are just about evenly divided. Man and wife, indeed, work together in the plantations as tappers and as field workers. That was at the root of the matter bothering the British overseer of the plantation I visited.

"One family now makes six dollars a day," he exclaimed to me. "What is it all coming to?"

The most reactionary force in Malaya is the Chinese and British industrialist or businessman. They knew Malaya when the empire was at its zenith. They saw Malaya as the place where fortunes could be made. The Britisher often looks back to the halcyon days of empire with great nostalgia and hopes against hope that the clock will be turned back. Some of them blame America for their present plight. "If it hadn't been for Roosevelt, England wouldn't have lost Asia," one said to me explosively.

"How did Roosevelt lose Asia for England?"

"By constantly harping on freedom for people."

"You mean Roosevelt started the revolutions in Asia? They hadn't been under way before then?"

"Roosevelt fomented them," he fairly shouted. "Roosevelt made the people unhappy with their lot. Now look at the fix we're in."

This is the British imperialist who used labor on a temporary basis, preferring a fluid rather than a permanent labor market to draw upon, with all the advantages of exploitation which that offered.

The Chinese coolies who worked the tin mines came to Malaya under conditions as unconscionable as those which originally enslaved the Indian rubber tapper. The Chinese coolies were ruthlessly exploited under a contract labor system, described in Purcell, *The Chinese in Malaya*. The coolie "worked out" not only the expenses of his recruitment and the cost of his transportation from China, but the profit of the broker as well. It was therefore common for the coolie to receive only food and clothing for the first six months and only nominal wages for the next six months. This contract system was known as "pig business." If he deserted and was caught, he was brought before a British court and fined. Then the fine had to be "worked out" by the coolie. As Virginia Thompson in *Post Mortem in Malaya* relates, this "pig business" was so callous of human rights that anti-foreign riots broke out in some of the Chinese ports where coolie labor was recruited for shipment to Malaya. Both the Britisher and the Chinese used this labor without conscience or restraint. But of the two, the Asian employer probably was the worse both as respects the amount of wages, the hours of work, and the conditions of labor.

Such reforms as have been achieved by Malayan labor have been over the opposition of the British and Chinese business interests. Malayan business today is highly vocal against trade unionism. It denounces trade-union leaders as Communists. It stands squarely against the trade-union movement. Its strength is considerable.

These days Malayan rubber plantations are in a true sense armed camps. Their own police patrol them by day, and floodlights guard them by night. The labor force lives on the plantation in huts furnished by the plantation. The children of the workers are educated in schools run by the plantation and extending through the sixth grade. But their attendance is not compulsory. The plantation has a store, where the workers shop, and nowadays a dispensary. The company towns of the Malayan rubber plantations are the company towns that American labor has known. Some are miserable places, hardly fit for human habitation. Some are bright, spick, and modern, like the labor lines of the Changkat Serdang Estate near Taiping, which is run by George de Lavenant-Clifford, an enlightened Frenchman, and his wife, a vivacious, warmhearted Irish lady. But they are the exceptions. Most of the Indian labor lines that I saw are depressing places. They have the atmosphere of slums; most of them give little opportunity for escape through educational opportunities; many are hostile to organized labor. Armed guards stand at the gates. And many rubber plantations have standing orders not to admit union organizers.

The British and Chinese employers were to pay heavily for their easy manipulation of the cheap labor of Asia. The immigrants, who were used to exploit the rubber and tin of Malaya, brought along the ideas of revolution that were sweeping India and China. These ideas were mostly political rather than economic. They drew inspiration from the political ferment at work in India and China. There were, of course, strikes in Malaya for better wages and working conditions, for better housing, and for better schools in the company towns. Strikes sometimes were called when the plantation owners put water in the milk that was furnished the labor lines or adulterated the food. But there were also other kinds of strikes.

What was happening in India had its reflex in Malaya. The slogans of the Indian National Congress resulted in strikes in Malaya, strikes that had political as well as economic aims. One strike demanded that Gandhi's portrait be hung in the labor lines. Another that the Congress flag fly at the estate entrance. There were strikes for equality of political rights, strikes for the grant of land to workers so that they would not be solely dependent on the fluctuating world price of tin and rubber. These are some of the ways the politics of India entered the Malayan labor field.

The politics of China entered when followers of Sun Yat-sen sought refuge in Malaya in 1910. By the mid-1920's Chinese nationalism was rampant in Malaya and the Communist influence began to be felt. When Japan invaded Manchuria, the China Relief Fund sponsored by the Kuomintang became active in

Malaya. The Relief Fund identified itself with Malaya's labor movement, whipped up anti-Japanese sentiment, and revived the spirit of nationalism among Malaya's coolies. The Chinese Communist Party became increasingly active. It promoted Chinese societies that became cells of Communist activities. Prior to Stalin's pact with Hitler, Malayan Communists promoted peace in the ranks of labor in order to gird Malaya for a struggle against Japan. When the Soviets made their pact with Germany, the Communist influence in Malaya was immediately thrown on the side of strikes and violence.

But whether the inspiration was Chinese Communism or the Kuomintang, the effect was somewhat the same. For China always claimed the loyalty of her nationalists wherever they might be; and they in turn seldom tried to give up their Chinese citizenship. The result in Malaya was an increasingly turbulent labor force that looked overseas for guidance, inspiration, and protection.

Malaya's labor force—long exploited and dangerously discontent—had few labor unions of responsibility to provide the leadership. It was mostly unorganized labor, inspired by men with political motives, that led the struggle. The struggle was bitter, and there was a special reason for the bitterness.

The laboring class with the revolutionary ideas made up a majority of all the wage earners in Malaya. Not only had they imported their revolutionary ideas; they themselves were aliens. The agitators for reform were "foreigners" whose race was alien, whose culture was strange, whose politics were borrowed from other lands. These facts increased the social and political tensions between the classes. These facts made the labor movement easily suspect, easily discredited. These facts helped draw racial prejudices and racial hates into the Malayan conflict.

Shortly before World War II the British gave Malayan labor numerous concessions in the form of progressive social legislation. But both the government and business conceived of the new legislation more as a means of controlling labor than of fostering its development. In 1941 the government, under the pressure of the tin mines and the rubber plantations, declared all strikes illegal; and troops and armored cars were turned against the strikers.

After World War II the Communists, who had successfully managed the underground against the Japanese, started immediately to organize Malayan labor. By September 1945 they had tin miners, rubber tappers, typists, clerks, cabaret girls, and practically every other type of labor unionized. Most of them were united in an over-all federation, the Pan Malayan Federation of Trade Unions (PMFTU), that was tightly controlled by the Communists. The law required the registration of all unions. By the end of 1947, 277 unions, with a total membership of about 200,000, had registered. Of these, 214 were dominated by the Communists; and they included the rubber workers, the tin miners, and the dock workers. These Communist unions were so strong that they could bring all of Malaya to a halt. And once or twice in the spring of 1948 they did just that. They whipped the country with strikes and made their power felt in almost every aspect of Malayan life.

Measures were taken to counteract the Communist influence in the ranks of labor. The British promoted trade unions that were free from the Communist taint. In 1946 they brought John Alfred Brazier, a locomotive engineer from London, to Kuala Lumpur for this purpose and made him the Trade Union Adviser. Brazier, short, stocky, and middle-aged, has spent his life in the trade-union movement. It is to him a career—a dangerous one at that, for he today is a marked man. Brazier brings to his job the determination of a bulldog jaw, and he lightens it with the bragging, the tall tales, the humor of the Cockney.

Brazier is a natural leader of men. He knows how to inspire them, unite them, and fill them with zeal. When he reached Malaya in 1946 the Communists already had the union movement under tight control. Brazier had no existing organization to work with. He had to start from scratch with men who knew little or nothing of trade unionism. Brazier, however, worked wonders.

In eighteen months he had organized non-Communist unions (mostly in the government and on rubber plantations) and had them in a fair competitive position with key Communist unions. As a matter of fact, Brazier was so effective that in the first six months of 1948 the Communist unions lost half of their membership. The magnitude of his educational program is indicated by the fact that it had to be conducted in four languages—English, Malay, Tamil, and Chinese.

On June 12, 1948, a law was passed requiring that every officer of a union, except the secretary, be of good character, actually employed in the industry, or one who has had three years of such employment. The law also prohibited federations of unions except among those in similar occupations or industries. This law made PMFTU illegal and also many of the other Communist-controlled unions. In July 1948 the government outlawed the Communist Party. The Communist union leaders (most of whom were Chinese) thereupon took the union funds and returned to the jungle, some of them taking their Chinese mistresses with them.

Brazier's educational program is continually expanding. He has training schools for union officers, and those who finish there are sent off to the United Kingdom for more training. His educational program includes vocational training for union members, citizenship courses, procedures in collective bargaining, and lectures, slides, movies, and plays for workers on remote rubber plantations.

Malaya has about one million workers in all industries. Of these, Brazier (who works very harmoniously with Templer) had organized 121,626 by June 1952. These included government workers, rubber tappers, harbor workers, and a few tin miners. They also included dance-hall hostesses, many of whom are prostitutes; and for these Brazier has negotiated contracts that give them free medical care. Brazier's unions numbered 210 by the middle of 1952, each of which was solidly anti-Communist.

Brazier's unions cut across all racial lines. He himself has a special respect for the Chinese, their organizing ability, their potential leadership in trade unionism. The multi-racial character of his unions promises to be a cohesive force that will help make one friendly community out of several antagonistic ones.

Trade unionism is largely unknown to the tin industry. The wages of the workers are in fact set by the Malayan Mining Employers Association. In 1952 the average daily wage of unskilled workers in European tin mines was 80 cents (U.S.) a day or $2.35 (Malay). The wage in the Chinese tin mines was even lower.

The bulk of Brazier's efforts to date has been directed toward the rubber plantations. There are 500,000 workers on the rubber plantations that are scattered the length and breadth of Malaya. Brazier has organized about 50,000 of them. It was their labor union that, with Brazier's help, I came to know.

The officers and most of the members of the Rubber Tappers Union are Indians. The head of it is thirty-year-old P. P. Narayanan. One afternoon in Kuala Lumpur, Brazier and I sat with him and six other officers of his union—J. Emanuel, K. P. Govindia Navi, M. Suppiah, R. Raju, N. S. Dawood, and H. K. Choudhury. These men were hungry for news of trade unionism in America.

What does a man who works in an orchard in America make per day?

Do women get a lower wage for the same work?

What wage does a truck driver in America get?

Do women get the same minimum wage as men in America? The same hours of work? Time off for childbirth?

Are Communists in control of any labor unions in America?

Do employers in America call all union leaders Communists whether they are Communists or not?

These seven men were members of a committee engaged in collective bargaining for their union. A few years earlier the union had agreed to a contract that hitched wages to the price of rubber. A formula had been worked out in arbitration proceedings which paid a wage in one quarter that was related to the price of rubber in the previous quarter. All went well while the price of rubber rose or fell within the price limits of the contract. But

in the summer of 1952 the price of rubber had fallen below one
dollar (Malay), and that eventuality had not been covered by the
contract. The planters insisted that the wages be reduced. The
union objected, insisting that the minimum wage be fixed at that
point.

In July 1952 wages were reduced to reflect the declining price
of rubber from $1.00 (Malay) to 90 cents (Malay). The wage
scales were:

Contract tappers	$3.40 (Malay)
Check-roll tappers	2.90 (Malay)
Field workers	2.20 (Malay)

The price of rubber continued to decline, dropping below 90
cents. New negotiations were undertaken. When I was in Malaya
a deadlock had been reached; and the dispute went to arbitration.
As a result wages were set as follows for periods when the price
of rubber ranges between 80 and 90 cents (Malay):

Contract tappers	$3.15 (Malay)
Check-roll tappers	2.75 (Malay)
Field workers	2.10 (Malay)

And lower wage rates were set for periods when rubber might
average between 70 and 80 cents (Malay) and 60 and 70 cents
(Malay).

The Communists meanwhile are active underground. They
print and distribute literature criticizing the union leaders in
scathing terms. Wages have declined with the fall of the price of
rubber. The wage decrease is due to the union contract, for
which the union officials were responsible. With that leg to stand
on, the Communists flay Narayanan unmercifully. They call him
a tool of the imperialists, a Running Dog. They pour on him and
on his associates calumny and hate. They have marked him,
Brazier, and other union officials for assassination.

The situation is so tense that Narayanan has to move surreptitiously about the country. His work takes him constantly to the

field. Surveillance of him is so close that he dares not tell even his secretary where he is going when he leaves his office. To avoid ambushes he makes no appointments in the field but goes about his organizing work on an irregular schedule. Only when he is ready to leave a property that he is visiting does he telephone his staff, advising them of his whereabouts.

This fear of Communist terror is not an idle one. The Communists strike with vengeance against Brazier's men. In 1952 they killed thirteen union officers. These were mostly men who were making the rounds of rubber plantations, collecting dues. One victim was a forty-year-old Indian by the name of Subrammaniam. While he was collecting dues from rubber tappers on the Effingham Estate near Kuala Lumpur, the guerrillas swarmed out of the jungle and seized him. They tied him to a rubber tree; his hands, high above his head, were bound fast to the trunk. They called the tappers and field workers to gather around. And shouting, "This is what happens to a man who collects dues for unions that are tools of the imperialists," they cut off his hands with a sharp machete and left him there to die.

In Malaya union officials and plantation owners serve today as allies in a common cause.

CHAPTER 7

DELIVER US FROM EVIL

Between 1786 and 1824 the British acquired sovereignty over three areas in Malaya—(1) the island
of Penang in the northwest, together with a piece of the mainland
opposite Penang; (2) the island of Singapore in the south; and
(3) Malacca, first a Portuguese and later a Dutch settlement on
the southwest coast. These three became the Straits Settlements,
a British Crown Colony. Later the British began to intervene in
the Malay states to protect British trade with the interior. As a
result of this intervention and as a result of wars and feuds, the
nine Malay states between 1874 and 1909 became British protectorates. Each Sultan signed a treaty by which he agreed in
substance to accept British advice in all matters except those
pertaining to religion (the Malays are all Moslems) and those
concerning Malay customs. The British ruled the country through
the Malayan Civil Service, which was made up mostly of British but containing some Malays, a few Indians—but no Chinese.

The Chinese first came as merchants to the Straits Settlements,
and some of them acquired British citizenship. But most of the

Chinese came in the late nineteenth and early twentieth century, when tin assumed world importance and when it was discovered that rubber trees from South America would flourish in Malaya. As I have said, the manpower to work the tin mines and to man the rubber plantations came mostly from China and India. Today the population of the Federation is roughly six million, of which 45 per cent are Malays, 45 per cent Chinese, and 10 per cent Indian. And in some states—notably Penang, Perak, Selangor, and Johore—the Chinese far exceed the Malays in number.

The Malays are an easygoing people who enjoy farming and fishing and who to date have largely disdained trade and commerce. They are a friendly, relaxed people who settled the country against the claims of the aborigines. As I have said, they live largely on the streams and along the seacoast, leaving the jungle alone. They did little to develop the country. They have a society that is simple and uncomplicated and largely democratic. They are passionately devoted to their culture and to their Moslem religion. They look upon the Chinese as those who would disenfranchise them of their heritage.

The present rate of increase of the Chinese is greater than that of the Malays and second only to the Indians. That is one reason the Malays worry. Moreover, in earlier days the Chinese were in Malaya on a temporary basis; they went there to make a stake and then return to China for their declining years. That attitude gradually changed over the years, until today most of the Chinese in Malaya probably do not expect to return, partly because Communist China is no haven for them, partly because their roots have become deeper and deeper in Malaya over the years. The Chinese of Malaya through 1952 remitted faithfully about three million dollars (Malay) a month to their families in Red China, an amount that in 1953 dropped to two million a month. But nowadays they plan to make Malaya their home.

The Chinese are shrewd and industrious. Today they own the wealth of Malaya. They own most of the tin and most of the rubber. They have banks and great mercantile houses. They have the restaurants, the shops, and the truck gardens. Malays and British own many rubber plantations; but the bulk of the latex (poured into molds made from kerosene tins cut in half and then rolled into thick, black slabs and dried) is in the hands of Chinese middlemen. Malays may do the fishing, but they sell their fish to a Chinaman. The truth is that one Chinese fisherman's guild has more wealth than any one of the nine Sultans of Malaya.

Not all the Chinese wealth has been taken out of the hides of the Malays. But the Malays have a strong feeling that it has been. Behind that attitude are years of sharp dealings by the Chinese and discriminations against the Malays. When a Malay went into the rice business, the Chinese who owned the trucks necessary to get the rice to market would raise the rates so high as to drive the Malay from business or force him to buy trucks of his own. When the Malays undertook to form rice-mill co-operatives, the whole force of the Chinese community was directed against them by boycott. The owner of the fishing boat, the net, or the trap operated by a Malay was often a Chinese fish dealer who had a monopoly of the catch at a low price, making the Malay a low-paid laborer. Innumerable instances of this character have built in the Malay's mind suspicion, distrust, and envy of the Chinese that influence every action.

The material success of the Chinese in Malaya would make Horatio Alger stories. Chinese who came to Malaya as coolies ended up as millionaires. I met one in Ipoh who about thirty years ago worked as a day laborer in a tin mine. In the 1940's he ended up with many millions and with six mistresses. When the Japanese took over Malaya, he lost both his women and his wealth. But by 1952 he got his wealth back—and six new and younger mistresses.

The Chinese have outstripped the Malays in other ways too. Badminton is the national game of Malaya, played everywhere. I saw small children playing it; high school teams were in competition; older folks had their contests. Playgrounds at school, the lawns of private homes, vacant lots were busy with the game.

Malaya has the world championship of badminton; and the champion players are Chinese.

Though the Indians in Malaya have been heavily exploited, they have not become an acute problem. Unlike the Chinese, they have remained largely in the laboring class; they are still migratory to a great degree; they have not developed a prosperous middle class nor a group of millionaires. Numerically they are a much smaller group. Although they are more politically alert than the Malays, in the Malay mind they do not loom as dangerously competitive.

But there are other reasons also why the Indians present no serious threat to the stability of Malaya. Few Indians have joined the Communist guerrilla forces. The Indian communities do not foster and support them. The Indians, with their roots deep in the Hindu, Buddhist, and Moslem faiths, have ethical and religious values that the Malayan Chinese by and large do not seem to know. The Indians are struggling against the heavy yoke which time and circumstances have placed on them. But their struggles are in the democratic framework. In Malaya the Indian is emerging as an influential person, a respected leader, and an integral part of a multi-racial community.

Many of the wealthy Chinese of Malaya keep nine sets of books; and the one they keep for the government shows very little taxable income. Many Chinese businessmen in Malaya have numerous aliases. A friend of mine rents a house from one Chinaman at Penang but pays the rent to another Chinaman who runs the corner drugstore. The Chinese use wheels within wheels to conceal income. Little Chinese capital in Malaya is dedicated to the public good. Much of it has been acquired illegally, i.e., tax-free. Most of it represents wealth without a soul, power without any spiritual backing or direction.

Late one night at Ipoh I sat in a private club talking with a group of wealthy Chinese about Malaya's future. They made one serious point. Malayan tin producers operate in an open market as contrasted with the Bolivian tin producers, who have had a liberal long-term contract with the United States. Malayan rubber producers likewise have an enormous insecurity owing to our increase in synthetic-rubber production. "A fair price for a reasonably long term would eliminate the uncertainties at every level of Malayan economic and political life," these Chinese capitalists told me. Malaya's economic stability does depend in large measure on the United States. We therefore have some responsibility for the crises in that nation. We need to use our purchasing power rationally to lessen the risks which the Communist threat has placed on the land.

Other suggestions of these Chinese capitalists were less enlightened. Some thought the United States should send the Marines to Malaya to clean up the guerrillas. Some thought American capital should be poured into Malaya for industrial development.

These were the richest men in the world, men whose incomes were not taxed more than 20 per cent, asking for dollars from overtaxed America. These men were asking for American military aid, while their grandsons dodged the Malayan draft or joined the guerrillas. They were cold, calculating men paying tribute to the guerrillas with one hand and begging for American aid with the other.

At the end I fear I was rude and abrupt. I said that the Chinese should clean their own stables, that they were responsible for Malaya's condition, that if loans were to be made, *they* were the ones to establish an ECA and help finance *America*.

That evening these Chinese millionaires seemed as degenerate as the Buddhist temple I had seen at Penang on Malaya's west coast. It is a snake temple. It has a statue of Buddha, but the walls and floors crawl with vipers. One buys a stick of incense and uses the smoke to stupefy a snake. Then he picks up the live viper, wraps it around his neck, says a prayer, lights a candle, and leaves. It would be a revolting experience to anyone who knows the sublime nature of the teachings of Buddha and his "Noble Eightfold Path."

The Chinese capitalists at the private club in Ipoh were to me as callous and exploitive as the priests in the snake temple at Penang.

At times the entire Chinese community in Malaya seems to be in rebellion. In the spring of 1952 all able-bodied youths were called up for the draft. Malays and Indians responded. But 90 per cent of the Chinese draftees failed to report. They disappeared. Many went into the jungle; some returned to China; others were swallowed up in the clannish Chinese communities that dot the country.

The call of the guerrillas to the young Chinese is still strong in spite of strenuous efforts of the British, Chinese, and Malays. Boy Scout troops, youth clubs, athletic teams, and many other community projects have been promoted to catch the interests of the young people and to tie their loyalties to law and order. At Ampang, not far from Kuala Lumpur, a British Red Cross girl told me, "It should be easier to win these young men over to our side than to kill them after they have joined the guerrillas." And yet the tide still runs the other way. When the guerrillas killed loyal Chinese schoolteachers and brought terror to the classrooms, they were able to keep a tight hold on Chinese youth.

I never will forget another evening spent in Ipoh. Dato Panglimo Bukit Gantang, a forty-year-old Malay who is Mentri Besar of Perak and a lawyer of note, tendered me a delicious fifteen-course Chinese dinner. The food was served in bowls placed in the center of the table, each guest using chopsticks to pick out his portion. The fifteenth course was fish; and after it was finished, each of us was given a towel to clean his hands and face. During the meal there was a lively, continuous conversation. Malays, British, Chinese, and Americans covered a wide range of subjects. This evening the Chinese especially were gay, relaxed men who talked freely of their problems and their ambitions. Near the end of the evening the conversation turned to the large reservations of farming and forest land which the government had set aside exclusively for the Malays. I asked Leong Yew Koh, an elderly Chinese with a keen sense of civic righteousness, how the Chinese community felt about that. He said that he personally thought it was a prudent measure. I asked him why. His answer was most revealing.

"If that land were not set aside for the Malays, we Chinese would get it all."

Quick as a flash, another Chinese spoke up.

"What are you saying, Leong Yew Koh? You know we will get it anyway."

The feeling of the Malays against the Chinese runs deep. On our visit to Gaal Kampon, deep in the jungle in northern Kelantan, we came across a truck that had run off the narrow dirt road and was mired in the mud. Malay villagers hailed us, asking if we would pull them out.

"Is that a truck of a Chinese?" I inquired.

The villagers roared with laughter. "A Chinaman's truck? Do you think we would help pull *him* out of the mud?"

The Malays are not necessarily more civic-minded than the Chinese. Nor do they have a higher regard for culture, education, and integrity. The Chinese—hard-working, aggressive, capable, and prolific—have a high survival value acquired as a result of a harsh and competitive struggle for existence during many centuries. The Malays have great personal charm, owing perhaps to their less competitive heritage. They think the country is theirs, that the foreigner has no claim to it. They feel in the pressure of the Chinese a threat to their way of life.

As I moved about Malaya I came to feel the powerful opposition to the Chinese that fills the Malay's heart. It is not open or overt, but it lies in the subconscious, brooding and sullen. I felt it in the villages along the east coast, where the Chinese are in the minority and where Malay culture still flourishes—villages that are as empty of the hustle and bustle of a Chinese community as a Western town is empty of the hum of New York City.

The Malay fishing fleet goes out at dawn to the South China Sea—thirty-foot open sampans under white sail. Their bows carry figures symbolic of good luck. The entire fleet will occasionally make offerings to the sea gods. The ceremony starts on land with the sacrifice of a male goat and ends with a service and prayer at the mouth of the river.

Women weave at ancient looms in the simple huts that line the beaches and the riverbanks. They sit on the floor, throwing the shuttle back and forth through the warp by hand, weaving each year a few yards of heavy silk cloth.

The markets, which are mostly roofed over but open at the sides, are filled with strange fresh fruits—durian (that smells so awful and tastes so good), jack fruit, mangosteens, bananas, coconuts, langsat, and the prickly rambutan.

The dresses of the women who fill these markets are gay and bright with reds, yellows, and blues.

Many villages have huge rebanna drums—about three feet in diameter and five feet long, painted in gay, colored designs. There are two men to each drum, and they use either their hands or drumsticks, depending on the tempo and beat of the music. The drums are hung on poles between trees, and when a number of them are played together the sound carries for miles. They are used to summon villagers in case of trouble. They are a part of festive occasions. I heard them at the village of Melor, not far from Kota Bharu, where the villagers played them especially for me late one afternoon. In this group there were four drums that soon set up a rhythm with frenzy in it. I recorded the music, and when I play it now, I am once more in Malaya's jungle with primitive man. It is music for a mad orgy—music that is sensuous—music that loosens the muscles and stirs the animal in man—music that makes one want to stomp and whirl and shout.

There are warm hospitality and good food in a Malay village. Malay food is curry, but not as hot as Indian curry. There is the milk of the green coconut, particularly refreshing on a hot day, and exotic fruits in abundance.

In most Malay villages there are *pawangs* or wise men who cast charms of love:

In the name of Allah, the Merciful, the Compassionate!
Burn, burn, sand and earth!
I burn the heart of my beloved
And my fire is the arrow of Arjuna.
If I burnt a mountain, it would fall;
If I burnt rock, it would be riven.
I am burning the heart of my beloved,
So that she is broken and hot with love,
That giveth her no rest night or day,
Burning ever as this sand burns.
Let her cease to love parents and friends!
If she sleeps, awaken her!
If she awakes, cause her to rise and come,
Yielding herself unto me,
Devoid of shame and discretion!
By virtue of the poison of Arjuna's arrow,
By virtue of the invocation "There is no God but Allah
and Muhammad is His Prophet."

A *pawang* invokes the spirits for the protection of a person entering the jungle:

Genii of the forest,
Gnomes of the forest!
Harm not nor hurt my body!
May my teacher be potent to free me from evil!
Away from my body!
I would free all my body.
Mother with the long limp breasts,
Royal chieftainess of the earth to the north,
I pray thee let my life go free.

The *pawang* casts a charm to keep away the prowling tiger:

Ho! mighty Brahma,
Lord of the earth,
Take away thy cat!

> *Harm not nor destroy my body!*
> *May my teacher be potent to free me.*
> *Ho! mighty and powerful Ali!*
> *Bow low and love me*
> *Have love and affection for me!*
> *May my teacher be potent.*

With these incantations brews are often mixed, rituals performed, and ceremonies enacted.

A *pawang* can tell the shape of things to come by rubbing soot and coconut oil on the thumbnail, making incantations, and then using the nail as a mirror to detect future events as he chants:

> *Peace be upon Thee,*
> *Who revealest thyself in the skin of a magic dragon,*
> *Who sittest a hermit on Umbrella Mountain in Java,*
> *I ask of God the lord of magic,*
> *I ask that this my request to thee be granted,*
> *That thou descend and set foot,*
> *Showing the way of apparition.*
> *Show us what we desire,*
> *Set us on the right path.*
> *By virtue of thy miraculous favour*
> *Grant us thy revelation*
> *Which we desire*
> *By the blessing of God*
> *Creator of all the worlds!*

The *pawangs* are Moslems, and their only God is Allah. Yet the old spirits which ruled Malaya before Islam reached the peninsula are still remembered in folklore; and the *pawangs,* with a reverent nod to Allah, teach the people that these ancient gods have residual powers which should be respected.

The Shadow Play of Kelantan which I saw at Kota Bharu is an ancient Malay institution, antedating by many centuries the arrival of the Moslem religion to the country. Though the ancient gods were dethroned by Islam, the new religion did not materially affect the play. The Shadow Play is based on the theory that the ancient gods are still hovering somewhere in the background, alert to attempt a *coup d'état*, easy to arouse to anger and seek revenge. Therefore, the play salutes and honors them and extends to them the friendliest of gestures.

I saw the play twice at Kota Bharu. The first time it was a clear, cloudless night and I was the guest of W. F. Churchill, second cousin of Winston Churchill and able British Agent for Kelantan. The second time I saw the play I was alone, and I sat in a misty drizzle that followed a heavy storm. The performance starts at 9 P.M. and continues until midnight. It usually runs every night for seven nights, one play being put on each night, each being part of a serial.

The stage is a hut about four feet off the ground and about twelve feet square. The front of the hut has no wall but opens onto a lawn where the audience sits. The three walls are bamboo; the roof is thatched. The To' Dalang sits in the middle of the stage near the front. A white cloth screen covers the opening. There is a large lamp between the To' Dalang and the screen, covered at the back and lighting up the screen. The characters are painted in black and white on large transparent fans, and they are worked by the To' Dalang between the lamp and the screen so that they are seen by the audience as shadows.

Behind the To' Dalang is the orchestra, also seated on the floor. The instruments are two large gongs and two small ones in wooden frames, a clarinet, and six drums. Two drums are oblong, played with the hands. Two are large drums that sit slightly tilted on the floor. They are played with sticks. Two are vase-shaped drums with hide stretched across the broad end and with the narrow end open—an instrument played with the hands and producing high and dull sounds through the alternate opening and closing of the narrow end. It's an orchestra quite similar to the ones used in Indonesia (and on the New York City stage) for the Bali dances. It produces stirring, exciting music for the drama and humor of the Shadow Play.

85

The Shadow Play in Kota Bharu is not written. It has been handed down verbally from one generation to another. Its telling depends on the skill of the To' Dalang. The To' Dalang whom I saw at Kota Bharu had the skill and talent of Walter Hampden, Will Rogers, and Bob Hope.

The play opens with a ceremony honoring the four powerful spirits of the universe—earth, fire, air, and water. The ancient gods—many of whom now bear Moslem names—are saluted and pacified. Prophets and dragons, ghosts and giants, devils and vampires are all tendered propitiatory offerings. The offerings are composed of rice, cakes, water scented with jasmine, and betel-nut leaves. Between To' Dalang and the offerings is the smoke of incense rising from a censer of burning charcoal.

To' Dalang bathes his body in the smoke of the incense and invokes the spirits—the spirits of the East (the sun, the guardian of the sun in eclipse, the spirits of the rainbow and the moon); the spirits of the North (including the dragons at the navel of the ocean); the spirit of the South (including the spirits of the forests and the soil); the spirit of the West—Semar. Semar is not only the Supreme God of Malayan mythology; he is also the clown.

In the Shadow Play, Semar is the character known as Pak Dogah. To' Dalang calls for aid from Semar. "I am the first of the actors, the original dalang," To' Dalang recites. "Stay not far from me, you who stand erect on one leg with crossed arms on a black moss-green rock under the rose-red umbrella of the sun and on white earth. Drive away evil genii, the accursed spirits and gnomes of the soil, spirits of the water. Avaunt ye powers of evil."

Then To' Dalang lifts his head, shouts "Ha!" and throws a handful of rice across the room. At that moment the orchestra splits the air with a thundering outburst. To' Dalang continues to throw rice. Suddenly, with a deafening clap, the orchestra stops and there is a deep silence for a few moments. Then the screen is rolled down and the play commences.

The play has many characters. Raja Seri Rama is champion of Good against Evil. To' Maha Siku is the first of all medicine men. There are numerous demons—Hanuman, Rawana, Jin Pentra Kala. They show sharp teeth and fangs and terrifying grimaces and usually carry threatening swords. These demons are the aggressive type, harassing and tempting Good and threatening man. Their most worthy opponent is Semar, the god turned clown. He is bald-headed, short, stocky, and potbellied, and his navel protrudes. His face reflects the wisdom of the village elder. He's no weakling. On the contrary, he's rough and ready, outspoken, quick to attack Evil and defend Good. What impressed me most about him was his tremendous nose, slightly bent upward like an elephant's tusk, and the determined set of his jaw. Plainly he was not a man to tangle with. He is always attended by his follower, Wah Long, who is a half-sized duplicate of his master. Wah Long likes to move out front and taunt the enemy. But he is always the first to retreat, hiding behind Pak Dogah.

The audience adores this couple. Wah Long is the Lou Costello of the play. Pak Dogah is Sancho Panza and Falstaff. Though a clown, he has the wisdom of the ages. When demons threaten destruction, when the music indicates that disaster is near, when Wah Long cringes, Pak Dogah stands firm and quickly mows the demons down with a cutting remark. He counters their darts with puns, with ridicule, with shafts of insight into their motives. And all the while the orchestra gives him support. When the situation is beyond salvation, when all is lost, when Wah Long is in panic, Pak Dogah frightens the opponent by exposing his Achilles' heel. And the orchestra adds the exclamation point.

The audience loves Pak Dogah. It waits on his words and laughs at his every move. He is the villager who outsmarts the cleverest god. He is their champion against the world. He is common sense and village wisdom against the foreigner's chicanery. He's not only the average villager; he's the ancient Malayan divinity, the Supreme God to whom all Malays, in the name of Allah, pay the greatest respect.

I too loved Pak Dogah. I missed many of his thrusts, but I caught the theme of the story and his strategy. The To' Dalang was skillful in building the tale to crisis after crisis. When the moments were dark and it looked as if the evil characters that poured in from the right of the stage were about to overwhelm Pak Dogah, I found myself anxious for the hero. But when the tenseness reached the peak, Pak Dogah, with a casual drawling remark or with a sharp command punctuated by the orchestra, always saved the situation. The little man with the protruding navel and monstrous upturned nose had the hearts of all of us. And much of his wisdom was no more profound than "Go soak your head!"

The legend of Pak Dogah is deep in Malay folklore. One day, when bathing, the Supreme Divinity scraped the dirt off his body, rolled it into a small ball, and buried it in the mud, just like paddy seed is planted in the muddy rice field. Out of the planting Pak Dogah arose. One day Pak Dogah, while bathing, scraped the dirt off his body, rolled it in a ball, and planted it. Thus Wah Long was created.

Semar or Pak Dogah is the most important symbol in northeast Malaya. Semar is the name for young nursery rice plants. The ancient god Semar survived the conquest of Islam because of the potency of his symbolism. Though the Shadow Play presents him in the rough character of a clown, he has the most important role. It is Pak Dogah who always saves Good from being destroyed by Evil.

The shrewd, powerful, and wise Pak Dogah can deliver the Malays from the evil demons of the spirit world. But delivery from the evil of the Chinese monopolist takes more than charms, incantations, and prayers. That has been undertaken by the Rural and Industrial Development Authority (RIDA), some of whose projects I visited with Bill Bangs out of Kota Bharu.

RIDA supplies what Malays have never been able to accumulate—*capital*. Winstedt, in *The Malays, A Cultural History*, gives three historical reasons why this was true—the communist inclination of the tribe to enrich it, not the individual; the tendency of chiefs in the old patriarchal states to confiscate the wealth of those who waxed rich; and the Moslem law against interest. These customs are changing fast. But they have handicapped the Malays in competition with the Chinese, who knew no restraints on capital accumulation.

As I have said, the Malays built their villages along the riverbanks and seacoasts—settlements that were self-supporting rice-growing and fishing communities. The interior of the country was little developed, not only because of the jungle but because of the water supply. In Malaya the red and yellow clays hold water in colloidal form; there is no water table. Thus the people are dependent on river and surface water rather than on springs. The Malay settlements today follow the pattern of old; the river valley shapes the political and social units for the people.

This often means that the villagers are far from the markets where their crops must be sold. RIDA builds narrow jeep roads that bicycles and carts can travel. RIDA furnishes timbers for bridges and pontoons that serve as connecting links in a chain of improved communications for the Malay villager.

RIDA, in order to break the monopoly the Chinese have had in rice milling, helps finance rice-mill co-operatives for Malays. In the state of Kelantan, of which Kota Bharu is the capital, RIDA has now organized twenty-seven such co-operatives. I visited some of them. They are operating smoothly and successfully; the profit that once went to the middleman now accrues to the farmer. (The Malays, like Americans, polish their rice white. The husks that contain the precious vitamins are fed to stock.)

RIDA is introducing tractors on dry paddy land, financing the replanting of small rubber plantations with high-yielding trees, and promoting central latex processing plants that will perform the wholesale marketing function and by-pass the Chinese middleman.

RIDA is helping Malays acquire fishing boats with deep freezes so that they can reach distant fishing grounds. It is financing boatbuilding yards for Malays, fish curing for Malays, fishing gear for Malays.

RIDA is building demonstration ponds where fresh-water fish can be reared both for the market and for village consumption.

RIDA finances small business: coconut-oil co-operatives; arts and crafts societies that market silverware, silk cloth, and other products of cottage industries; small textile factories; tile plants; furniture factories.

I visited the furniture factory of Ismail Ysoff of Kota Bharu financed by RIDA. Ysoff, an able, industrious Malay, had been put out of business by the Chinese furniture factories, for he had to work by hand while they had saws, lathes, and other power-driven machines. RIDA loaned Ysoff $6,000 (Malay) to install modern machinery. His place is now a thriving establishment with a half dozen employees. Thanks to RIDA, Ysoff is back in competition; and his grin that reaches from ear to ear acknowledges his gratitude.

RIDA is financing water-supply projects for the Malay villages. It is training rural leaders in a wide range of skills necessary for rural development. It is constructing schools in villages, teaching girls domestic science, installing playing fields for children, and building community centers where meetings, plays, movies, and lectures may be held and libraries kept.

Some of these projects have Chinese as beneficiaries. But in large measure they are designed for Malays. The plan is to help the Malay enjoy his inheritance. RIDA wants to deliver him from the domination of foreigners who now own the country and lay siege to it through terrorists whom they finance and support.

RIDA is Pak Dogah in the industrial and agricultural field.

CHAPTER 8

THE MELTING POT

The British and Malays share some of the blame
for the rebellion in the Chinese community. The
Chinese have long been aliens in the land—grandfather, son, and
grandson. They have been a political minority with few civil
rights.

Some sultans have let a few Chinese own land. Yet by and
large landownership has not been available to them. Very few
political offices have been open to the Chinese. They have not
qualified for the Civil Service.

Voting rights have largely been withheld from all the people.
There have been no elective offices at either the federal or the
state level. Some municipal elections have been held, but these
were few in number and relatively unimportant. Yet even in them
most Chinese had no vote, for only a small fraction of them were
admitted to citizenship.

In the Federation of Malaya—the union of the nine Malay
states—the British have full appointive power. There is a Federal
Legislative Council of seventy-five members, most of whom are

appointed by the High Commissioner. This Council has legislative functions subject to the large residual powers of the High Commissioner. The qualifications for seats in the Council have been so drawn as to guarantee the Malays a majority. In practice the Chinese have always been granted a minority of seats—in 1952, fourteen out of seventy-five. And only one out of the eleven government departments has been allowed the Chinese.

Political discrimination against the Chinese is one reason why that community sits glowering at the government. It owns the country but is not welcome in its councils. That is why it lends an attentive ear to the Communist underground, whose constant propaganda is racial equality and the elimination of any discrimination against any group on account of its nationality.

At Ipoh I discussed this problem with several prominent Chinese in a long after-dinner talk. One elderly millionaire—his tongue loosened by brandy—was bemoaning the lack of opportunities open to the Chinese in Malaya.

"Opportunities?" I exclaimed. "Why, you *own* the country."

"But we have no political opportunites. A Chinese boy who reaches maturity finds he is barred from all civic posts, from owning land. He's an outcast in the country where he was born. That's why he turns to the guerrillas. For the guerrillas promise that under Communism all races will equally inherit the country and equally run it."

"These are sons of wealthy Chinese?"

"Many of them. You see, it takes four generations of Chinese to produce a guerrilla."

He went on to explain that the coolie who came from China worked out his heart in the tin mine. His son, however, owned the tin mine. His grandson multiplied the ownership manyfold. His great-grandson rebelled at the system whereby the people who owned the country had nothing whatever to say about its management.

The resentment of the Chinese has endless manifestations. The University of Malaya, founded several years ago, announced the establishment of a Chinese department with instruction in English. In reply the Chinese community announced early in 1953 the raising of funds for the creation of a Chinese University. And so the competition between the races goes.

Templer is alive to the danger of keeping the Chinese a political minority and denying them civil rights. And he has taken important steps to eliminate that discrimination. One of the most dramatic is his program for Kinta Valley, which he adopted against heavy pressure from the British and Malays. As I have said, Kinta Valley is the heart of the tin industry of Malaya; and it also harbors a virulent breed of Chinese guerrillas. The bandits, generously supported by the Chinese community, have thrived there. Leong Yew Koh and other civic-minded Chinese were tired of the guerrillas and ashamed of the way in which the Chinese tin miners have been their accomplices. Templer challenged them to clean their own stables. They responded by putting up several hundred thousand dollars to raise, equip, and maintain fifteen hundred Chinese troops to hunt down the Communist guerrillas in the Kinta Valley and liquidate them.

I stood with Templer as he addressed these trainees. It was not a complimentary talk. He did not praise them for their valor or courage. He did not comment on the excellence of their record on the target range. He spoke mostly about the Chinese in Malaya, the great opportunities Malaya had offered them, the record of their industry and ability. He was brutally frank in saying that the guerrillas were a Chinese product—manned by Chinese, supported by Chinese, protected by Chinese. He said that the Chinese have a great role to play in the new Malaya of tomorrow, that they must be citizens of Malaya, not forever owing their allegiance to an outside power.

"It is time, however, for the Chinese to assume some civic responsibilities," he concluded.

"This is your chance. Will these carbines find their way into guerrilla camps or will they be used to kill guerrillas? Have Malayan Chinese the capacity for citizenship? Some say no. I

93

say yes. I am trusting you. If you fail in this, the Chinese cause in Malaya will suffer greatly."

When Templer's fighting words had been translated into Chinese, the young trainees cheered him to the echo. There was no doubt that these Chinese youngsters now had a cause for which to live and, if necessary, to die.

On my visit to this camp I met two young Chinese officers in charge of the training program—Lieutenant Huang Chong Sen and Lieutenant Yee Tien Song. They had asked to see me. And we talked for a half hour or so in the doorway of a spick-and-span bamboo kitchen where six Chinese cooks were preparing fish for dinner. It appears that these officers were trained by the American Army in India near the end of World War II. They sought me out to express their gratitude to America for the training they had received. After the formalities were over, we discussed Kinta Valley and Templer's program. I asked these two Chinese officers if it would succeed in the Kinta Valley. There was the light of crusaders in their eyes when Sen answered, "We Chinese will clean up this mess—if Malaya will only trust us and give us time." And Song broke in to say, "These trainees are good boys. You can tell America she will be proud of what we do in the Kinta Valley."

Templer realizes that political therapy may often be more effective than military tactics.

He has announced the formation of a multi-racial Federation Army in which Malays, Chinese, Indians, and Eurasians will serve.

He has stood against the colonial attitude of reserving clubs for the white man exclusively. In attacking the color line at one club in Kuala Lumpur he stated that the things for which men of different races and different colors were fighting in Malaya "transcend any differences there might be of skin or color or custom."

Templer has promoted and encouraged the Boy Scouts, whose ideals cut across all racial lines and who teach a citizenship in which all nationalities have a stake. He is promoting a medical-care program for rural areas that serves all races. He is behind an educational program that does not discriminate against any nationality but treats them all as equals.

He has promoted village councils—elective bodies chosen by the villagers with a large degree of local autonomy and powers of self-government in matters of schools, roads, health, sanitation, and the like.

Most important of all, Templer has fashioned a law which lowers the barriers to citizenship. Very few Chinese—less than a third—had ever been eligible for citizenship. In September 1952 he and the sultans of the nine Malay states caused a new code to be promulgated, admitting many Chinese and Indians to citizenship in the Federation of Malaya. Any person who was born in Malaya and one of whose parents was born there has been made a citizen by operation of law. It is estimated that by that provision about 60 per cent of resident Chinese (1,200,000) and 30 per cent of the resident Indians (180,000) have acquired citizenship.

Now that Chinese and Indians have a broad base of citizenship in the country, Templer is opening the Civil Service to them. For every four Malays in the Civil Service, one non-Malay Asian will now be admitted.

The attainment of citizenship by these large alien blocks has stirred new political activities. Malaya has had four main political parties. Two are organized along racial lines—the United Malay National Organization (UMNO) for Malays and the Malayan Chinese Association (MCA) for Chinese. These parties have not been entirely parochial. The slogan of MCA, headed by Sir Cheng-lock Tan, has indeed been "one country, one people, one government." He has wanted the Chinese to transfer their loyalties to Malaya. And he has urged the Malays to give the Chinese equal rights, starting with landownership. "A land title," he maintains, "is the hoop that holds the barrel together." And the progressive element in UMNO has been willing to accept members of other races as full nationals, if they in turn are willing to pledge their loyalty to Malaya.

Two other political parties have cut across all racial lines and opened their membership to people of every race—the Independence for Malaya Party (headed by a distinguished Malay, Dato Onn Bin Jaafar, who was the founder of UMNO) and the Pan Malayan Labor Party, patterned after England's Labour Party. These latter two have been quite inactive.

What will be the shape of things to come, no one knows. In December 1952, when seven municipal elections were held, UMNO and MCA joined forces to defeat the Independence for Malaya Party. They carried five of the seven towns for their alliance candidates—Kuala Lumpur, Malacca, Batu Pahat, Muar, and Johore Bahru.

The Malayan political pot has begun to boil with fresh demands for the independence of the nation. Tungku Abdul Rahman, head of UMNO, has called for conferences of all Malayan political parties to discuss plans for independence. In late 1952 he said, "Some Malays consider that other races have no right here. But I say Malaya has sufficient wealth and resources for fair distribution to all who need them."

Certainly Malaya will have her independence. That is desired not only by the Malays, the Chinese, and the Indians, but by most of the British as well. The time when that can be achieved will depend on the efficiency of the melting pot.

The moral of Malaya is, indeed, the moral of the melting pot. The story of the great American melting pot where people of many tongues, many races, many religions were welded into one united nation is a story so well known as to be almost forgotten. In America we have always assumed that a Pole could be a halfback or a congressman, that a Jew could run for governor or be a judge, that a Negro could hold office or be the champion boxer. We are all Americans with equal rights and equal responsibilities. The first generation of immigrants might be clannish, living aloof from the community and resisting absorption into it. But the second generation is quickly swept into the stream of American life.

There have been two main reasons for our success. First, each person has had a stake in the country; there has been equality of opportunity regardless of race, creed, or color; political rights have not been reserved for a select few but have been enjoyed by all the people. Second, we have had a public school system. The public school has been our real melting pot. There one language, one history, one culture were taught. The teacher ignored racial prejudices and enlisted students of different colors, different faiths, different races in one cause. The teachers of our public school system have indeed been the real evangelists of Americanism.

Malaya shows what will happen if people of several races have neither equality before the law nor the unifying influence of a common education. The tensions grow and grow, tearing the country apart. Templer knows this. And there is an increasing awareness of it among the Malays, who long tolerated the Chinese and Indians as alien residents but withheld from them most of the political rights.

One afternoon in Kuala Lumpur I talked with Dato E. E. C. Thuraisingham about the problem. He is a heavy-set, middle-aged Indian with gentle manners and a brain of fine texture. He is Member for Education in the Federation of Malaya. He spoke with feeling about the broad social program the British have for Malaya and the necessity for giving political equality to each race. Great advances would be made if everyone had the right to vote, if all discriminations in the laws were eliminated. But more than that was needed, he maintained. If the school system of Malaya were not reorganized, the races would never be united in one national cause.

I have referred earlier to the vernacular schools in Malaya. Each race has its own vernacular school. The Chinese have theirs and teach only Chinese language, Chinese history, Chinese culture. They orient the students not to Malaya, but to China. They teach the glory of China, not the promise of Malaya. These schools total close to seventeen hundred, and practically all of the Chinese children attend them.

The Malays have vernacular schools of a distinct religious character.

The Indians have vernacular schools too. But the Indian schools, unlike the Chinese, do not instill in the young a loyalty to a foreign country. Nehru—statesman that he is—has made it clear to the Indians in Malaya that those who permanently reside there should not look to India as their fatherland. No Chinese government in Malaya's long history has ever done the same.

Thuraisingham reviewed Malaya's vernacular school system for me. And then he said:

"The salvation of Malaya must be found in the public school system. Education must be compulsory. The vernacular schools must come to an end. All students—Malays, Indians, Chinese—must be taught one language. They must be taught pride in their communities, pride in their states, pride in this nation."

Leaning forward at his desk, he raised his voice to say, "If *all* the children attend multi-racial schools, we can weld *one* nation out of these different races."

Today Malaya is not one nation but an aggregation of racial groups. The tensions are so great that the British cannot leave for the time being. If they withdrew at this juncture, chaos would probably result. Then the Communists would certainly take over.

There is still talk of colonialism in Malaya. The British record in Malaya has its seamy side. Britain today has important stakes in Malaya. It is estimated that Malaya makes the largest dollar contribution of any of Britain's colonies to the sterling pool—an amount that has been running close to $500,000,000 a year. In other words, Malaya, though acquiring dollars with its rubber and tin, is not allowed to spend them for steel, cement, and other needed materials. Five of its six dollars go into the sterling pool.

If this were a permanent vise in which Malaya was held, it would present political problems as serious as those which most colonies have had. The crucially important consideration is the direction of British thinking and the nature of British policy for the future. The British have an enlightened program for Malaya, and the leadership of Malcolm MacDonald and Sir Gerald Templer is liberal and progressive. They contemplate independence for Malaya and political equality for all her people. In other words, Britain not only plans independence for Malaya; she is taking progressive steps in that direction. Her interim management is essential if the Chinese Communists are not to win by default.

Templer and MacDonald speak of the day when Malaya—rich, strong, unified, and independent—will be a proud member of the British Commonwealth. An increasing number of Malays have the same desire. More and more Chinese and Indians are making Malaya their fatherland. Communist terror still grips the land. But the civil conflict is becoming more and more manageable as political therapy is used to cure the basic ills of the nation.

The Communist propaganda continues to demand equality of all races and to promise it to all nationalities the day the Communists win. There is no reason why equality among the races cannot be acquired the democratic way. There is no reason why national independence cannot be achieved. But it can be done if—and only if—Thuraisingham's words are heeded and the secret of the melting pot, discovered in America, is rediscovered in Malaya.

PART **2**

THE HUKS OF THE PHILIPPINES

CHAPTER 1

MANILA BOY

I sat in a Philippine Army camp not far from Manila talking with thirty-two-year-old Tomas Santiago, alias Manila Boy. He is short and slight, even for a Filipino. He combs his shiny black hair straight back with a flourish. He stood barefooted before me, looking me in the eyes. His trousers were ragged; his shirt was open at the throat; his brown coat showed patches at the elbows. His eyes flashed as he spoke, and his words came with the rapidity and force of machine-gun fire. He was speaking of the plight of the Philippine peasants, of his aversion to Communism, of his devotion to Ramon Magsaysay.[1]

Ramon Magsaysay—Secretary of National Defense since 1950 and the one who introduced me to Manila Boy—was the man Manila Boy came to Manila to murder. Luis Taruc, thirty-eight-year-old Communist leader of the Philippine Huks, had given him that assignment. Manila Boy was glad of it. For months he had been Taruc's faithful bodyguard; for months he had listened with excitement to Huk plans for seizing the Philippine Government.

[1]Pronounced Mawgh-Sigh-Sigh.

103

He had lain in wait for ambushes; he had been a loyal and fervent aide in the Huk cause. He was with the Communist high command as they sat around small campfires in the jungles of Luzon talking of the complaints of the peasants and the injustices of the government. This assignment to murder Magsaysay pleased him no end. Now he was to be the instrument for writing a glorious chapter in Huk history.

But Manila Boy on the road to Manila—like Saul on the road to Damascus—was converted. The man who resolved to kill Magsaysay became his apostle. Today he is an evangelist in Magsaysay's cause.

Manila Boy told me the reason for his conversion. At Taruc's command he had come down out of the hills dressed as a simple peasant. He carried grenades, and pistols were concealed in his loose clothing. In a few days he reached Manila and by discreet inquiry located Magsaysay's office. When he got within two blocks of it, he passed a group of Philippine peasants engaged in animated conversation. They were discussing Magsaysay; and what he heard made Manila Boy turn back and join them. They were praising Magsaysay, calling him a hero. They said he was the people's friend, that he would punish any soldier who harmed a peasant. Manila Boy, who had seen with his own eyes the cruelty of the Philippine Constabulary, challenged these statements. But the street-corner group lashed him with their tongues. Then an ex-Huk among them recognized Manila Boy, took him aside, and asked him to talk with Magsaysay.

The next morning Manila Boy and the ex-Huk walked into Magsaysay's office. They sat and argued for an hour. At the end of that time Manila Boy gave his hand to Magsaysay, emptied his pockets of grenades, handed over his pistols, and said:

"I came to kill you. Now please, let me work for you."

Magsaysay made him face the charges that the law had against him.

"If the charges are true, plead guilty. If they are not, stand trial."

Manila Boy took his medicine; he received a sentence, was paroled to Magsaysay, and today works for and worships the man.

I talked with other ex-Huks who had had similar experiences—twenty-five-year-old Manuel Cayod, alias Commander Amat; twenty-one-year-old Juan Suerte, alias Commander Roger; seventeen-year-old Francisco Aguilar, alias Pering; eighteen-year-old Jose D. Aguilar, alias Peiping. I sat in Magsaysay's office and saw dozens upon dozens of dirty and bedraggled young men from sixteen to twenty-five years old walk in and renounce their career of crime and violence. In each case Magsaysay made them face the charges against them. They would be back shortly, paroled to him. Some would be assigned to squads who were ferreting out Huks in the hills; some would be made intelligence agents for the Philippine Army; some would undertake bold espionage projects against the Huks. Others would be rehabilitated and returned to civilian life.

Today the ranks of converted Huks are swelling. A hard core of Communists (about four thousand) remains in the hills under the command of Casto Alejandrina, faithful to death to the creed of the Kremlin. But their followers are trooping to the other side.

Manila Boy goes about the countryside, talking to the villagers. Though diminutive in size, he has a force and energy that explode in sharply punctuated words. He knows about Communism and the way Soviet Russia uses it for empire building. He knows that the Communists in the Philippines would create a new order of serfdom for the people. He tells the people these things. He also tells them how opposed the Huks are to the Church, how they violate women, how they degrade marriage. He tells the people of the disrespect the Huks have for priests. And then he emphasizes an idea that impresses the freedom-loving Filipino:

"Why make the Islands a tail to Russia's kite? The Philippines must be independent—free of all foreign domination. We can run our own affairs. We have the votes. We can pass the laws. We can make the Islands a decent place for everyone." His brown eyes flash as he builds to the climax.

"Magsaysay will see to it that no one starves. Magsaysay will put an end to injustices. He's one of us. Let's put our trust in him."

CHAPTER **2**

THE LADY WITH THE TWO BASKETS

In 1950 these Huks numbered at least twenty thousand. They were armed and under the central command of an astute Politburo operating from Manila. These twenty thousand armed Huks had at least two million Filipinos in reserve. In large areas they had the people on their side. In western Luzon in Zambales Province they controlled several towns, even to the collection of taxes. They ruled by force and terror. In those days all they had to do to control an outlying city was to kill a man, leave his body in the street with a tag reading, *He resisted the Huks.* The city was terrorized; the mayor was told to do what the Huks said—or else. A Catholic priest who spoke up in protest was made an example. A rope was tied to each leg, and each rope was tied to a carabao. Then the carabaos were driven in opposite directions, tearing the holy man in two. Thus did the Communists use terror to fasten a hold on the Philippines. Their hold became more and more paralyzing. More and more villages were cowed into submission.

The internal conditions in the Philippines were ideal for disaster. The Armed Forces were corrupt, inefficient, and demoralized. In some areas the Huks were acting in the role of the constabulary. Trucking firms were paying toll to the Huks in order to keep their trucks rolling. The Huks were managing huge affairs—they were smuggling arms and war matériel from the Philippines into Formosa, China, Indonesia, and other parts of Southeast Asia. (The northern tip of Luzon is only six hundred miles from the Chinese mainland.)

The Philippine Government seemed unable to cope with the emergency. The treasury had a large and mounting deficit, with taxes covering only about 60 per cent of expenditures. Schoolteachers were not being paid. Agricultural and industrial output was below the pre-war level, although the population had increased by 25 per cent. The standard of living of the people was falling. The real wages of workers had dropped in some instances below 50 cents a day. Exports had fallen; the country was living on imports; but the end was in sight, for its foreign exchange was fast being drained away. The peso was depreciating on the black market, dropping from two to an American dollar to four.

There was a real inflation, prices being on the average three and a half times as high as pre-war. Inequalities in income—always large in the Islands—had become increasingly great. While the poor got poorer, the profits of the wealthy people multiplied, owing in part to the inflation. The United States poured two billions into the Islands at the end of World War II. On that largesse the rich got richer; huge fortunes were made.

The inflation, fed by large budgetary deficits and excessive creation of credit, promised to get worse. Inefficiency and corruption in government were rampant.

Chinese immigration visas were selling for from two to three thousand dollars. Only the poor paid taxes. The personal and corporate income taxes were miserly. It was common talk in Manila that for a few hundred dollars a millionaire could arrange to pay no taxes. Businessmen feared a collapse of the peso; agricultural and industrial workers were full of despair; unemployment was mounting; the public had lost confidence in the government.

Then came the election of 1949. The election was notoriously dishonest.

Time magazine reported that the Filipinos had learned about government "from Hague and Pendergast as well as from Madison and Jefferson." Voting lists were manipulated so that when a man appeared at his precinct to vote, he was advised that his new precinct was miles distant, too far for him to reach that day. Ballots were forged; ballot boxes were burned; election officials were bribed. The election was managed in such a highhanded fashion that even Filipino employees of the American embassy who lived at Cavite, adjoining the American naval base at Sangley Point, were barred from voting. Elpidio Quirino, running for President on the Liberal ticket, defeated Jose Laurel, running on the Nationalista ticket. Though the margin of victory was great, many Filipinos felt the election had been stolen. Discontent rode high; there was a rumbling in the villages.

By 1950 conditions were worse. The new Quirino government was halting and indecisive. When I visited Manila in the late summer of 1950, disaster seemed imminent. Drastic measures were needed, but there did not seem to be courage and character for the occasion. Men like Myron Cowen, American Ambassador to the Philippines, were alert to the dangers. The Quirino government finally agreed to the appointment of an American Survey Mission headed by Daniel W. Bell of the American Security and Trust Company, Washington, D.C. Its report, dated October 9, 1950, was blunt in its criticisms, specific in its recommendations, and sober in the alarms it sounded.

In the fall of 1950 many who spoke reassuringly in public were frightened at heart. It seemed that this young Asian republic, which had received its independence on July 4, 1946, was doomed.

The Huks became more and more the invisible government. The plan was thoroughly conceived and well laid. The Politburo would seize the Islands in the spring of 1952. There were some

Americans in high positions who feared that by 1950 the situation had deteriorated so far that the Huks could actually have taken over the government at that time, had they realized their own strength and the weakness of the Quirino regime.

At this time Magsaysay was in the Congress but not well known to the Filipinos. He was known, however, in Manila circles; and he had a high reputation there for honesty and courage. He had been a guerrilla against the Japanese during their occupation and came out of the underground untarnished by any Communist influence. A small group decided that he was the man of the hour, the one to reorganize the Army and restore its prestige.

Some say the American Ambassador was the moving spirit behind the project. However that may be, a strong group of Liberal senators spearheaded the drive for Magsaysay. They knew that the forces of disintegration were fast at work in the Islands. The Huks were striking more and more frequently; their terror was making itself felt in the arteries of communication; main roads were becoming more and more insecure; railroads were constantly interrupted; the widow of the late Manuel L. Quezon was cruelly ambushed. The Huks seemed able to strike at will. The Army was not able to cope with the situation. No matter how severe the police measures, violence flourished.

President Elpidio Quirino was persuaded to name Magsaysay as Secretary of National Defense on September 1, 1950. From then until his resignation February 28, 1953, Magsaysay rendered brilliant service.

The top command of the Huks had such confidence, it decided Magsaysay should die the day he took office. No more effective propaganda could be designed for the Huk cause than announcement to the world that the Huks could kill top government officials as and when they pleased.

The Huk plan to murder Magsaysay was well laid. One Rizal— a young Filipino who had joined the Huks as an escape from a scandal—was to make an appointment to see Magsaysay at ten o'clock on the evening of September 1. Two other Huks were to

110

follow Rizal in a jeep and interrupt the conference to fill Magsaysay with lead.

Rizal is a glorious name in Philippine history. Jose Rizal was a famous Philippine revolutionary hero of the nineteenth century, and this young Rizal was his grandson, as Magsaysay well knew. Young Rizal's voice on the telephone was serious and filled with concern; he had important messages to deliver to Magsaysay; the conference would have to be secret, for if it were known, even Magsaysay's life might be endangered. And so the rendezvous was laid at an unsuspicious residence on the outskirts of Manila.

Magsaysay appeared at ten o'clock. He stayed an hour and reached home untouched. Within a few minutes after he had left the rendezvous, the two assassins arrived. They had been delayed by jeep trouble. They were anxious to have Rizal make a new appointment with Magsaysay. But Rizal, while pretending to co-operate, used various excuses. While the days dragged on, Magsaysay was making a convert out of Rizal.

The conversion started the night of the rendezvous. Young Rizal took a liking to Magsaysay, and Magsaysay spotted at once young Rizal's vulnerable point. It was the grandson's pride in his grandfather, the man who gave his life in 1896 for the independence of the Philippines from Spain. Magsaysay gave young Rizal an insight into international Communism. He explained what it is and how it works. The loyalty of a Communist, whether he be a Huk in the Philippines, or a guerilla in Malaya, or a comrade in North Korea, is to the Russian fatherland first. Russia today is empire building, using fifth columns within the various countries to destroy existing governments. Why make the Philippines a colony of Russia? Why not make the Islands independent of all foreign powers?

While Magsaysay was educating Rizal, Rizal was educating Magsaysay on the viewpoint of many of the Huks. As the two men sat in secret conferences day after day young Rizal poured out to Magsaysay all the woes of the Philippine underdog.

Shortly the two men became friends and allies, pledging each other support against the Communists. Magsaysay at once asked Rizal for help. No solution of the Huk problem would be complete until the underground Communist Politburo was liquidated. Who made up the Politburo? Where did the members live?

Rizal, who was a trusted agent of the Communist high command, put Magsaysay on the road to discovery. One morning he had Magsaysay stand concealed in his apartment when an old lady with two baskets came to the door. One basket contained meat, the other bread and vegetables. These were rations which she was distributing to the top command of the Communist Party.

"Follow her, and in a few days you will know the names and addresses of each member of the Politburo," Rizal whispered to Magsaysay.

She was followed, and the next week at three o'clock one morning, Military Intelligence Service (MIS) raided numerous residences simultaneously. Each member of the Politburo was arrested. To Magsaysay the greatest surprise was Jose Lava, the head of the Politburo. He was a quiet university professor with whom Magsaysay had innocently been having lunch every week or so. It was this unobtrusive professor who had planned Magsaysay's death.

The raid went off so swiftly, its secret was so well kept, that MIS found the records of the Philippine Communist Party intact. They contained a mine of information that was invaluable—clues that were promptly used to smash the backbone of the Huk organization. So it was that the man whom the Huks planned to murder the day he took office managed by good luck and astute maneuvering to have the Politburo in jail in less than two months. They were tried on charges equivalent to our crime of sedition, and on May 11, 1951, each was convicted and sentenced either to death or to life imprisonment.

CHAPTER 3

THE HUKLINGS

The Huks trace back to the Socialist Party formed in the 1930's by Pedro A. Santos, who was bent on agrarian reform. Luis Taruc was indeed associated with Santos in that party. During the Japanese occupation the Huks became an underground group working for Philippine independence, as Benjamin Appel describes in *Fortress in the Rice*. Their name Hukbalahap is an abbreviation of five Tagalog words meaning the People's Army against the Japanese. Taruc organized the Huks in 1942 and under that banner recruited 100,000 Filipinos during the Japanese occupation. They were responsible for the death of about 20,000 Japanese and Japanese collaborators.

There were two other underground groups operating in the Philippines at that time. One was a group commanded by Magsaysay. Another was the Wachis, an affiliate of the Communist Party in China, and commanded by a former Chinese shopkeeper, Hwang Chieh. The Wachis (who, so far as I could learn, no longer operate in the Philippines) were all Chinese. They were the ones primarily responsible for converting the Huks into Communists. During or shortly after the Japanese occupation the top Huks became Communists, and they have been under Communist command to this day.

Once the Islands were freed of the Japanese, the Huks changed their tactics and their name. They became the HMB—the People's Liberation Army; and, Communist-style, they set forth on a program of force, violence, and propaganda designed to overthrow the Philippine Government.

The Huks remained almost exclusively an organization of Filipinos. Some foreigners, however, joined them, including quite a few Chinese Communists and a handful of Americans. Ronald Dorsey left the U. S. Navy to become a Huk officer. Another was the American Communist, William J. Pomeroy of Rochester, N.Y., who served in the Philippines in the U. S. Army during the war. On his discharge he returned to the Islands, married a Filipino girl, and joined the Communist high command. Pomeroy was the intelligentsia in the Communist cause. He was a thoroughgoing Marxist, trained in dialectical materialism.

Up to the time of Pomeroy's enlistment in the Huk cause, the Huks had had more brawn than brains. Pomeroy undertook, among other things, to teach them the Marxist creed, to instill in the youngsters a passion for class warfare, to develop in them a fanatical faith that would lead them through torture, machine-gun fire, and starvation to the new world of Communism. To this end Pomeroy helped set up Stalin University. It was a roving university that followed the Huks wherever their advances or retreats might carry them. Sometimes it met in a clearing on a remote hillside; sometimes it had a grass hut for a classroom. Its location was always temporary. It met wherever the fortunes of the Huks might lead.

Its lessons were the writings of Marx, Lenin, and Stalin. There were no optional ones. This university offered a standard curriculum. Only straight Communist dogma was taught—class warfare, the doom of capitalism, dialectical materialism, guerrilla tactics, the Red flag, and the *Internationale*. It taught "American imperialism," "Catholic fascism," and "Russian democracy." The course lasted about four months.

The students were hand-picked by guerrilla units. They were chosen for their qualities of leadership, for their intelligence, for the likelihood that they would make zealous converts. Those who graduated were given positions of responsibility. I talked with Huk men and Huk women who had taken the course. They had almost invariably been put in command of troops. They almost unanimously praised their American teacher. This American teacher, who now is in a Philippine prison serving a life sentence, produced hundreds of leaders for the lower echelons of the Huk organization. I found them to be almost invariably staunch, dyed-in-the-wool Communists who would make no compromise, who would give no ground. They had the light of fanatics in their eyes, a light that would burn brightly through long years in a dark dungeon.

Such a person is Andrea de los Reyes, alias Commander Bulaklak. She commanded troops in Quezon Province, Luzon. When I talked with her she was at Camp Murphy (near Manila) in a barbed-wire stockade built for female Huks. There were dozens of women there. Some were wives of Huks, with babies in their arms, who had been caught up in a dragnet and not yet screened. Others were camp followers of the Huks. But Andrea was a hardened Communist guerrilla. She had commanded troops, and from the swagger of her walk one could tell that she carried authority well. She said she surrendered; but the records show she was captured in battle. I was relieved that the guard who accompanied me into the stockade had left his gun outside. For there was tenseness in the air as a dozen of these female guerrillas under Andrea's leadership gathered around. Here was a woman who might quickly disarm a guard and who would without hesitation kill all of us for the cause.

When at last the women were separated and Andrea sat alone on her cot, she told me her life story. She was now in her early thirties. She had been to Stalin University and had been converted

115

to Marxism by Pomeroy. She told me she had joined the Huks because her father had been killed by the constabulary. She knew no other way to get revenge, to see that justice was done. She went to the Huks with a heart overflowing with hatred for the police; she was made to order for Communist indoctrination.

As she talked about her Communist exploits her face became hard, her jaw firm. There was a resolute look in her eyes. Her bare feet hung motionless over the side of the cot. When the questions became pointed, when the answers might be incriminating, she took an old-fashioned comb, placed it between her big toe and her second toe, and sawed vigorously. Now her eyes were fixed to the ground. Now she was a tigress who was cornered. Now she was savage in her determination to give no ground in the cause that was holy to her.

She was part of the hard central core of Huk leadership that would never be converted. Rizal, Manila Boy, and the hundreds of others who were flocking to Magsaysay's leadership were misguided youth who, seeing the error of their ways, were eager to march under a noble banner. But Andrea, like Taruc, was a mad dog of the jungle. That kind would have to be tracked down and killed or kept behind bars. The virus of Communism had infected them and made them immune from reason and from compromise. They had one mission in life, and that was to destroy the existing order and supplant it with a new one.

The resoluteness of these Huk Communists is shown by the story of the Huklings. The Huklings are babies of the Huks picked up by the Army and constabulary on their raids of Huk jungle camps. Magsaysay has established a nursery for these babies at Camp Murphy. There they are taken and washed and given clean clothes. Then they are baptized and given names. I was at the nursery when some troops came in with two young Huklings about eighteen months old. They had been picked up in a raid on a Huk camp near Katanawan, Quezon Province, on August 4, 1952. We called one Carlito and the other Pablito. Little Pablito had been caught in the crossfire and wounded in his arm. Magsaysay and I stood watching the nurses take care of them. Turning to me, he said:

"This marks a new era in the fortunes of the Huks."

"What do you mean by that?"

"Up to now, whenever we raided a Huk camp we found no babies. The mothers and fathers took their babies with them when they fled. Now they leave them behind."

"What is the importance of that?"

"In the first place, it means that we are closing in on the prey, that they are not advised of our coming, that they do not have much time to escape. In the second place, the orders have come down from the top to leave the babies behind."

There was a long silence broken only by the cries of little Pablito as the bandage was being removed from his arm. Turning to me, Magsaysay said:

"A woman who will obey an order to run and leave her baby behind in the woods must be a rabid Communist."

"How many mothers show up later at the nursery to claim their children?"

"Only one out of fourteen. That shows the hold Communism has on *some* of our people."

CHAPTER 4

THE ARMY AND THE PEASANTS

One of Magsaysay's first undertakings was the re-organization of the Army and the constabulary. The Armed Forces, designed to protect the people against domestic and foreign enemies, were fast becoming as dangerous to the peasant as the Huks. A villager awakened at night by Huks who demanded food had no alternative but to feed them. Yet if he were apprehended by the police, he would be killed, his house burned, and his property confiscated. Hundreds of people who were victims of the Huks became in turn victims of the police. One night in Laguna 50 farmers who were attending a dance were lined up and shot by the constabulary because they were *suspected* of being Huks. On Good Friday 1950 the Army, in revenge for the killing of an officer, massacred 100 men, women, and children in Bacalor, Pampanga, and burned 130 houses.

The police were indeed worse terrorists than the Huks, for the Huks seldom killed a peasant. The Huks sought their victims from among the police and government officials, from among those who drove sedans, not bullock carts. Since government was more and more oppressive, the Huks became in the eyes of the peasants more a savior than a persecutor. Moreover, many peasants joined the Huks to escape the police or, as in the case of Andrea, to get revenge for some actual or imagined injury.

The Army and the constabulary were oppressive in other respects too. They were almost always on the side of the landlords against the peasants. They were often in the pay of the landlords. A landlord would give them a commission to help him collect an exorbitant and unlawful rent from the tenant. On rent day the hapless tenant would find his farm visited by soldiers. There would be a bayonet at his back as he measured out the landlord's share of the rice. The law said the landlord could not get more than 30 per cent. Even the 70 per cent that the law reserved for the tenant was often not enough to live on. Yet the landlords, under the pressure of the Army's bayonets, usually got over 50 per cent.

The Army and constabulary were both oppressive and corrupt.

"They were supposed to be the people's defender," Magsaysay told me, "but they were as much an enemy as the Huks themselves."

Magsaysay and General Calixto Duque cleaned out the Army and constabulary from top to bottom. Any soldier who accepted money or other bribes from a landlord, any soldier who shot a villager for aiding a Huk, any soldier who burned a house or who stole or raped or plundered was punished. Magsaysay's threats were made good. He showed by a few examples that he meant what he said. He found idealistic leadership among young officers. He weeded out the unethical. Magsaysay and Duque, with the help of General Leland Hobbs of the American Army, produced a new Army and a new constabulary within a few months—two of the best I have seen—and trained them to be on the side of the people against all predators—whether they be landlords or Huks.

Magsaysay, son of a blacksmith, was born in Zambales Province forty-five years ago. He is nearly six feet tall, large-framed, and rangy. He is a Filipino with both Chinese and Spanish blood.

During the years in the jungle while he was harassing the Japs, he learned the trials and tribulations of the guerrillas—their sufferings and ordeals, their anxieties, their psychology.

"When you were a guerrilla, what was the thing you feared most?" I asked him.

"Dogs," he answered briskly. And his eyes lighted up as he told me how he trains dogs to hunt down the Huks and the great success he has had with them.

He also tracks Huks down with the aid of ex-Huks. He lays ambushes along their customary routes of travel. He uses tricks and subterfuges to entrap them. Once he paid a Huk a handsome price to give a picnic to twenty-six die-hard Communists who would never surrender. They had to be killed or captured. The picnic was held in a remote jungle rendezvous often used by the Huks. The feast was spread and the Huks were gorging themselves on it, when the host stepped momentarily out of the circle. The ambush was well laid; the twenty-six unsuspecting Huks were mowed down by machine-gun fire.

Magsaysay trained the Army in guerrilla warfare and sent them into the jungles to hunt down the Huks one by one.

Magsaysay placed a price on the heads of the Huk leaders (the price on the head of Taruc, the leader in 1952, was 100,000 pesos or $50,000). These rewards often bring valuable leads. Sometimes Magsaysay gives a curious twist to the reward. He places a higher price on the head of a lieutenant than on the chief himself. This creates jealousies in the ranks of the Huks, and often followers of the chief take it out on the lieutenant by turning him in or giving valuable clues to his activities or whereabouts.

Magsaysay presses hard on the Huks in another way too. He induced Quirino to suspend the writ of habeas corpus, an action which the Supreme Court later upheld. Now he can hold men in protective custody for months on end. It's a stern measure which many defend as a necessity. But others who cherish civil liberties rail against it; and there is much grumbling that Quirino and Magsaysay abused this absolute power.

Magsaysay offers amnesty to Huks who surrender. In radio talks and in printed propaganda he emphasizes his leniency. He promises that a surrendered Huk, after he has faced legal charges, will be paroled to him and that he, Magsaysay, will see to it that he gets a job or is settled on a farm or is set up in business. Hundreds take his terms and give themselves up. Some of these have prior criminal records; most of them joined the Huks merely in revolt against some injustice. One Moro chieftain, who, when I was in the Philippines, trooped down from the hills with 200 men and surrendered to Magsaysay, had turned renegade a few years earlier in protest to the treatment of his people by a corrupt judge of a Philippine court. These Moros were not Communists; they were rebels in the best American sense. Magsaysay dealt with them accordingly, taking their arms and sending them back to their villages to lead peaceful lives.

By 1951 the ranks of the ex-Huks were swelling, but the converts were not yet numerous enough to satisfy Magsaysay. To turn the tide permanently against the Huks he needed to enlist the enthusiastic support of the people. What he needed was a new and bold program that would dramatize the issues and show the peasants that he and the Army were really on *their* side.

He found the issue in the oppressive practices of the landlords. In central Luzon landlords actually evict tenants who insist that the law, which places the rent ceiling at 30 per cent of the crop, be enforced. These tenants are ignorant and helpless. The weight of society—including the legal profession—is against them. They have no ally in the courts. They are victims of the influential landlords, who long have controlled the government, the courts, and the police. Magsaysay did an unprecedented thing. He ordered the Judge Advocate's department of the Army to go into the courts and defend the tenants against eviction. The Army on the side of the tenants! The Army against the landlords! An unheard-of thing!

But it was true. Army lawyers stood in the courts and pleaded the cases of the tenants. When they lost, they took the cases to

121

the Supreme Court. The word spread throughout the Islands that justice had at last come to the peasants. The Army, which once was a locust that devoured them, was now their champion. The word spread to the jungles. Manila Boy and the other orators whom Magsaysay had enlisted in his cause spread the word. Magsaysay was the Liberator, not the Oppressor. Magsaysay would see to it that the peasant got justice. Magsaysay was the people's friend.

That single act of sending the Army into the courts to defend the tenants against the landlords was probably more responsible than anything else for swaying the tide of public opinion over to Magsaysay. Since that time the Huks have lost much of their popular following. The hard core of the professional Communists remains. But its steady liquidation is under way.

CHAPTER 5

LANDLORDS AND LAND SPECULATORS

Magsaysay does more than advocate the cause of the peasant. He is engaged in a program of rehabilitation of the Huks who have surrendered and forsworn the Communist creed of terror and violence.

—Huks while serving sentence or while paroled to Magsaysay are given vocational training, mostly in carpentry and leather work. They are paid in cash for their labor.
—Magsaysay has an appropriation from Congress out of which loans to small business may be made. Many an ex-Huk under Magsaysay's supervision is becoming a Main Street merchant and a member of the hated bourgeois against whom the Communists rail.
—Magsaysay has an employment program to find work for ex-Huks.
—Magsaysay has a rural rehabilitation program for the grant of land to the ex-Huks and their resettlement on farms.

It is on the last of these—the land problem—that any true solution of the Huk problem depends.

123

Landlordism has placed a curse on most of the Middle East and Asia. The Philippines are no exception. The landlord problem is indeed as acute in the Philippines as in any country in the world. Where the landlords are the most numerous, there the Huks are the thickest. Take a map of the Philippines and place blue pins on the heavy landlord holdings; then place red pins on the concentration of Huks. The blue pins and the red pins will form close clusters. The Hardie Report (Philippine Land Tenure Reform, Analysis and Recommendations), prepared in 1952 by the Mutual Security Agency, gives the details.

On a national basis 35 per cent of all Philippine farms are operated by tenants. But that cold statistic does not tell the whole story. In 16 provinces 40 per cent of the farms are operated by tenants; in 7, 50 per cent; in 4, 60 per cent or more. It is in these provinces that the strongholds of the Huks are to be found. Their great fortress has been in Pampanga Province in Luzon. Mount Arayat—3,367 feet high and thickly wooded—north of Manila and not far from Clark Field, is a stronghold of the Huks. Nearby is the Candaba Swamp containing thousands of acres. The mountain and the swamp provide good hiding. The nearby villages are sources of food. They also have been good recruiting grounds for the Huks. For this is the heart of landlordism: *here 70 per cent of the farmers are tenants; here 2 per cent of the people own 98 per cent of the land.*

There are some large estates in the Philippines—40,000 acres, 80,000 acres, and even larger. As many as 30,000 tenants work for one landlord. Most of these huge holdings are sources of evil, for they are held by absentee owners and managed by local agents who feel none of the responsibilities of ownership.

Not all large ownership, however, foments social discontent. Jose Yulo owns extensive acreage about an hour's drive from Manila. His tenants have modern houses, schools, hospitals, and doctors. They even cook on electric stoves. Their standard of living is high. No one has ever left those villages to join the Huks. And as Yulo told me with a twinkle in his eye:

"Me control their votes? Listen, my tenants are an independent lot. I'm a Quirino man; but in the last election they all voted for Laurel."

But civic-minded Jose Yulo is the exception among the large landlords. Moreover, the curse of Philippine landlordism is found not so much in the large holdings as in the smaller ones. These are absentee landlords—merchants, doctors, lawyers—who have purchased ten, twenty, or thirty acres as an investment. They lease the land to sharecroppers (90 per cent of all tenant farmers in the Islands are sharecroppers). *The landlords collect on their investment from 20 to 22 per cent a year.* That is a handsome return. It is so handsome that very little capital is available for any other purpose. Everyone wants to put his money in land. Where else can one get a better investment? Where else will capital be safer? The capital of the Philippines, in fact, is mostly in the land. It lies there idle—*rentier* capital unavailable for the industrial development that the Islands badly need. The 20 to 22 per cent annual return is from the hides of the peasants who writhe under a burden of rent and interest and eke out a bare subsistence.

The living costs of the *average* farm tenant family are estimated at $313 a year. The gross income of the *average* tenant family will be no more than $180 a year for rice land and no more than $160 on sugar cane.

The truth of the matter is that there are in the Philippines today one and a half million farm families below the subsistence level. Several factors contribute to that condition:

(1) Over 50 per cent of all farms are less than two hectares,[1] which in the Philippines is too small a unit to support a family, even though only 30 per cent of the crop is paid as rent.

(2) Tenants pay as a minimum 30 per cent of the crop as rent. But the majority pay 50 per cent or more.

[1] One hectare is 2.471 acres.

(3) Interest paid by tenants on loans would make our loan sharks wince. Tenants are commonly bound by usurious transactions to their landlord under loans that bind the father, the sons, and the grandsons to perpetual indebtedness. The tenant becomes the serf subject to the landlord's control. The landlord owns and controls him; the tenant farmer is beholden to his master even when it comes to voting. It is the landlord's pleasure that the tenant must serve if he is to survive. I have talked with Filipino farmers who pay 200 per cent interest or more a year. That rate is not uncommon. One hundred per cent interest a year is customary. Farmers out of necessity borrow money each year. They never get caught up; they pay interest on interest. If the creditor is not the landlord, he will be the crafty Chinese moneylender.

(4) The absence of all-weather roads puts many farmers out of contact with the markets at critical periods. The absence of adequate and economic storage space for farm produce forces the farmer to sell in a low and to buy in a high market. The absence of co-operative marketing and buying facilities puts the farmer at the mercy of the Chinese middleman. There are very few co-operative rice mills. The Chinese capitalist or the landlord takes his toll there too. And there is no such thing in the Philippines as a floor under farm prices.

This miserable condition of the Philippine farmer breeds a dangerous virus. The main industry of the Philippines is agriculture. It accounts for 58 per cent of the national income. Over 70 per cent of the people in the Islands derive their livelihood from it. But the system of land tenure is so vicious that it threatens to destroy the great civilization for which the Philippines are famous.

Land reform was the campaign platform of Luis Taruc, the Huk. He ran for Congress in 1947 and was elected; and in 1948 he was shouting for land reform. It looked for a while as if Quirino was making progress with the Huk problem. He was Vice-President under Manuel Roxas, and thus came to the presidency when Roxas died of a heart attack in 1948. In 1946 Roxas had negotiated with Taruc for a settlement of the Huk question. But it fell through. When Quirino succeeded to the presidency he offered amnesty to Taruc and the Huks. Quirino promised them a program of "social amelioration" consisting of land grants to peasants, public works, relief for the needy, mobile health clinics, agricultural credit, and freedom of speech and the press. But Quirino's program never was realized; and Taruc's co-operation was not long-lived. In the late summer of 1948 Taruc repudiated Quirino's offer and returned to the jungle after announcing, ". . . the Communist Party of the Philippines, of which I am a member, besides fighting for the eventual achievement of socialism, is also fighting for land for the peasants and other agrarian reforms and for the full and complete independence of our country from all forms of foreign domination. . . . I have instructed my men to . . . refuse to submit to a fascist peace imposed by imperialist-feudal guns and bayonets."

Taruc's change in plans was not happenstance. The Communist Conference in Calcutta had directed the resumption of jungle warfare throughout all of Southeast Asia by the fall of 1948. And Taruc, Communist that he is, was obeying the voice of his master.

Magsaysay knows how the Communist command in the Philippines leads back to the Kremlin. But he also knows that the political leverage of the Huks comes not from conversion to Marxism, but from the desire of people to escape their awful plight. He knows, in other words, that the great power of the Huks derives from the people's misery and that the land-tenure system is the source of most of it. Families impoverished from generation to generation, young people facing a future of misery, of malnutrition, of illiteracy, of serfdom—these are the ones who follow the Huk leader with his promise that they will inherit the earth.

Magsaysay has done something about the land problem. He and others in the Armed Forces, particularly Major Ciriaco V. Mirasol, organized the Economic Development Corps of the Army (known as Edcor) and started land-resettlement projects on Mindanao—the southernmost island of the Philippines. Unoccupied, unclaimed land was set aside at two places—Kapatagan and Buldon in northern Mindanao. This is flat land, traversed by many small winding creeks and covered by second-growth forest. The forests provide trees for lumber and rattan for furniture. The soil is good for rice, corn, and various root crops. Bananas, papaya, and other fruits flourish there, as do coffee, sugar cane, and tobacco.

Huks who have neither been indicted nor convicted by the courts and who want a farm of their own are sent down there. Each settler is assigned a farm of six to ten hectares. The Army helps them put up a house and clear the land. The settlers are on Army rations until their crops come in. The Army also puts up schools, nurseries, dispensaries, chapels, and co-operative stores. The Army furnishes each farmer with a carabao, the faithful work animal of Southeast Asia. The farmer gets the land free after he has operated it for a year. He then starts to pay back the advances which the Army has made, including the cost of the carabao.

These communities are modern, healthy, and happy ones. Many people have thought they were the answer to the land problem of the Islands. But good as they are, they amount only to a drop in the bucket. By late 1952 less than 300 families had been resettled here. The rehabilitation of 300 families out of one and a half million impoverished farm families is a minor contribution to the basic problem of the Philippines. Moreover, resettlement is not a panacea for the pernicious land system which the Philippines inherited from Spanish days. It supplements land reform but does not take its place. There is the unwillingness of people to pull up all community roots and go to a new and distant

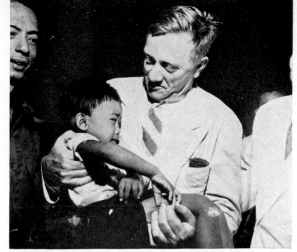

Little Pablito had been
caught in the crossfire
and wounded in the arm.

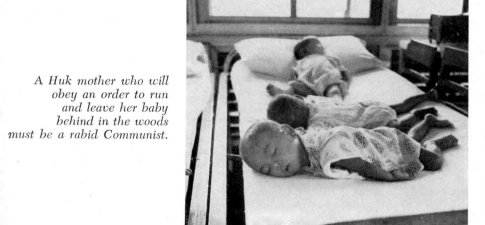

A Huk mother who will
obey an order to run
and leave her baby
behind in the woods
must be a rabid Communist.

Magsaysay has
the energy and drive
that the Philippines need.

I remember
the breakfast with Quirino
in August 1952
at Malacanan Palace.

Benvinedo had cleared
this valley land
with his own hands.

Manila Boy
spoke of his devotion
to Ramon Magsaysay.

area. There is the heavy cost of forcing mass migrations of people. Moreover, in the new region, as in the old, the ancient vices quickly appear and the new settler becomes the victim of the old system.

I saw some illustrations of this on a visit I made to the island of Mindanao in 1952. I went by air to the Koronadal and Allah valleys, where the government has resettled almost 10,000 families. The resettlement agency is called Lasedeco (Land Settlement and Development Corporation). In August 1952, 6,000 additional families were there, awaiting resettlement. But this project—worthy as it is—has bogged down. The local officials are bright, earnest, and industrious. But somewhere high above them fraud, dishonesty, and inefficiency have crippled the undertaking.

Mindanao, the southernmost island of the group, contains vast, undeveloped resources. There are fertile valleys that have hardly been touched. Thousands of acres could be turned into model farms. That was the purpose of Lasedeco, and there is still hope among the local officials in Mindanao. But the resettlement efforts have been grinding slowly to a stop.

When the word spread that these valleys would be open to settlement, hungry speculators filed claims to the land and by that act placed a cloud on the title to every acre in the project. Higher-ups in Manila co-operated with them to keep their claims alive. They succeeded in paralyzing the whole operation. Before titles can be given, surveys must be made. Lasedeco has been operating twelve years and few surveys have been made; no titles have been issued. The speculator stands behind the government official, controlling his action. The speculator wants money to have his cloud to the title removed; and the public official, directly or indirectly, supports him in this position. Quirino has taken some measures to crush graft. But corruption is still rife. Many Philippine officials still believe in rehabilitating themselves before rehabilitating the country.

One of the best cases in point is Benvinedo Atenzor of Banga, whose farm was among those I visited. He came to Banga from

Iloilo, Panay, in 1940 because he heard of an opportunity to own a farm. He was assigned eight hectares of the rich black soil in the Allah Valley. He built a sturdy house on stilts and thatched it with palm leaves. The house—spick and span—has two rooms for living and sleeping quarters and a porch for cooking. Benvinedo has a wife and seven children. He has one carabao, several pigs, and numerous chickens. He has pineapple, bananas, coffee, and papaya in his yard. Within two years of his arrival his rice fields were in full production. By Philippine standards Benvinedo has prospered. His income, over and above food for his family, is about 3,000 pesos ($1,500) a year. Benvinedo has prospered because he is smart, industrious, and freed from the hold of a landlord. He has also been shrewd enough to escape the toils of the Chinese moneylender. But in spite of his industry Benvinedo Atenzor has not been able to get a deed to his farm. In halting English he let loose the rage that was seething in him.

"I will not pay anyone any money," he screamed at me. "This place is mine; I made it with my hands from the jungle."

I went with Benvinedo through his orchard. He had planted each of the trees and now touched them gently, as though they were old friends. We walked into his rice paddy that was lush and green. It stretched several hundred yards to the north, joining other fields that seemed to run to the horizon. A south wind touched the grain and sent soft ripples rolling across it.

Far in the distance were low-lying hills—perhaps 3,000 feet high. They had a purplish tinge this afternoon as they lay against a sky that was brewing a black storm. My plane had skimmed over them on the flight to Banga, and I had seen the thick and tangled jungle that covered them. That was the kind of jungle Benvinedo had cleared from this valley land with his own hands. He had risked cobra with his bare feet in thick grass. He had lived on thin rations as he rooted out trees, encountered disease, fought pests. The struggle with the jungle never ceases. The jungle is always the aggressor, ready to invade and take over quickly if man sleeps too long. That is why Benvinedo is up at dawn, manicuring his few hectares until dusk each day. The years of work have made these hectares a part of him, him a part of them. They have his anguish, his sweat, his worries, his hopes.

While we walked the edge of his rice paddy, Benvinedo told me again the story of his struggles to carve this farm out of the wilderness. He turned, looking at me full face. Several front teeth were missing; a scowl was on his face; his right hand with its callused fingers and bulging knuckles scratched his stubble. There was anger in his voice as he asked me, "Why cannot I get my title?"

Benvinedo Atenzor has waited ten years. Others have waited longer. Benvinedo, by Allah Valley standards, is well off. In Allah Valley it costs a farm family at least 800 pesos ($400) a year to live. Many—probably most—of the farmers there do not have that much income. Like the starving farmers of Luzon, these Mindanao farmers do not make enough to buy clothes for their families and procure the necessary medicine. They are a poor, miserable lot.

Lasedeco provides some doctors and dentists whose services are free. Banga has a hospital which I visited. Like the homes, it is on stilts as a protection against water and reptiles. It is a primitive structure with a thatched roof. It has twelve beds and an operating room. The operating room is an old truck bed (with the axles still attached) that has been raised up on poles to the level of the hospital and attached to it as a wing.

Banga has primary schools that go through the sixth grade. I visited them with Florderico V. Loreta and Jose Parreno of Lasedeco. The buildings, built by parent-teacher associations, are long, high, thatched structures cut up into rooms holding about thirty students each. Because of the warm year-around climate, the walls are drafty and there is an open space by the eaves for ventilation. Photographs of Quirino, Rizal, and other Filipino heroes hang in the classrooms. And each room that I saw had a large sign facing the students: "Be Honest."

Banga's schools have seats for about 80 per cent of the children.

School attendance is not compulsory, because the need to have children for work in the fields is too great. And the high school— a good Catholic institution that charges tuition—is beyond the reach of most families.

Though these farmers have been settled on land, they still are victims of the Chinese moneylender, who in the spring advances four units of rice in return for ten units payable in the fall. There is no form of agriculture credit that is non-usurious. There are no co-operatives. The farmer, though he owns his own land, is in a weak and vulnerable position as a businessman. Being illiterate, he is a prey to every exploiter who comes along.

Back in Manila, I talked with Magsaysay about this problem. He cursed the inefficiency and corruptness that prevented the surveying of the land and the issuance of titles in the Lasedeco projects. Exactly the same conditions almost defeated his resettlement program with Edcor. Magsaysay adopted bold and energetic measures. He sent the Army engineers out to make the surveys; and by shouts and threats he forced the issuance of land titles without payment of tribute to anyone. Magsaysay, honest as he is courageous, said to me:

"The Mindanao land-distribution project is a scandal. There should be a house cleaning, starting from the top."

The sum of the resettlement projects is plus, yet they do not add up to much. The bulk of the cultivated land is still held by absentee landlords; there is no agricultural credit bank, no marketing agencies, no guarantees against usurious interest, no price protection whatsoever for farm produce. The absentee landlords and the Chinese moneylenders feast on the land. The man who works the land, who takes his wife and children to the fields to make enough to hold body and soul together—this man is as poor and as miserable today as he was when the liquidation of the Huks began.

There is knowledge of this fact in the rice fields. The peasants —and those who move among them and work with them—know that no matter how many Huks are killed, the virus on which

Communism feeds continues to flourish. Some tenants are beginning to organize to protect their rights. I talked with representatives of one Peasant Union that had at one time as many as 2,000 cases in the courts, involving the rights of tenants against landlords. Ceferino Inciong, their spokesman, told me:

"We have the best government and the best laws. But we also have the worst landlords. Unless our landlords will follow the true Christian faith and adopt the principle of the golden rule in their dealings with the tenants, nothing will save us from Communism."

CHAPTER 6

NEGOTIATING WITH THE TIGER
FOR HIS FUR

One day in Formosa my thoughts returned abruptly to the Philippines and its scourge of landlordism. I had been visiting farms out of Taipei, talking with the farmers, and learning something of the problems of landlordism that had long laid a heavy hand on that island. An official of the Formosa Government was explaining the land-reform program that had been promised the island by Chiang Kai-shek. This program was a gradual one, starting with rent reductions and ending with land distribution. In the summer of 1952 Formosa was still in the early phases of the program; the breakup of the large estates had not begun.

I asked the reason for the delay, pointing out that delay, delay, delay in that basic reform on the mainland was one reason for the political default of Chiang Kai-shek and for the victory of Communist Mao Tse-tung.

"With that lesson clear and vivid, why the delay in land reform on Formosa?" I asked.

The Chinese to whom I addressed the question is a soft-spoken, gentle soul who in his sixty-odd years has been witness to the great turbulence in Asia. He has been on intimate terms with politicians who by words promised reforms and by deeds lined their own pockets instead. He has seen many land-reform programs halted or subverted by officials who had been "reached." He has seen the influence of landlords in politics so strong as to stop all land reforms; he has been a witness to their corrupting influence.

There was a long pause before he answered my question.

"Why the delay in land reform in Formosa?" he asked teasingly. He seemed to delight in coining the answer:

"Negotiating with the tiger for his fur—that's the reason."

Negotiating with the tiger for his fur! The expression took me back to the Philippines and my several visits there. I remembered the breakfast with President Quirino in early August 1952 at Malacanan Palace, where huge chandeliers, hung with hundreds of pieces of cut glass, tinkle softly in a warm breeze. We sat on a second-floor veranda eating sweet papaya, omelet, and wheat cakes while we talked of the social discontent that makes the Philippines rumble.

Some eminent Filipinos had formed the Philippine Rural Reconstruction Movement (PRRM), of which Conrado Benitez is the chairman and Domingo Bascara is the executive director. Dr. James Yen of the International Mass Education Committee (of which I have been a member) had come to the Philippines to help PRRM launch an intensive reconstruction program in one or more of the provinces. Dr. Yen, Mr. Benitez, and I, together with other members of PRRM, were with Quirino at this breakfast; and our discussion of ways and means to get the program under way covered a wide range.

Schools were needed, schools in adult education—and teachers to run the schools.

Public health centers were in demand—and technicians to train nurses, midwives, and first-aid dispensers.

New methods of seed selection, new species of rice, cross-breeding of hogs, vaccine for livestock, control of diseases in poultry, and other methods of scientific agriculture were needed—and men and women to run demonstration centers.

Marketing co-operatives, credit co-operatives were sorely needed—and able, honest men to manage them.

The villages of the Philippines also need recreation halls, sanitary engineering, all-weather roads, hospitals, doctors, and the material comforts of the city. The list of needs is long, and the items that would be underscored as emergency ones are numerous. But there is a basic need that underlies all these; and it is land reform.

Land reform in other countries is having an impact in the Philippines. The land distribution effected in Japan by General Douglas MacArthur beginning in 1945 has had profound repercussions. What was just for the Japanese tenant is just for the Filipino. Even Ireland's and Mexico's experiments in land reform have had influences in the Philippines. And every word of progress in land reform on Formosa is a stimulant in the Philippines.

Our breakfast discussion kept returning over and again to the land problem.

If agricultural production were increased, the dividends would accrue mostly to the landlords. Are the landlords to be the primary beneficiaries of this rural reform program?

If marketing co-operatives were organized for the share of the crops the peasant now receives, he still would not make enough to live on in view of the oppressive sharecropping system that enslaves him.

Public health measures will lower the infant mortality rate and increase the life expectancy of everyone. Look at what happened in Puerto Rico, where public health measures increased the pressure of people on the land! If fewer Filipino babies die as a result of the work of PRRM, there will be more mouths to feed. There are already one and a half million families below the subsistence level. Unless something is done about land as well as public health, the number of starving families will increase.

Industrialization would help raise the standard of living of the people. Today it is very low, the *average* per capita income in 1951 being about 250 pesos or $125. A very small number of Filipinos receives the lion's share of that income. Disparities in individual income are as great in the Philippines as anywhere in the world. So the *average* income of 250 pesos ($125) a year does not fairly reflect the miserable lot of the Filipino at the bottom of the pyramid. Population is increasing 2.4 per cent a year (about 500,000 people). There is new, unused land that can be opened to cultivation, and it will absorb the new population for a while. If modern methods of agriculture are introduced, the required labor force would be cut substantially. Even if primitive methods of agriculture are employed, there is at present an excess farm population to operate the existing cultivated areas. Industrialization programs are sorely needed to take up unemployment, to raise the national income, to avert the severe revolution that will come if existing conditions continue. These programs require capital. But the bulk of Filipino capital is in the land. It lies there idle, paying the owner a magnificent return, as I have said. And to the owner it looks safe and secure, come the revolution. But if the country is to be saved from the ultimate tide of Communism, that system must be changed. Filipino capital must be taken out of the land and put into factories, if there is to be enough work, enough food, enough peace and security for everyone.

And so this breakfast discussion of social discontent in the Philippines, like every discussion of it, focused largely on the land problem. Quirino, astute politician that he is, knows better than anyone that land reform lies at the root of the Huk rebellion. As I have said, their stronghold is in Pampanga Province of central Luzon, where 2 per cent of the people own 98 per cent of the land.

"Let's move into Pampanga Province," Quirino said at this breakfast meeting. "We'll clear Candaba Swamp, distribute the land, bring in new settlers, and erect model villages. We'll carry a program of political action into the heart of Hukland."

Pampanga proved too lawless, too turbulent for PRRM. They went instead to Nueva Ecija Province and Rizal Province. Nueva Ecija has been a stronghold of the Huks. There is much unused forest land there. President Quirino has ordered the opening of 50,000 hectares of public land for landless farmers and the cooperation of various governmental agencies in the promotion of the rural reconstruction program of the PRRM. Quirino, in making such promises, is sincere. I think he's convinced that unless land reform is accomplished the Philippines may be violently unstable.

But in the Philippines as elsewhere there is a long distance between political talk and political action, especially when it comes to land reform. This is a matter Dr. Jose P. Laurel and I discussed one afternoon in 1952 at his home in Manila. Dr. Laurel, head of the Nationalista Party, is President Quirino's great rival. Dr. Laurel is a distinguished Filipino who is not only able but honest. He has been in public life for forty years and still has only a modest income. He is short, slight, and wiry; and he does not show the sixty-nine years he has lived. Many honors have come to him. He was once Justice of the Supreme Court and later Minister of Justice. He was one of the men whom General Douglas MacArthur and President Manuel L. Quezon left behind to be the steward of Philippine affairs during the Japanese occupation. Laurel became President under the Japs, and for that act was condemned by many as a puppet and a collaborator. He was particularly denounced for the announcement of "a state of war" against the United States in the fall of 1944 during the days of the Japanese occupation. He went to trial in 1947 for treason on account of his collaboration with the Japanese. But on January 28, 1948, before the trial finished, President Roxas, who had served with Laurel in the government under the Japanese, granted him amnesty.

The story of his administration under the Japanese is too long to relate here. Knowing the man, I am convinced that whatever he did that had the appearance of sympathy with the Japanese cause, he did under compulsion. He told me that he took the presidency under the Japanese because he thought he might alleviate the plight of his people. He has been a storm center of Philippine politics and a highly controversial figure. Today he is the elder statesman, much loved by the Filipinos. There are dozens who were there in the occupation whose lives he saved or whom he protected against the Japanese and who testify to his loyalty to the Filipinos.

The people of the Islands have shown their respect for him in a tangible way. In 1951 honest Ramon Magsaysay and his reorganized Army saw to it that the election was an honest one. There were nine of the twenty-four Senate seats up for election. Laurel's candidates won all of the nine. There were forty-five provincial governors elected, and of these Laurel's candidates won twenty-three. "The jury's verdict of confidence in me," Laurel told me in 1952.

Laurel admires Magsaysay though they had different political origins. He suggested to Quirino that both step aside so that Magsaysay could be elected President in 1953 on a coalition ticket. Quirino refused. Magsaysay (still a poor man) resigned as Secretary of Defense and joined Laurel's party in preparation for the presidential race.

Laurel knows the Huks. He admired their stand against the Japanese and deplored their domination by the Communists. Laurel feels that the detention camps in the Philippines are oppressive, that they hold many innocent people. He rages at Quirino for the suspension of the writ of habeas corpus on October 22, 1950. It was Laurel who challenged the constitutionality of the suspension on behalf of a person who claimed to be unjustly detained. The Supreme Court, in *Montenegro* v. *Castaneda,* 48 Off. Gaz. 3392, held that the writ had been constitutionally suspended for Filipinos accused of "invasion, insurrection, and rebellion," though not for those accused of "sedition."

In Laurel's view the bulk of the Huks are victims of Communist propaganda, too ignorant to know what Communism really is, and ready followers of anyone who promises to get the landlords and moneylenders off their backs. This afternoon in his study he summed it up to me over the teacups.

"Most of the Huks are filled with discontent because of unemployment, land tenure, and the heavy rent and outrageous interest they must pay."

Laurel agreed that no real and abiding answer to the Huk problem would be found unless the land problem was settled.

"What are the chances of land reform?" I asked.

The answer was slow in coming; Laurel, now on in years and perhaps too tired for another try at politics, spoke from the heart; and both what he said and the tone in which he said it carried dark predictions.

"The legislature is controlled by the landlords; it is very difficult for a candidate to be elected without landlord support. And no landlord is going to legislate himself out of business."

On New Year's Day 1953 Quirino eloquently illustrated Laurel's point. Quirino denounced the Hardie Report, which demanded basic land reform in the Islands, as American "interference" in the domestic affairs of the Philippines. That outburst was a measure of the power of the landlords in Quirino's government.

Once the United States had a chance to settle the problem. Landlordism was almost as acute when we took the Islands from Spain as it is today. But we did little about it during our long rule. None of the governors from William Howard Taft on down tackled the problem seriously. Today Laurel and other Filipinos speak of the "invisible power of America" in Island affairs. Today American officials are strongly on the side of Philippine land reform. Admiral Raymond A. Spruance—our present Ambassador in Manila—is wise and fearless. He stands firmly for land reform. Many Filipinos believe that it will take the full exertion of American influence to bring about the change, to put a land-reform program through the Congress.

140

Meanwhile the rural discontent is as great as ever. Meanwhile Magsaysay moves more and more into a strategic position. Unless he falls victim to political assassination, he will head the government someday soon. Magsaysay to date has used a magnetic personality, sincerity, and a record of individual honesty to swing the popular tide against the Huks. Yet what has been done to remedy the basic social conditions on which the Huks have grown strong has been trivial.

That is why Magsaysay paces nervously up and down in every conversation. That is why Magsaysay—who is only in his mid-forties—carries the worries of millions of people. That is why Magsaysay looks to the future with hope clouded by apprehension.

For the one question that keeps pounding in his head—the question that pounds in the head of many a Filipino liberal—goes to the very heart of Philippine policy:

How long can we keep killing Huks for the benefit of the landlords and the Chinese moneylenders?

It was on that basic issue that Magsaysay broke with Quirino early in 1953.

There is the ability and promise among the Filipinos to solve the crucial land problem the democratic way. One of the most powerful influences is the quiet, soft voice of a lady. She is Mrs. Asuncion Perez, who is a member of the PRRM and Commissioner of Social Welfare in Quirino's Cabinet. In my view she ranks with Eleanor Roosevelt and Madam Pandit as one of the great women of this century.

Mrs. Perez, short, slight, middle-aged, and graying, was in the underground during the Japanese occupation. One evening in Manila, at a dinner in the home of Ambassador and Mrs. Spruance, she told me about an arduous mission she performed. The guerrillas had planned to kill Laurel. She carried a message from Manuel Roxas in Manila to the guerrillas eighty miles distant in the hills, saying that Laurel was not a traitor, that his life should be spared, that he was trying to soften as much as he

141

could the heavy blow of the Japanese rule. Shortly thereafter she and her husband, Cirilo B. Perez, were picked up and interned. Her husband was executed. She was kept in prison for months and questioned daily for hours on end. Her food ration was a handful of rice once a day. Sometimes squash was added, but never salt or sugar. When she was released, she was down to sixty-two pounds—a waif, a walking skeleton.

Mrs. Perez has seen the depths of the misery in Asia; she has experienced its poverty; she knows the cruelty in the exactions of the moneylenders and the landlords. Mrs. Perez knows that the Filipino peasant is as much a slave as his faithful carabao—that governments of the landlords, for the landlords, and by the landlords will never alleviate his conditions. Mrs. Perez knows that under the existing system the peasant will be eternally bound by debt, by poverty, by unconscionable sharecropping. She has been as vocal, as insistent, as unequivocal about the need for land reform as anyone. On the side of reforms her voice has been as loud as the voice of Taruc, the Communist. But she rejects Communism as a creed or platform.

What she told me this night reveals, I think, the Filipino soul. She and I were sitting in a corner of the veranda, drinking our after-dinner coffee. Her words were so low I had to bend close to hear her.

"During the Japanese occupation we learned that the value of life is in the happiness one can help another achieve. We learned in those trying days that there is good in most people. We learned that with patience people can be rallied to a cause. We learned that misery and poverty are common grounds for welding people together, for uniting them in a crusade.

"Foreigners who travel the Islands often see only the miserable conditions under which our peasants live. They do not see the soul of the Filipino. They view the misery and poverty with despair. They see only a bottomless pit with no solution except force and violence. But our misery and poverty—why, they offer us exciting opportunities. Look at the beautiful garden God gave us.

It's not a garden for a select few of the people. It belongs to all of us. We are brothers and sisters together. The suffering of one is the suffering of all. Something of great beauty will rise from the misery of our people, something fine and decent and fair, something that is just to peasant and landlord alike. If we will remember that we are our brother's keeper, we can fashion a society more glorious than the Communists ever dreamed."

Mrs. Perez finished with a triumphant note in her voice. But there were tears in her eyes too.

Magsaysay has the energy and drive which the Philippines need. Even if he may not know finance, export-import controls, taxation, industrialization, and the other technical aspects involved in raising the national income, a "brain trust" of competent technicians can be supplied. Yet technical competence is not enough. Idealism is needed too—standards of conduct that reflect the conscience and soul of the Filipinos and make for fairness and decency in human relations. This idealism will in large measure come from the frail little woman, Asuncion Perez, who from the dark depths of a Japanese prison saw the bright destiny of her people.

PART **3**

VIETNAM
—A NATION IN DISINTEGRATION

CHAPTER 1

A PHANTOM ARMY

Rugged mountains with a tumbled mass of peaks rising over 7,000 feet form the northern and western borders of Vietnam. Their dense vegetation, harsh limestone cliffs, and narrow defiles have made them somewhat of a barrier against the invader, somewhat of a refuge for minority tribes. But these mountains have never been much of a protection against China on the north. They have passes which served as the pathways for the human migrations which peopled the countries of Southeast Asia. They have long been the traditional haunts of tigers, elephants, panthers, and malarial mosquitoes. Now they are also the refuge of Communist guerrillas. Today they furnish Red China and the Communists of Vietnam (the Viet Minh) the staging grounds for an unrelenting military action. Red China has secretly united with the Viet Minh to drive the French out of Vietnam and to take over the government. It is from this mountain stronghold that strong Communist forces make their great assaults.

These mountains are the source of the Red River and many

147

other fingers of water that run southeast to the Gulf of Tonkin. The Red River delta is rich in rice. Wherever one looks there is wet paddy. The rice fields run to the horizon—unbroken except for an occasional lone tree and clusters of villages. From the delta the mountain strongholds of the Communists look like the low broken hills of western Connecticut. Their lines are soft; and on a clear evening they stand silhouetted against the sky like relics of ancient ranges.

Up to the fall of 1950 the French held most of these hills by a line of forts along the Chinese border. But the Communists drove them out. Today the Viet Minh occupies them and from that strategic position commands most of the delta. The Red River delta is a narrow coastal plain, hemmed in by mountains on the west and on the north. The French have placed their uneasy lines at the head of this delta. Should the Viet Minh break through, all of Vietnam might fall. For there are not many natural defense positions to the south.

Far to the south are other Viet Minh forces. They are scattered through the rich delta near the mouth of the Mekong River in Cochin China.

The Mekong, which rises with the Yangtze and Salween in southeastern Tibet, flows 2,800 miles to the sea in southern Vietnam. Its rich delta of swamps, rice lands, palm trees, and mangroves gives ideal hiding grounds to the guerrillas. These guerrillas are smaller in number and weaker in strength than those up north. They are far from the Chinese border and are therefore more on their own. But they are strongly entrenched, and re, cently they have extended their operations into the neighboring state of Cambodia.

There are strong political as well as military reasons why the Viet Minh concentrates its efforts on the Red River delta in the north and the Mekong River delta in the south. Those are the two rich areas of the country, the Mekong River delta being one of the richest rice-producing regions in all of Southeast Asia. The Red River delta in the north and the Mekong River delta in the south are the food baskets of Vietnam. They hang, as it were, on either end of a long pole, the pole being the range of Annamite Mountains that runs north and south for the length of the country.

When I was in Vietnam the Mekong River delta was deep in floods, so I did not visit it. I traveled instead the Red River delta, far to the north.

A macadam road, built high to serve as a dike in time of floods, streaks north from Hanoi. It is pock-marked from the pounding of trucks and from land mines. When I traveled it in August 1952, it was heavy with traffic. Dozens of American-made trucks filled with soldiers were moving north.

Up front were white-kepied French Legionnaires (mostly Polish and German) with hard-bitten faces. I had seen some of them on leave in Hanoi, carefree, relaxed, swaggering. I had talked with some in the lounge of the Hotel Metropole, and they were sure this business of war would be over and done with in a year and that they would be on their way home. And when I had asked, "The French will win in a year?" there was only a shrug of the shoulders.

Next in the caravan came young Vietnamese troops, as nondescript and as expressionless as the peasants in the rice fields.

In the rear came truck after truck filled with Senegalese troops. They wore broad-brimmed hats. And their smiles were almost as wide. I had seen them on guard at bridges outside Hanoi. They were always smiling or mimicking. Once when I stopped to take a picture of a sentry, he dropped his gun, held his hands above his head, and, feigning solemnity, said, "I surrender, monsieur." The Senegalese who were present had roared with laughter. About the only smiles I had seen in this country were the smiles of the Senegalese. They have roots perhaps deeper in the country than any other foreign race. Many of them in the Tonkin area have almost become members of the peasant families. They serve the role of big brother. Their attachments are close and enduring. And this day they waved and shouted at me from the trucks which carried them to the front lines a few miles north—the thin lines that stand between Hanoi and the Viet Minh army.

We were slowed to a few miles an hour by this caravan of trucks until we came to a left-hand fork in the road a few miles out of Hai Duong. There we bore off to the northwest, leaving the troops. The day was hot and muggy; not a breath of air stirred; no ripple touched the high stand of brightly green rice; paddies were empty of people and of animals. The rural scene was as peaceful as any New England could offer.

But war and peace are a strange mixture in Vietnam. What seemed to be a calm and placid countryside quickly exploded with violence. As I rounded a curve in the Jeepster I was right in the middle of a battle. A dozen French soldiers were charging across a field toward a squat mud hut by a lone palm tree. A half dozen men opposed them, rising from the grass and firing. One man fell, a wisp of smoke floated above him, and then the sound of the guns was lost in the screech of my tires.

Vietnam knows war as few countries have known it. She has been in the throes of bloody civil war for six years. Ho Chi Minh, the tubercular Communist who has had a more powerful hold on the people than any leader in modern times, has been a fugitive since late 1946. Since then he has been hiding in the mountains on the Chinese border, organizing his army and marshaling his propaganda. The Chinese set up military training schools for him. Russia sent instructors from Czechoslovakia, many mortars, and some 2½-ton trucks. China supplied carbines, machine guns, bazookas, anti-aircraft guns, mortar, and artillery —much of it American equipment that originally had been given Nationalist China or that was captured in Korea. China has had no tanks, no planes, and only a few trucks to give Ho Chi Minh. But she has been furnishing 3,000 tons of ammunition a month. And recently she has started to supply political commissars to Ho Chi Minh's army.

This war material has to be carted over the mountains from China. There is little motor transport and only primitive roads.

Ho Chi Minh answered that problem in logistics through the mass use of slave labor. He has conscripted all men between eighteen and forty-five for the army and for his labor battalions. With China's help he has mustered as high as 600,000 coolies for some of his operations. They are his supply line, moving hundreds of miles over the mountains with food, supplies, and ammunition for the Viet Minh army. Yet without much motor transport Ho Chi Minh waxes strong. Opposed to him are nearly 400,000 troops (150,000 French) with tanks, planes, artillery, and all the modern implements of war. But Ho Chi Minh's armies, though vastly inferior in arms and equipment, are a stand-off to the French and Vietnamese. They are so strong that for the most part they hold the initiative. Their estimated total is 300,000 men, with a central unit composed of 50,000 hard and seasoned troops. These soldiers are probably as good as any in Asia. Ho Chi Minh carefully conserves them. He has committed them to battle only twice. He holds them in reserve, using unorthodox warfare to undermine the opposition.

(1) There are few direct assaults. The tactics are one of infiltration behind the lines in an effort to harass and annoy the opposition and to keep it off balance.

(2) The Communist orders are never to meet a superior force head on, but to give way. These orders go further and direct the soldiers to dissolve before a stronger force, to conceal their weapons, to take off their uniforms and assume the role of peasants, and days or weeks later to reassemble at a designated point.

(3) Troops seldom move in the classical way. There is no convoy, no body of men marching down a road, no sweeping movements of mechanized troops. The soldiers travel at night—behind or in oxcarts, across rice paddies on foot, or in unsuspecting trucks. They may also move by daytime in the guise of peasants. A cart full of grass may conceal their carbines; loads of banana wood may contain sticks that have been hollowed out and filled with hand grenades. Thousands of soldiers often sift

through a countryside silently and mysteriously, suddenly to appear far in the rear of their enemy.

(4) In the hills the troops are dug in, and the defense runs miles in depth. There is no "front line" in the conventional sense. Dugouts twenty feet or more deep hold a few men. These dugouts are so widely dispersed and so well concealed that they offer no military target either for artillery, mortar, or aerial bombs.

(5) Dispersion extends to supplies and ammunition dumps. For example, aerial reconnaissance will show no enemy artillery within range. Yet under cover of night thousands of coolies pull guns dozens of miles to points within range of the "front" and before dawn wheel them back again.

The success of these tactics depends primarily on two conditions. First, there must be great reservoirs of expendable man power. Second, there must be a sympathetic, co-operative community of the same race as the enemy army. In other words, the enemy must have popular support far to the rear of the lines that are supposed to defend the nation.

The army of the Viet Minh employs the tactics Mao Tse-tung used in China. It never attacks until it has a vastly superior force in the field. It gives way before overwhelming power, its army becoming peasants. Until the strategic hour to strike arises, it harasses the opposition, infiltrates his rear, keeps him constantly off balance, and takes a heavy toll of his men.

The battle I passed through this August day, though a minor skirmish, was illustrative of these Communist tactics. It took place about twenty miles behind the French lines. How contact happened to be made I do not know. A handful of Viet Minh troops was apprehended deep in French territory where under cover of night it had been wreaking destruction on communications.

The examples of this operation are frequent and dramatic. Hué, a town of about 30,000, is some 300 miles south of Hanoi and over 100 miles below the Viet Minh stronghold in the provinces of Thanh-hoa and Vinh. It is the ancient capital of Annam. On August 26, 1952, the day before I reached there, a regiment of

Viet Minh troops (about 3,000) suddenly appeared below Hué. Their appearance was more startling than General Jubal A. Early's arrival at the back door of Washington, D.C., on July 11, 1864, during the Civil War. Early had brought his cavalry cross-country through Maryland on a hard, fast ride. These Viet Minh troops traveled silently and quietly. They drifted down from the north singly and in small groups, traveling at night and sleeping in huts of sympathetic villagers by day. It took them days on end to work their way south of Hué, where a rendezvous had been arranged. Yet in spite of the time it took, the necessary reliance that was placed upon the villagers along the way, the distance covered, the number of people who must have known of the movement, not a word of the intelligence reached the French. The first the French knew of the episode was when the Viet Minh regiment moved into action south of Hué. The French at once dropped para-troopers into the region, and the news account was that the Viet Minh suffered a severe setback. The truth of the matter is that the great majority of this regiment—well over 2,000—melted safely away in the jungles and the rice paddies to work their way to some rendezvous.

This type of operation is frequent and amazingly successful. As this account is being written in the winter of 1952 the news is full of these episodes. Unless one reads carefully, the impression is likely to be created that the French have had resounding suc-cesses in quelling the assaults of the Viet Minh. The truth is that the French positions are constantly infiltrated; the French "vic-tories" are often engagements with Viet Minh forces far in the rear of the French lines. By military standards it is usually the Viet Minh that is strong. The Viet Minh keeps the French pretty much in fixed positions. Then it goes around the flanks, suddenly appears far in the rear, or turns up in the midst of a French stronghold. Its troops come and go with apparent ease, disap-pearing as mysteriously as they arrive, melting away in the rice paddies like a phantom army. The Viet Minh is, indeed, so mobile that it seems to be everywhere in the country.

The French would welcome an all-out engagement. But the Viet Minh is not accommodating. When the French take the initiative and move in force against the Viet Minh, the results are usually meager. The Viet Minh, though everywhere, seems to be nowhere.

In late August 1952 the French moved 10,000 troops into the heart of Viet Minh country in an all-out drive against a supposed stronghold. They used tanks, artillery, mortar, and planes. This movement, designed to operate as fast as lightning, struck with great force and speed. For twenty-four hours this powerful wedge drove deep into Viet Minh territory. The results—no Viet Minh captured, no Viet Minh troops engaged. One Vietnamese was killed by artillery fire, but whether he was a Viet Minh soldier no one knows. As one French officer said, "It's like trying to hit mosquitoes with a sledge hammer." The Viet Minh forces gave way before the assault, avoiding any engagement. They proved again that they are a phantom army. They showed the Vietnamese that the French cannot trap them or encircle them. They showed the peasants up and down the land that French troops, American armor, and all the skills of modern war are futile against them. When that happens, the Vietnamese—whether he is a Communist or not—smiles to himself and boasts to his wife. He is secretly proud of Ho Chi Minh, the underdog, who can make the French look silly. For it is the French that every Vietnamese hates or distrusts. The anti-French attitude is Ho Chi Minh's greatest asset. That strong feeling against the foreigner cuts deeper in Vietnam than even the misery and poverty of the peasant.

In the winter of 1952–53 the Viet Minh won an important military victory not wholly reflected in the news. It pushed west into the edge of Laos, skirting strong French positions. It now is in position to command the Mekong River that runs the length of the Associated States and pours into the China Sea south of Saigon. Once it controls the Mekong, its forces north and south can join hands; and all French positions in Vietnam will be outflanked. This maneuver may not be completed until the winter of 1953–54, or perhaps a year later. For the Viet Minh, Communist-style, precedes its military movements with political action. It is now indoctrinating the Mekong River valley with discontent and high promises. When it is adequately "softened," the Viet Minh army will move.

Meanwhile, the French forces hold fast at impregnable bastions. In Vietnam the Maginot Line psychology still dominates French military thinking. It is perhaps natural, since the French missed participation in the military strategy that won World War II. There is none of that experience in their background. But the impregnable bastions of the French in Vietnam are proving to be forts easily outflanked. The French have not learned the Viet Minh guerrilla tactics. And in spite of the great disaster they have experienced in Asia they still seem oblivious of the fact that political action is sometimes even more effective than military might.

CHAPTER 2

IMPERIALISM—FRENCH STYLE

The French first came to Indo-China in the early
seventeenth century not as exploiters or imperialists
but as missionaries. The Catholic priests, mostly Portuguese and
Spanish, had been in the country since 1550. After 1659 many of
the Catholic missionaries were French; and their work and the
work of their successors produced close to two million Catholics
in this Buddhist and Confucian country. By the beginning of the
nineteenth century some French missionaries had become involved in local politics. Between 1825 and 1833 the government,
encouraged by China, promulgated harsh decrees against them
and their converts. Numerous incidents occurred, including persecutions and murders of the clergy. Most of the ports were closed
to Europeans, and immigration of Europeans was drastically
limited.

Long after the persecutions started, Louis Napoleon dispatched
a fleet, ostensibly to protect the clergy. But he had other reasons
as well. The French coveted the wealth of South Vietnam. Moreover, the ports of China were largely monopolized by other

European powers. Indo-China seemed to offer a natural outlet for the riches of southwest China. The French fleet captured Saigon in 1859. Chinese troops aided the Vietnamese in resisting the invasion; but the French broke the support of China by a blockade. Then the French Army undertook to subjugate all of Indo-China. By 1893 the French Army had consolidated its hold on the entire country. Cochin China (South Vietnam) became a French colony. Annam (Central Vietnam) and Tonkin (North Vietnam) became French protectorates. So did Cambodia and Laos.

Today three countries make up Indo-China—Vietnam, Cambodia, and Laos. Vietnam is composed of the former colony of Cochin China and the two protectorates, Annam and Tonkin. Though Vietnam comprises only 40 per cent of what was Indo-China, it has about 85 per cent of the twenty-five million people.

Vietnam had known the invader before. The northern provinces, where the main part of the war is being fought, had been ruled by the Chinese for over a thousand years—from 111 B.C. to A.D. 939. There were during this period great uprisings and short periods of independence. From then until 1427 there were powerful Chinese invasions which were repulsed by long and hard efforts. The Chinese power ebbed and flowed until the fifteenth century. Repeated invasions were made; repeated rebellions against the Chinese were undertaken. Vietnam was profoundly molded by Chinese culture and its institutions were adapted to the Chinese way of life. Yet China did not engulf Vietnam nor destroy its personality. After the Chinese rule ended, the country was cohesive, unified, and tenacious in the retention of its own way of life. It was then that the Nguyen dynasty, of which Bao Dai is the present ruling member, was founded.

Political organization followed the Chinese pattern, with the Emperor at the top, and below him governors who ruled over provinces. The commune, an organization of village notables, was the smallest administrative unit. It owned roads, woods, and pastures. This property was collective. It was redistributed every three years in equal parts among the inhabitants of the village, one part (sometimes a tenth) being set aside for some public benefit such as the support of students, the care of the aged or the orphans, and the like. The political institutions of Vietnam were not democratic in our sense of the word, but they were not dictatorial nor bureaucratic like the French colonial administration that was to follow. The King, as well as the officials and the people, were governed by moral obligations. The King held a mandate from Heaven which was revocable if he proved himself unworthy. The voice of the people was the voice of Heaven. The government member in his official capacity had to conduct himself as one who was performing a religious rite. As an indication of their attachment to ancient customs, especially property rights, villagers still say, "The King's law does not override village custom."

The chief administrative officers were mandarins who were selected on the basis of national scholastic examinations. These examinations were open to all on a competitive basis. The son of a peasant could take them and, if he were successful, could reach the highest administrative post in the land. The notables of the communes administered village regulations; the mandarins, the laws of the central government. But before an individual suffered the death penalty, the Emperor had to approve.

The advent of French rule brought a change. The power of the Emperor was reduced to Central Vietnam. South and North Vietnam became protectorates. France destroyed almost all of the self-government in Vietnam, leaving to the Vietnamese the collection of direct taxes, the performance of some police functions, and the administration of "native" courts.

France did not encourage perpetuation of the ancient culture of the Vietnamese. Rather, it adopted the policy of reducing the Vietnamese to colonial people and giving them a second-class citizenship. Vietnam had a distinct educational system. Each province and each district had a school of advanced learning with public examinations for degrees. They were abolished by the

French. The French established libraries, research centers, technical schools, and in 1930 founded a university at Hanoi. These institutions disseminated French culture; and in many ways the French colonizers attached the highest importance to learning the French language and revering French institutions. But for the Vietnamese the French created an inferior educational program which suppressed the humanities.

The French made very little contribution to elementary education. In fact, they made it available for only 2 per cent of the people. They created no secondary schools for Vietnamese until 1919, and then they made them available for less than 1 per cent. Though the French romanized the complicated Sino-Vietnamese language and made it easier for everyone, they kept over 60 per cent of the people illiterate.

Only the lower government posts were open to Vietnamese, and then only to those few who had become French citizens. The higher administrative posts were for the French exclusively. The pay of the French official even at the lower echelons far exceeded any income a Vietnamese, trained as a professional man, could make. The perquisites of the government were for the French, not the Vietnamese.

The French imported the Napoleonic Code into the south and displaced much of the native law in Central and North Vietnam. Vietnamese judges sat in the lower courts in Central and North Vietnam. But when Frenchmen and French interests were involved, the judges were French. Thus a case concerning the rights of the rice distillery (a monopoly granted by the government) was tried before a French judge. So also were cases involving taxes laid by the central government. In the south and in the north the French tried to destroy the democratic spirit of the commune and make French agents out of the notables. In that effort they stirred tremendous opposition and resentment.

On the face of the record it seems that France did much for Indo-China. It constructed over 3,000 kilometers of railroads, 32,000 kilometers of roads, 3,000 kilometers of canals, 16,000 kilometers of telephone lines. It increased rice production from 300,000 tons in 1865 to 3,180,000 tons in 1945; rubber production from 200 tons in 1911 to 76,000 tons in 1941; coal production from 250,000 tons in 1900 to 2,500,000 tons in 1940. The French did much to stop land erosion; and they built many reservoirs and dikes for irrigation, especially to serve French landed interests. During the eighty years of their occupation they have invested about two billion dollars. But the people of Indo-China got only the crumbs; the French, the feast.

The exploitation of Indo-China was cold and calculating. Indo-China was a source of food and raw materials for France and a market for French goods. France imposed a preferential tariff on Indo-China, cutting it off from Asian goods which were lower in price than the French. French capital was used to exploit Vietnamese mineral and agricultural resources and to open rubber and coffee plantations. Few factories, however, were built. It was the policy of France to ship the raw materials home for processing. It was also French policy to create dummy corporations that would lay claims to all the wealth of Vietnam against the day when the riches might be developed through concessions or otherwise.

The stories of French exploitation are legion.

Rubber-plantation companies that paid Vietnamese workers a few francs a day would make a 50 per cent return a year on capital.

Anthracite companies that paid coal miners 750 francs a year showed returns on capital up to 60 per cent a year.

The monopoly in alcohol that was granted a French company destroyed the native distilling industry; the monopoly in opium helped degrade the people.

French textile industries paid wages averaging about 600 francs a year. The dividends in 1939 on each 1,250-franc share was over twice that amount.

The laborer in Vietnam was chronically oppressed. Even during the best years he could save nothing. The average income of

*I sat outside a Buddhist pagoda near Hanoi
—as tranquil a spot as I could remember.*

The village notables at Dong Khe
stood in a group to meet the governor.

At Dong Khe we met the village elders
—their faces so serious as to be sad.

At Giang Bo each family got a mat
of lotania leaves, a can of condensed milk,
and about two quarts of rice.

the Vietnamese laborer prior to World War II was 49 piasters a year! He lived from day to day, ate well only at harvest time, and eked out a bare existence. Virginia Thompson, in *Notes of Labor Problems in Indo-China* (1945), gives the bitter details.

Prior to the French occupation the indigenous economy was based primarily upon small farms and artisan industries. Many villages supplemented agriculture by artisan activities. There were villages of weavers, of distillers, of carpenters, of blacksmiths, and the like. These artisan industries were largely wiped out by the French by means of protective tariffs and other devices.

The population of Indo-China rose from eleven million in 1885 to twenty-seven million in 1946. The French contributed to the increase by vaccinating against epidemic diseases. But they lowered rather than increased the standard of living of the people. The rice paddies tell the story. About 95 per cent of all owners own about 29 per cent of the rice paddies. Slightly over 5 per cent own about 60 per cent of the rice paddies. (The rest is communal land.) The 95 per cent own on the average 1.73 acres per proprietor, while 60 per cent own less than 1 acre. These people for years have not made enough to satisfy their hunger. As a result of the loss of artisan industries more and more fell victims of usurious loans, lost their small holdings, and became share tenants. Many of the details are supplied by Jacoby in *Agrarian Unrest in Southeast Asia* (1949). In South Vietnam particularly, the French favored the establishment of a landed class in control of 80 per cent of the rice fields. There 200,000 landless families work as sharecroppers.

Rice export was made a monopoly and was granted to a few colonial societies. It returned fortunes to the exporters while the Vietnamese peasants who grew the rice lived in poverty and whole sections of the country starved. A family of five averaged between 1,300 francs and 1,510 francs a year from their rice paddies.

The French encouraged the development of a small group of Vietnamese capitalists. They admitted some of them to the boards of directors of French corporations. But by and large they restricted them to investments in agricultural land. They feared the Vietnamese as competitors in industry. Industry, commerce, and finance were preserves reserved exclusively for the French. If there were to be outsiders, they had to be foreigners who, if too enterprising, could be expelled from the country. Thus even the Vietnamese middle class was small in size and restricted in operations. And they were the only ones in the entire country on whom the French had any claims to loyalty and friendship.

This policy had a profound effect on the revolution that was to break in Indo-China. There was no substantial middle class out of which a resistance movement could grow. India had its Congress Party which represented the non-Communist core of resistance to the British. But the economic practices of the French allowed no such political development in Indo-China. The 80 per cent of the population earning their living as peasants or fishermen and living in misery and poverty furnished the leadership for revolution. The Vietnamese capitalist gave them, rather than the French, his sympathy.

The attitude of the French toward the populace was domineering. A native would be addressed with the familiar *tu* rather than *vous*. Liberty, equality, fraternity—the proud boast of the French Revolution—were forgotten in Indo-China. Those who took up the cry of the French revolutionaries were exiled. Simple peasants speaking out for reforms were beaten. Civil liberties were harshly suppressed. Political prisoners were commonplace. Books and pamphlets deemed proper in Paris were incitements to revolution in Indo-China and therefore unlawful. Free speech was denied the natives. Disagreement with the authorities was the equivalent of sedition. Even a verbal protest of a Vietnamese to a Frenchman cost him dear.

The French suppressed all Vietnamese organizations. As a result the present generation has not learned how to unite its efforts. The people forgot how to organize an opposition and make their influence felt. That by-product of French policy is now working against the French. The Vietnamese now more easily succumb to the highly organized Communist movement.

The French built almost three times as many prisons in Indo-China as they built hospitals. The chronicles are filled with records of cruel and inhuman punishments of the accused. The vengeance of the French ran to communities as well as to individuals. Before Hitler conceived the infamous episode at Lidice the French in Indo-China wiped out whole villages in retaliation for the misdeeds of "rebels." In 1930 one village was wiped out by incendiary bombs because it was supposed to have granted asylum to insurgents.

The French bureaucracy became the symbol of special privilege; the French police became the symbol of terror; the Frenchman became the symbol of exploitation. The popular Parisian phrase—"the radiance of French culture and thought in the world"—brings only a scornful, bitter laugh in Vietnam.

Young Vietnamese who studied began to see how the ideas of revolution could be used against the French in Indo-China. The republican ideas of the French Revolution never took hold. The democratic ideas of the American Revolution and the Marxist ideas of the Russian Revolution had some effect. But the fermenting ideas of freedom came from the Chinese and Japanese. For Vietnam throughout history has been a part of those zones of culture.

CHAPTER 3

THE REVOLUTION

The first revolutionary was not a peasant but a king.

He was Emperor Ham Nghi, who signed the treaty that gave France the protectorate. A few months later he fled and called upon the people to revolt. He waged guerrilla warfare for five years before he was captured. The revolt went on. The local heroes were many. A man of letters—Phan Dinh Phung—was one. He organized the guerrillas (1893–95) and set up a base for their operations in the mountains of Central Vietnam. Another was De Tham, who was finally captured twenty-eight years after the French protectorate. He was the last of the old resistance leaders.

But the revolution did not die. The leadership passed to new hands, and soon it was to be lodged in one who was steeped in the Marxist creed.

Ho Chi Minh—slight, thin, with a skimpy mustache and stringy beard and the mark of tuberculosis on his face—was born in the 1890's.

Before World War I he went to Hong Kong, then to England, and afterward to France, where he worked as a "retoucher" of photographic plates. He was first a Socialist. At the break between the Second and Third Internationals he decided for the latter. In the 1920's he went to Moscow and then to Canton, where he became the attaché to Chiang Kai-shek's Soviet adviser. In 1927 he founded the Revolutionary Youth of Vietnam—an organization which was Communist-supported and which used Communist tactics. It became the Communist Party of Vietnam in 1929. In 1941 Ho Chi Minh formed the Viet Minh (the Vietnam Independence League) to operate against the Japanese.

When the Japanese entered Indo-China in 1940, the Vietnamese believed the French would fight and that turmoil would fill the country. A new wave of resistance against the French arose. But the French at once made a compact with the Japanese whereby the Japanese guaranteed French sovereignty in Vietnam and the French agreed to furnish the Japanese with transport, food, and other supplies needed for their conduct of the war against China. The French and Japanese then brought their full force against the guerrillas inside Vietnam.

Ho Chi Minh had been arrested by the Chinese sometime after the outbreak of World War II; but since they concluded he was only a vagabond, he was released. He went to Kunming, capital of Yünnan, and made contact with the Allies. He then began the spread of propaganda in Vietnam through tracts. In 1944 he created an Army of Liberation, and our OSS dropped supplies and ammunition to help it carry on guerrilla activities against the Japanese.

Ho Chi Minh fought the French and the Japanese not only with guns but with propaganda. He wrote articles and pamphlets and distributed them among the people. He was hunted by every French policeman, yet never found. He was a phantom, a ghost, who seemed to move at will, casting an ominous shadow over the French regime. Peasants spoke of him in whispers; young and old rallied to his call; the hopes of thousands of miserable people went with him wherever he moved. But he is a man who always liked to surround himself with mystery. He probably was not back in Vietnam from the time he first left it until the Japanese defeat.

"My party is my country" was his slogan. His main cause was independence from the French and Japanese. But he also had a broad program of domestic reform for the country.

—Abolition of absentee landlordism and usury
—Guarantee of a living wage
—Production of enough rice and clothing to provide each citizen with his bare needs
—The teaching of everyone how to read
—The guarantee to everyone of "democratic liberties"
—The abolition of the hated head tax
—Equal rights for women and for minorities

Ho Chi Minh is a name well chosen by this man who had been known until the war years as Nguyen Ai Quoc. It means Ho of the Chaste Intentions, which permits the surmise, "Yes, I belong to the Communist Party, but you know my real intentions."

On March 9, 1945, the Japanese, sensing disaster, eliminated the French and offered control of Vietnam to Emperor Bao Dai, who had stayed on the throne during the occupation. The Japanese, to curry popular favor, also released 10,000 Vietnamese political prisoners who had been held by the French. Ho Chi Minh answered by renewed violence. By June 1945 he had acquired control over areas of the nation that included four fifths of all the people.

Soon it became apparent that the Allies would be victorious. So Bao Dai (on Japanese orders) declared his independence of France on March 11, 1945. But that was not enough to save the country from Ho Chi Minh. In August 1945, Ho Chi Minh called for a general insurrection. As a result of the turmoil that followed, Bao Dai abdicated and the pro-Japanese government resigned. On August 25, 1945, Ho Chi Minh proclaimed the Vietnam Democratic Republic and made Bao Dai his "Supreme Adviser." A week later Ho Chi Minh entered Hanoi as the head of the new government—a coalition government composed of numerous parties or blocs from the Communists to the Catholics. Retaining Bao Dai was a clever move. The King was bereft of prestige. His suppression would have enabled a pretender to rally the opposition to Ho Chi Minh's insecure regime.

The new government proclaimed its Declaration of Independence on September 2, 1945. The Declaration opened with a quotation from our own Declaration of Independence of 1776: "We hold these truths . . . that all men are created equal, that they are endowed by their Creator with certain inalienable Rights, that among these are Life, Liberty and the pursuit of Happiness."

The Declaration paraphrased the French Declaration of the Rights of Man of 1789: "Every man is born equal and enjoys free and equal rights." And it proclaimed the principle of equal rights and self-determination of peoples sponsored by the United Nations.

The Declaration accused the French, as we in 1776 accused George III. It listed the grievances of the people, from the stifling of public opinion and the suppression of liberties to the exploitation of workers and the appropriating of the wealth of the nation for the foreigner.

A parliament of 400 was elected in January 1946. Eighty-two per cent of all men and women over eighteen years old voted. The election was orderly, since it was policed by Ho Chi Minh. But there is evidence that it was controlled so that Ho Chi Minh would win. Minority parties won some seats in the Parliament, but the majority was won by the Vietminh.

Ho Chi Minh was elected President. He immediately started an illiteracy drive. Signs on the walls at Hanoi read, "Illiteracy is no less a crime than theft." There were night and day classes conducted by volunteer teachers. Recalcitrants were fined. A three months' course was offered all citizens in learning the romanized script the French had introduced.

This program was handled at the village level. There were village committees elected for a six months' term, all races being proportionately represented on them. The committees met once

167

a week; and every two months they called the entire village to a meeting to account for what had been done and to lay future plans.

There was a famine in 1944–45, caused in part by the requisitioning of food by the French and the Japanese and in part by the Chinese. The surrender of the Japanese north of the 16th parallel had been left to the Chinese Army. The Chinese bled the north country white. The famine that resulted claimed about one million victims. Ho Chi Minh took vigorous action to feed the people. The French and Japanese had laid on the country the enforced cultivation of jute, castor beans for oil, and poppies for opium. Ho Chi Minh substituted sweet potatoes, maize, and soybeans in the Tonkin (northern) area. These were crops that came to maturity before the harvest of the rice.

Ho Chi Minh repaired the system of dikes that had been badly damaged by the flooding of rivers.

He took all fallow land and gave the use of it to anyone who would work it. The land reverted to the owner, but the cultivator kept the crop. This compulsory loan of property extended to water buffalo and farm implements, as well as to land. The total of all these measures increased the food of the Tonkin area by 373,000 tons and saved the people from death by starvation.

There was order throughout the land—from south to north. Public utilities functioned. The new government opened the prisons and let loose all the political prisoners. A new excitement filled Vietnam, the excitement of the creation of a government freed from foreign control.

On November 9, 1946, the National Assembly adopted a constitution which had conspicuous democratic overtones. It was based upon the "union of all the people without distinction of race, clan, creed, wealth or sex"; the guarantee of "democratic liberties"; the establishment of a "true people's government." It guaranteed freedom of speech, press, assembly, religion, residence, and travel. It provided for compulsory public education and equality of all Vietnamese citizens "in the economic, political and cultural fields." It granted the right to vote to all Vietnamese who were eighteen or older, "without distinction of sex." It provided for a parliament to be elected every three years, every 50,000 people having one representative. The President (as well as the Vice-President) was to be chosen from the members of the Parliament for a term of five years, with no limitation on the number of terms he might serve. All judges were to be appointed; there was a provision for jury trials; and the torturing or ill-treatment of persons accused or of prisoners was to be forbidden.

But this new government had telltale signs of Communist influence. Ho Chi Minh created political police to search out non-conformists. He also had a Political Bureau, composed of notorious Communists, which produced many brochures of Communist propaganda. And the flag he adopted had a red field with a yellow star in the middle.

How the new government would have developed, no one knows. Certainly the resistance movement was by no means entirely Communist. Ho Tung Mau, Ho's oldest friend and staunch collaborator, was not a Communist. He had long counseled Ho Chi Minh against the Communists. But Ho Chi Minh temporized. Both men became outlaws; both ended with the Viet Minh forces, supported by Red China. And only last year Ho Tung Mau, perhaps as a gesture of his basic integrity, committed suicide. The elimination of colonialism might have removed the one powerful stimulant which Communism had in Vietnam, caused the eclipse of Ho Chi Minh, and set the course of the new government in another direction. The answer will never be known. For there were cruel events in the making—events, partially under the American influence, which destroyed the dream of Vietnam independence by reintroducing French colonialism.

It was agreed at the Potsdam Conference, held in July 1945, that all of Southeast Asia was in the British sphere of influence. The British were to occupy Indo-China up to the 16th parallel, the Chinese above it. They were to restore "law and order" and remain until the 200,000 Japanese soldiers in Indo-China were

169

disarmed and repatriated. In the north the Nationalist Chinese armies took "law and order" to mean recognition of the Ho Chi Minh government. In the south the British construed it as requiring the overthrow of Ho Chi Minh and particularly the restoration of the French. The first British representatives to arrive in Saigon were greeted by the Vietnamese; several hundred thousand paraded in honor of the occasion. As the parade was breaking up, a shooting incident between French and Vietnamese occurred in which several Frenchmen were killed.

The welcome given the British was ill-spent. The British refused to deal directly with Ho Chi Minh's government, claiming it was a puppet of the Japanese. Rather, the British communicated with the Viet Minh only through the Japanese headquarters. The British declared martial law; they closed Vietnamese newspapers; they armed French troops who had been interned by the Japanese; and they ordered disarmament of the Viet Minh. The British moved Viet Minh officials out of some posts in Saigon; and on the night of September 23, 1945, French soldiers raided Viet Minh headquarters in Saigon, arrested many leaders, and took over the seat of government. The French offered Viet Minh leaders a limited autonomy under French control. The Viet Minh demanded full independence. There was no agreement. Fighting spread. The French landed reinforcements. And after attacks and counterattacks the French fastened tight their hold on Saigon. In 1945–46 the United States was not on the side of Asian nationalism. The official attitude of our State Department was that "this Government does not question French sovereignty" in Indo-China.

The Japanese were those whom the British were supposed to disarm. But they turned the Japanese Army and Air Force loose on the Vietnamese and used them to restore "law and order." Not until the Japanese had helped the British restore southern Vietnam to the French did Japanese disarmament start in earnest. In October 1945 the British turned command over to the French. By December 1945 the French had over 60,000 troops south of the 16th parallel and were ready to complete the "pacification" of the country.

Up north the Chinese, while fostering and protecting the nationalist movement, encouraged the development of an opposition to Ho Chi Minh. They gave their protection to newspapers that attacked Ho Chi Minh and his regime. But the Chinese had no precise plan for overthrowing Ho Chi Minh. They were indeed more interested in drawing off the wealth of the country, sucking it dry.

Once the French had gained control of the south, they approached the Chinese for evacuation of the north. That was agreed upon by treaty in February 1946. By that treaty Nationalist China obtained from the French a surrender of rights of extraterritoriality, a railroad in Yünnan, free passage of Chinese goods through the port of Haiphong. France obtained a withdrawal of Chinese troops from Indo-China. Thereupon the French prepared to take over the north. But when the French undertook to send troops there the entire country rose against them. The spirit of revolution possessed the north and the revolutionaries were deeply entrenched. There were signs or slogans everywhere—"Independence or Death"—"Death rather than return to Slavery." The Vietnamese took down all French signs, all French names on the streets. Vietnamese names took their place.

The French thereupon changed their tactics. They negotiated with Ho Chi Minh. In March 1946 an agreement was reached. The French recognized Vietnam as a separate state and agreed that it was to have a parliament and an army. Ho Chi Minh agreed to permit 15,000 French troops to be stationed in the country for five years. He demanded that South Vietnam (the rich delta the French first possessed and always coveted) be included in Vietnam. The French refused. So it was finally agreed that the issue of South Vietnam was to be left to a plebiscite.

Then started a series of futile negotiations. Ho Chi Minh demanded that a referendum be held in South Vietnam. The French said there could be none until that part of the nation was "pacified." Ho Chi Minh responded that the way to pacify it was to have the referendum. The French, always anxious to keep South Vietnam, refused. Ho Chi Minh wanted his government to have independent diplomatic representation abroad as do the members of the British Commonwealth. The French refused.

At this juncture the French persuaded Ho Chi Minh to go to Paris for further talks. The French say that Ho Chi Minh at Paris made a peaceful settlement impossible. Ho Chi Minh can be denounced for being a Communist, for such he was and is. But he cannot be denounced for the failure of the Paris conference. While he was en route there, the French High Commissioner— Georges Thierry d'Argenlieu—in violation of the agreement made with Ho Chi Minh, suddenly proclaimed the autonomy of South Vietnam as the Federation of Cochin China. The French thus acted unilaterally on an issue that was on the agenda for discussion at Paris. The Paris conference was therefore doomed to failure, and it failed. But contrary to the French propaganda, the failure was due to the French, not to Ho Chi Minh.

Ho Chi Minh was in the hands of the French and had to return to Vietnam on a French warship. Under the pressure of those circumstances, he made certain concessions. Prior to his departure from Paris he undertook several engagements in order to prevent a coup by the French. He agreed to accept piasters issued by the Bank of Indo-China as legal tender, which meant that Ho Chi Minh, who had already issued his own money, would no longer be able to control his finances. Moreover, Ho Chi Minh agreed to the general formula of a customs union. Thus he would not be able to export goods. And even though he wanted to, the French had a fleet which stood guard at the ports.

The French took one more step which removed any basis for negotiation with Ho Chi Minh. After he had departed from Paris the French adopted on October 27, 1946, the Constitution of the Fourth Republic. That Constitution included a provision for the French Union, which was defined unilaterally in a colonial sense. Ho Chi Minh had understood the French Union to be a cultural bond with some sort of vague military alliance. He and other Vietnamese nationalists had insisted straight along for national independence. When the French Union was unilaterally defined so as to create a virtual colony out of Vietnam, the French repudiated the nationalists' ambitions.

After Ho Chi Minh returned to Hanoi numerous provocative incidents occurred. The French wanted to control the port of Haiphong and met minor opposition from a small military unit of Ho Chi Minh's. The French suffered twenty casualties. Thereupon the French fleet opened fire, calculated to produce terrorism. The French fleet bombarded the entire civilian population of the port of Haiphong, killing at least 6,000 civilians.

Distrust of the French had always been deep in the hearts of the Vietnamese. By December 1946 this hatred became a livid, leaping thing. Ho Chi Minh produced a murderous plan. He made his arrangements with great care. On December 19, 1946, his men moved into action. They invaded every French home in Hanoi and killed men, women, and children. Some accounts say that thousands were killed. Actually forty people died in the awful massacre. Others, who were kidnaped by troops of Ho Chi Minh, were later released.

The French moved into the north in force. Ho Chi Minh fled Hanoi and went to the hills on the China border. There he is to this day—six years later—unless, as rumor has it, he died in September 1952. From the jungles he organized armies and propaganda. His government was recognized by Red China on January 18, 1950, and by Russia on January 30, 1950. Through the Viet Minh radio at Bakan (near the China border) he broadcasts to the people. And his message is one of hate and hope—hate for the French, hope for the independence of his people.

In 1945 and 1946 Ho Chi Minh was probably not too popular with the people. Since then they have suffered greatly. There have been six years of guerrilla warfare; thousands of peasants have been impressed into service by both sides; their farms and villages have been trampled over. Today the people are sick and tired of war. Yet even so, Ho Chi Minh has probably increased in popularity. The heavy hand of the French is still on the land. The resistance movement is stronger than ever; and Ho Chi Minh is the outstanding symbol of it. There is little doubt that in a popularity contest Ho Chi Minh would still lead the field.

CHAPTER 4

A HOUSE DIVIDED AGAINST ITSELF

Dong Khe is a small village of North Vietnam, sixty miles or so northeast of Hanoi in the rich and strategic Red River delta. The Red River delta is a rice-growing region. Wherever one looks there is wet paddy; and in August fields of rice, rippling in the hot wind, stretch to the horizon. In the north are low hills with lines soft and broken. Those are the hills held a year ago by the French and today by the Viet Minh.

The village of Dong Khe, not far from them, has changed hands several times since Ho Chi Minh unleashed his forces in the winter of 1946. In August 1952 I visited it with Pham Van Binh, then Governor of North Vietnam, and General de Brigade René Cogny of the French Army, the day after it had been freshly taken by the French. Vietnamese troops patrolled its muddy streets. They also walked the low dikes that extended far out into the rice fields surrounding the village, as if they expected the Viet Minh to rise suddenly from the paddies and make an assault. And one solitary Vietnamese soldier stood guard over a nearby swamp ablaze with the beautiful Japanese hyacinth.

A rehabilitation unit had arrived ahead of us and was busily engaged. This was one of the GAMO teams organized by the French to follow on the heels of the Army. I had heard of the work of the GAMO in Southeast Asia before I reached Vietnam. I had been told that its influence on the side of rehabilitation had done much to help heal the scars of civil war. In Saigon I had talked with the President of Vietnam about it. Nguyen Van Tam was appointed President by Emperor Bao Dai in June 1952. Tam, fifty-seven years old, is a slight man with great energy. He works quietly and unobtrusively. Yet he is bold and direct in his words and deeds, and is a good executive. Once head of the police, he is today a "strong" man feared by the people. He is feared because of his record. He obtained French naturalization and for years aided the French cause in helping arrest and repress nationalists and Communists alike. He is known best for his cruelty in torturing political prisoners.

I asked Tam about GAMO. He spoke feelingly of it. It was a poor system, he thought. He had opposed it and had tried to convince the French not to use it. His own system was much better, he insisted.

"What was your system?" I inquired.

"Stern justice for the Communists and their sympathizers," he replied.

Stern justice for the Communists and their sympathizers in the context of Vietnam meant only one thing—ruthless extermination of anyone who dared protest an injustice. I can only believe that GAMO, a creation of the French, also knows the technique of terror. One phase of its operations deals with ferreting out Communists from the conquered villages. I stood in a damp and dingy room while some suspects were being questioned. They had the flame of hatred in their eyes; they looked at me, not as hunted men and women who were finally cornered, but as militant crusaders who would never surrender their cause. Whether that cause was nationalism or Communism I could not discover. But I felt in the little village of Dong Khe the intensity of the feeling behind the revolution. And I believed from that moment the stories I had heard that GAMO was as insensitive to the distinction between a rebel who was a patriot and a rebel who was a Communist, as the French had always been.

GAMO is not, however, purely a police measure. At Dong Khe it had one unit organized for the dissemination of anti-Communist propaganda. There were banners and placards on display. There were booklets for distribution. There were comic strips showing Ho Chi Minh as a weak, ineffective, miserable creature supported by a big, bloody, and rapacious villain called Red China.

There was one unit that had collected all the currency of the Viet Minh. The coins were in a half-bushel basket—dirty coins made of a lightweight metal and poorly stamped. There were bills printed on cheap paper and impressed with pictures of peasants. And the central figure on both the coins and the paper currency was the head of Ho Chi Minh. This GAMO unit was setting up a food-distribution center and arranging for the issuance of ration cards.

But before any villager could get a ration card he and his family had to be vaccinated for cholera. They stood in line—mostly women and children—their left arms bare. Vietnamese nurses sat in the open at tables loaded with medical supplies. Without looking up they wiped a spot clean on the arm in front of them and injected the vaccine. Dozens of people went through the line. Children cried, women who were new to the experience closed their eyes, others turned their heads and suffered the agony of anticipated pain. At other tables Vietnamese nurses dispensed salve for ugly sores on the children's heads. The heads were first clipped short and then the salve applied with daubers.

I had been witnessing for a half hour or so the operations of the GAMO when a young Vietnamese took me aside.

"It's all a fraud," he explained.

"What's a fraud?"

"The medical care the French are dispensing."

"What's fraudulent about it?"

"That's not real vaccine in the syringes."

"What is it?"

"Probably water."

"Why do you say that? Do you know for sure?"

"I do not know for sure. But I know the French; and the French cannot be trusted to do anything good for the country."

"You mean this GAMO operation is put on as a stunt for my benefit?"

"Exactly."

"The GAMO does nothing good?"

"Nothing—except of course to punish anyone who dares speak against the government."

I do not believe that broad indictment of GAMO. It has done good work in the rehabilitation of some villages. But I came to know that in this war-torn country of Vietnam there was one group more hated, more suspected, more reviled than any other; and that group was the French.

Dong Khe had changed hands so fast that there was a stunned and paralyzed look in the eyes of the inhabitants. Today it was the French and Vietnamese who were there. Yesterday it had been the Viet Minh. Who would be their masters tomorrow?

The village notables or elders—the administrative group that in Vietnam manages the commune—stood together in a small square to greet the Governor. This square was fifty feet across and lined by the low, one-story peaked huts with thatched roofs that distinguish the villages of this area. Most of the notables were dressed in white trousers, long black gowns, and black skullcaps. Their faces were so serious as to be sad. Their high cheekbones were emphasized by pinched cheeks and skimpy beards. It was a muggy, steaming day with not a breath of air. Black clouds that promised relief from the heat were on China's border to the north. But Dong Khe was suffocating. A young man dressed in white stood in the sun and gave an address of welcome, sweat streaming from his face. The then Governor, an energetic, idealistic man in his forties, stood in the shade and replied. And then the notables gathered around for a serious discussion.

The Communists had been there for months and had not treated the villagers harshly. But if the notables co-operated with the French, the Communists might kill them. Would the Governor leave the Army at Dong Khe for protection? Would the government defend Dong Khe in case it were attacked?

"You are here now. If we are here alone tomorrow, what will happen to us?"

That question runs through the minds of most people in Vietnam and expresses their feeling of insecurity. That one question is, indeed, symptomatic of the disintegrating influences that are loose in this ancient country.

These days everyone is on a tentative basis in Vietnam, unsure of his status, uncertain of his future.

The Bank of Indo-China. The Bank was established in 1875 and since that date has enjoyed many privileges in the country, the most prized perhaps being the power to issue money. It has throughout its history been closely tied to French financial interests. Its directors and officers have served as directors on the boards of dozens of corporations doing business in the Associated States. In this way and in others it has occupied a controlling position in most of the business enterprises in the country. In practice it loaned money to the French and Chinese, not to the Vietnamese. The French worked largely through Chinese agents who became their intermediaries in commerce and in speculation. Thus easier and more discreet combines were effectuated. The Chinese in turn made loans at usurious rates to the Vietnamese farmers. They were the ones who obtained the rice at cheap prices from the peasants and furnished it to the French monopolies for export.

The Bank's activities include not only the Associated States but other nations and continents. It has recently turned its primary attention to other areas of French colonial activity. The political trend in Asia and particularly the menacing uncertainties in Vietnam were the reasons. The result is that today only one eighth of the assets of the Bank are in Indo-China.

Vietnamese Intellectuals. The intellectuals are more than tired of the French regime; they are bitter in their attitude. They are convinced that the French even today have no desire or intent to quit Vietnam. They are suspicious of Ho Chi Minh, but even more, they are suspicious of the French. They are not sure that Bao Dai, their Emperor, has the ability to manage the crisis. They live day by day without much hope. They can find no counterforce to rally behind. Their lack of confidence in the Bao Dai government involves more than their appraisal of its ability. They believe it lacks basic integrity, for they think it is beholden to the French. They say that the ministers and other officials owe their professional status to the French. A majority of ministers are naturalized French citizens. Some have wealth that is the product of favors rendered by the French. Some have personal ties of loyalty to the French. Their distrust of the French is so great that their measure of a man is his degree of independence from the French.

Ngo Dinh Diem, brother of a Catholic bishop, is a hero in Central and North Vietnam, with a considerable following in the south too. From 1929 to 1933 he was provincial Governor of Central Vietnam. In 1933, at the age of thirty-two, he became Minister of the Interior. In July 1933 he resigned in protest to the refusal of the French to allow a National Assembly. In reprisal the French forced Bao Dai to strip Ngo Dinh Diem of all honorary titles. Twice he refused Bao Dai's invitation to form a government. Since 1950 he has been at Maryknoll College, Lakewood, New Jersey, studying American democracy.

Ngo Dinh Diem has long argued that Vietnam should have a

status analogous to that of India and Pakistan in the British Commonwealth. He insisted on that when Bao Dai asked him to form a government in 1949. On June 16, 1949, he published in the Saigon press a threefold declaration:

—Only a status comparable to that of India and Pakistan can satisfy the aspirations of the Vietnamese.
—Economic and social reforms must be achieved which respect the dignity of the individual.
—Members of the resistance movement must be admitted to positions in the government in accordance with democratic criteria (thus excluding Communists).

Ngo Dinh Diem told me that of these the most important condition was independence from France. Ngo Dinh Diem was not satisfied that Bao Dai would stand firm against the French and demand full independence. So he twice refused the Presidency.

Ngo Dinh Diem is revered by the Vietnamese because he is honest and independent and stood firm against the French influence. There are few officials in the Vietnamese government who have that reputation. Therefore, the Vietnamese intellectuals see little hope in the present administration.

The Refugees. Tens of thousands of refugees fill the highways and pile up in the villages.

I visited Aimo village north of Hanoi and saw 300 Vietnamese huddled together in the mud, cooking their rationed rice over small fires of straw and dung. They were mostly women and children. A trachoma team, financed and trained under our MSA economic aid program, was there examining eyes and painting the underlids. I saw another group of refugees in the village of Giang Bo near Hanoi. These refugees had just arrived and were being vaccinated. Then they were lined up for receipt of rations of food and supplies. Each family got a mat of lotania leaves, a can of condensed milk, and about two quarts of rice—all financed under the MSA program. In this village there were no men, only women and children.

"Where are the men?" I asked.

No one could say. Perhaps some were in Ho Chi Minh's army, some in the French Army. Perhaps some were coolies drafted by Vietnam or forced into labor battalions by the Viet Minh. Perhaps the husbands and sons of these women at Giang Bo were dead. Perhaps they were in hiding. One story was that they came out only at night and stayed concealed in the daytime to avoid being drafted. Only the women knew where they were; and the women would not talk.

The Vietnamese women these days carry the burden of the work of the country. I seldom saw a man in the rice fields. I seldom saw a man walking the highways or at work on them. Highway travelers and workers were almost always the women. They wore chestnut-brown cotton dresses. Some had green sashes and black turbans. Most wore the large, circular bamboo hat with the sharp peak. Most of them had coated their teeth with black enamel. Some chewed betel nuts. They usually carried baskets at either end of a pole that rested on the shoulder. These baskets carried water, food, fuel. When the load was heavy, the women had the quick, nervous trot peculiar to Asia—the pace that keeps the baskets from swinging.

These women never seemed happy and relaxed. Though many were beautiful, they did not seem to be aware of it. They went silently and glumly about their work, never talking even to each other. They walked as if they were under harsh orders.

The women in line for rations at Giang Bo were also grim and silent. They had no smiles for anyone. They kept their worries to themselves. Those worries concerned the safety and well-being of their menfolk. Their faces reflected burdens almost too great for the human body to carry. Yet their eyes showed the fire that would enable them to survive all adversity and to produce new life in the process.

A *House Divided against Itself*

To them Ho Chi Minh was only a nationalist bent on liberating their homeland from the French rule. He was one of them. He did not ride in splendor nor live in luxury; he slept under a tree and ate the same food as they did. When Ho Chi Minh, the commoner, occupied the government building in Hanoi, he walked the streets freely and at noon sauntered over to the café in the Hotel Metropole, where he sat and talked with all comers.

These women were too ignorant of Marxist doctrine to make a decision for or against it. But they could not believe Ho Chi Minh was an evil man. And they felt deep in their hearts that the French were.

These refugees often carry the wounds of battle. They almost always have the marks of hunger and undernourishment on their faces. They walk in rags, usually with no personal belongings except perhaps a ring or a pin or some other item of sentiment that can be concealed on the body. The Tonkin area is cold in the winter, the temperature frequently dropping to the freezing point. People in rags can sleep alongside dikes or in flimsy huts in the summer; but they need walls, and stoves, and blankets in the winter. The resettlement of these refugees is a major undertaking to which the United States through MSA is making a notable contribution. I talked with the members of the American MSA team that is working on the problem in Hanoi. One of them, a fine American Negro, Herman J. Holiday, told me about the enormity of the task. I asked him what was the most difficult aspect of the job.

"Getting these people to have hope for the future. Getting them to have confidence in someone, faith in some cause."

I went with one of the Americans, Dr. Warren Winkelstein, Jr., to visit a hospital in Hanoi. There were 960 patients in the hospital and 240 beds! There were four doctors for the 960 patients. One doctor for 240 patients! Four patients for every bed! Some of the patients had pneumonia; others, tuberculosis. Some had broken bones; others had ugly wounds. Some were heart cases; others had had major operations. No patient could stay in his

183

bed for more than six hours a day. Then he left it to make way for another. The next eighteen hours he slept on the floor or sat in the hallway or wrapped himself in a robe and tried to find a comfortable corner. I walked the wards of this hospital, my heart filled to overflowing. These 960 sick and suffering people raised their heads as I passed, their eyes filled with supplication, their tongues silent. There was something heroic and noble in their attitude. It was reflected in the voice of the young Vietnamese doctor who whispered to me, "I'm proud of my people. They are miserable and they suffer much. But they suffer in dignity."

Bao Dai has a huge palace in Hanoi, a three-story mansion set in vast grounds that have tennis courts lighted overhead for night use. The palace inside as well as out is worthy of a Louis XIV. Bao Dai seldom uses it. A caretaker told me that the Emperor used it perhaps three days a year. Some of the doctors in Hanoi tried to get the palace for a hospital for the refugees. But Bao Dai refused.

Rallied Forces. The "deserters" from the Viet Minh are called the "rallied" forces. Much is made of the fact that in the last year the number of "rallied" forces has increased. But the number is entitled to little weight. They are mostly people who have been held by the Viet Minh and then released. Ho Chi Minh releases them after their detention has served his purpose in order to avoid feeding them. Ho Chi Minh holds a densely populated area where the food supply is low and where he is plagued with inflation. He cannot afford to feed extra mouths. And he has few medicines to care for the sick.

On their return these "rallied" people usually do not take sides. They are mostly passive, waiting the turn of events. Most of them are not Bao Dai supporters. Many have seen Communism in operation and do not like it. I talked with some and learned from them what the Viet Minh is doing behind its own lines. The bulk of the people in the Viet Minh areas probably do not know enough about Communism to know what it is. The high command of the Viet Minh—numbering between 600 and 1,000—are dyed-in-the-wool Communists. The top command is a seven-man Politburo (Tong Bo). They have full command of the Viet Minh movement to such an extent that some Vietnamese say that Ho Chi Minh is their prisoner. However that may be, the Communists control the key posts in the Viet Minh government. They have organized their villages along Soviet lines. They have set about indoctrinating the younger generation in Marxist philosophy. The Viet Minh usually does not fasten itself tightly onto a village at once. It waits perhaps a year before showing its Communist character.

The Viet Minh distributes land to the peasant. But any improvement in his economic lot is questionable. Under the old regime his landlord took 50 per cent or more of the annual crop as rent, though by law he was entitled only to 30 per cent. Under the Viet Minh the tenant probably pays 70 per cent in one form or another.

Those who escape the Viet Minh know these things. They know the bite of Communism. Some think the particular bite is severe because of the dire economic straits the Viet Minh finds itself in during this war; they believe that Ho Chi Minh would take good care of the people in days of peace. Others think the severity of conditions under the Viet Minh is typical of Communism. But even some of these wonder whether that condition is any worse than Vietnam under the French and Bao Dai.

The Catholic Bishops. The anxiety and uncertainty that hang over the land have even affected the Catholics, whose anti-Communist record the world over is outstanding. The Catholics of Vietnam number nearly two million. Their roots are deep in the nation. A Catholic priest was indeed France's first emissary to this land.

In the northern delta there are two large dioceses administered by Vietnamese bishops. One is Phat Diem, with 150,000 Catholics, and the other is Bui Chu, with 250,000. When Ho Chi Minh came to power he announced a program to bring all spiritual, professional, and community organizations under a central command for the purpose of "saving the country." There was to be an organization of Catholics, an organization of Buddhists, and so on. The Catholics of North Vietnam adopted this idea. But they shortly discovered that, under Ho Chi Minh's plan, these organizations were to be indirectly controlled by Communists. The Catholic bishops then suppressed these organizations and created instead the National Catholic Federation.

Ho Chi Minh, knowing that the Catholics are strong and militant in their faith, treated the bishops tactfully. He sent them letters in which he stated that he considered them his "Supreme Counselors." But as time went on some of the Communist administrators in various localities sought to incite the Church by provoking lawsuits against the clergy, the Catholic laity, and the Catholic religious orders. Each time the Catholic bishops protested. And each time Ho Chi Minh sought to work out a peaceful settlement.

Ho Chi Minh finally decreed that each village was to recruit militia so as to be able to participate in the defense of the country. The Catholic communities in North Vietnam organized their militia, which referred themselves to the moral authority of the bishops. They bought arms from the Chinese troops and from Japanese deserters. These militia became a stabilizing force in the Red River delta.

In spite of that fact, General Jean de Lattre de Tassigny, the brilliant French officer who rallied Vietnam against the Viet Minh in the winter of 1950, abolished them. He acted in an impetuous moment. His twenty-three-year-old son Bernard, an infantry lieutenant, was killed in battle in 1951 near Phat Diem in the southern part of North Vietnam. General de Lattre suspected some militiamen of complicity. With lightning speed that was characteristic of the man, he abolished those armies of the bishops. Today the bishops have no militia. Their towns are therefore easy for Communist infiltration.

A subsequent incident at Phat Diem illustrates the awful decision confronting the bishops.

Phat Diem lies at the mouth of the Red River. It has long been the headquarters of a thriving bishopric that has several hundred churches whose tall spires dominate the rice fields for many miles along the China Sea. This bishopric had seven battalions of troops. It also had a small factory where grenades and bombs were made. It had been safe and secure from Viet Minh raids. But after its military force was taken away it was defenseless. The Viet Minh forces that had long raided other towns in the delta now raided Phat Diem. One day in 1952 they came in and took over. The villagers, fearful of the Communists, fled to the cathedral for protection. But the Viet Minh did not molest them. It did not pillage nor rape nor murder. It left the villagers alone. Shortly thereafter the Vietnamese came and drove out the Viet Minh; and when they occupied Phat Diem they ravaged the place.

As a result of this and other episodes, the prestige of the Viet Minh remained high for four years. Catholic bishops were treated well by the Viet Minh. Their church properties were not molested; they were left alone to preach their faith and minister to the needs of their people. Perhaps for that reason, perhaps for the sake of their own survival, the Catholic bishops in North Vietnam did not inveigh against the Viet Minh; nor did they rally, at least publicly, their people against Ho Chi Minh. In 1952 they signed a manifesto against Communism, but they carefully avoided any condemnation of the Viet Minh.

But in November 1952 the tactics changed. Monsignor Duc, the Vietnamese Bishop of Vinh, several priests, and hundreds of Catholics were arrested. A campaign of persecution and terror was laid against the Catholics in the Phat Diem area. The true colors of the Viet Minh were finally disclosed and perhaps their greatest political blunder made.

The Buddhist Church. I sat outside a Buddhist pagoda near Hanoi on an August morning. The three-tiered, tiled roof of the temple was curved at the eaves. Large, spreading trees—more expansive than our chestnuts and elms—put the whole place in shade. Rice fields, owned by the Sisters who ran the pagoda, stretched far on two sides. The quiet of the place, the deep shade, the bright green of the rice paddies made the spot the most tranquil one I could remember. Here was a place for meditation and prayer. It even seemed that here one could be on the edge of danger and yet secure in the isolation of his thoughts.

The Buddhist Church of Vietnam is indeed remote from the struggles of the people and the country. It is not like the militant church of Burma. It is a passive institution. It teaches very little social or community responsibility. It concerns itself mostly with devotions which women especially practice. The Buddha sits in the middle of the temple. On his right is the god of mercy; on his left, the god of punishment. There are tiers upon tiers of Buddhas looking down on ghastly scenes. There are many devils torturing men for the sins they committed—sawing the head in two, pulling out the hair, breaking the back, twisting the neck, cutting out the stomach, quartering the body, placing a person on spikes, burning him.

The Buddhist Church in Vietnam has been left very much alone by the Viet Minh. Its temples have seldom been destroyed. Its influence is neither pro-Communist nor anti-Communist. It exists strangely apart from the conflict that is tearing the nation apart. The simple peasant, noticing the respect that Ho Chi Minh shows all churches and all clergy and not knowing the fate which all religion suffers at the hands of the Communists, doubts if Ho Chi Minh is as evil as the government says.

Censorship. Bao Dai has imposed on the press as cruel a censorship as the French ever knew. Every printed word to be disseminated within the country or sent abroad must pass the censor.

The news accounts written for the local or international press must first receive approval. Editorials must have official sanction. It takes the local papers in Saigon from two to four hours to get an edition cleared with the censor. Editors often write their news columns several different ways, hoping to have another version that is acceptable if the submitted one is rejected.

I asked one editor what would happen if he published an editorial without clearing it with the censor. I had difficulty getting an answer because my question seemed preposterous. But when I pressed for a reply he said, "There would be punishment in any case. But if the editorial demanded a free press or was critical of the powers that be, I would go to jail and my paper would be confiscated."

There are editors in jail in Vietnam. A glaring example is a journalist whose name (known to Vietnamese patriots, including Ngo Dinh Diem) I dare not print for fear of endangering his life. He attacked the French Union. He attempted to show that America, the ideal democratic country, would help colonial people emancipate themselves. He was arrested and banished without trial to an unhealthy mountainous region, where he was kept for over a year before being released.

The Bao Dai government, like the French, has camps for "political" prisoners which I was not able to see. French law, unlike Anglo-American law and unlike the law that prevails in India, Burma, and Malaya, has no writ of habeas corpus. These "political" prisoners therefore languish indefinitely in prison.

But my editor friend went on to add hurriedly, "The Communists seem able to get out from those camps easier than the rest of us."

"Why is that so?"

"The Communists seem to be well supplied with money."

Newspaper correspondents have difficulty getting their stories cleared for transmission abroad. This last summer a friend of mine filed a story which said that two Vietnamese companies had been wiped out by the Communists. He had carefully checked

189

the story for accuracy. It was, however, rewritten by the censor to read that two Vietnamese companies had cleverly escaped a Viet Minh trap. My friend, indignant at the distortion of the news, protested. He asked to know if he had been inaccurate.

"No," snapped the censor. "But you were too damned objective."

As a result of this censorship, the news from Vietnam is to be mistrusted. All news is put in the most favorable light possible for the French and for Bao Dai. All news is slanted against the power and strength of the Viet Minh. One who reads the American press without knowing the geography of Vietnam will commonly think the French are enjoying tremendous victories. But in the winter of 1952 many of the stories about the "victories" were grossly misleading. They were often instances where the Viet Minh suddenly appeared far to the rear of the French. The French dropped paratroopers into the troubled spot and often contacted the guerrillas and captured or killed some of them. But I have personal knowledge of instances described as French "victories" in which the guerrillas escaped entirely or suffered only minor losses. The French "victories" were more often than not French defeats. One has to look at Vietnam from the inside and see censorship in operation to understand the treachery of the news that reaches the world.

Communist Cells. The Viet Minh has an organization that permeates the entire country. The household servant, the waiter, the telephone girl, the woman running the roulette table at the night club, the chambermaid, the taxi driver—all these may be working for Ho Chi Minh part time.

Women who trot quietly down a highway with loads of soft banana wood at either end of poles balanced on their shoulders may also work for him. The core of the wood may have been hollowed out to make room for hand grenades. Or their baskets

190

may contain ammunition. Carts of hay on squeaky wooden wheels pulled by cattle may contain guns or may even conceal soldiers. The men and women working in the rice paddies may be Viet Minh troops in civilian disguise, biding their time.

These innocent-appearing civilians often go out at night on solitary missions for Ho Chi Minh or assemble by prearrangement at some rendezvous. They put hand grenades with time fuses inside bicycle tires and leave the bicycle next to the house or door to be bombed. They place bombs under automobile hoods. At night they blow up strategic facilities.

On the night of August 30, 1952, when I was in Saigon, they blew up storage tanks containing 175,000 gallons of gasoline. The explosion, which was eight miles from town, was so severe it broke windows in the city. These Viet Minh agents often put on the dark green French uniforms at night and raid French stations or outposts. One night in late July 1952 a column of them in French uniforms descended on a rest center for French officers at Cap St. Jacques on the beach at the mouth of the Saigon River and killed twenty men, women, and children, wounding twenty-three more.

These guerrillas lay land mines at night, making strategic roads dangerous. I flew from Saigon to Hué in north central Vietnam. The Hué airport is nine miles from town. Each night that road is freshly laid with mines by the Viet Minh. This morning the road had to be cleared before we could leave the airport.

The tracks of railroads are constantly mined. These days a locomotive always pushes ahead of it at least two empty flatcars to take the shock of explosions.

The road that runs northeast from Hanoi to Haiphong is pockmarked from land mines that are laid in it nightly. The day I traveled it road crews of women were repairing the holes made by last night's mines. The chances are that some of those who work for the government in the daytime lay the mines at night. For when darkness descends the Viet Minh takes over.

Each town has a curfew. And the suburbs are often out of

191

bounds after sundown. Hanoi's curfew is 1 A.M. But the delightful lakes that lie at its edge and which have long been a favorite promenade are not safe for travel when the sun sets. The reason is that when darkness descends the Viet Minh organization comes out of the underground and goes about its business. It has a vast food-collecting corps; it passes along information to headquarters; it smuggles Viet Minh agents through hostile lines; it moves armies under cover of darkness. The food and supplies it moves are tremendous; the military maneuvers it completes are startling; the destruction it wreaks is appalling.

There is a large measure of truth in the saying that the country is Vietnam by day and Viet Minh by night.

The tentative commitments, the temporary alliances, the fluid loyalties that characterize Vietnam came home to me on my visit to Hanoi. I called on Pham Van Binh (who until late 1952 was Governor of North Vietnam) in his office in the massive building opposite the Hotel Metropole. The office building, like the hotel, is a product of ugly French architecture. It has a small courtyard in front, heavily guarded by troops. I walked up one flight to the Governor's office and sat with him, sipping champagne and discussing the affairs of North Vietman. His eyes were warm, and his black hair glistened as he talked. He is a nervous, able, amiable man—a personal friend of Bao Dai and an executive with a record for good administration. He talked freely of the problems and plight of Vietnam, and he spoke with considerable objectivity of the Viet Minh. I asked him if he knew Ho Chi Minh personally. He said that he did, and he gave me his appraisal of the man. He stopped to light a cigarette, and as he looked up there was amusement in his eyes.

"You speak of Ho Chi Minh. When he was President of the Republic, he lived in Hanoi. His office was in this building. In fact, Ho Chi Minh's office was in this very room where we are now sitting."

"When he left did he take his staff with him?"

"Oh no. His staff remained behind. Everyone in this building—

*The River of Perfume
is a wide, purling river,
reminiscent of our Mississippi.*

*The Queen Mother
is a power in the land.*

*In Giang Bo there were no men,
only women and children.*

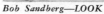

Bob Sandberg—LOOK

*Dong Khe
had changed hands so fast
there was a stunned
and paralyzed look
in the eyes
of the inhabitants.*

Bob Sandberg—LOOK

*In the village
at Giang Bo, near Hanoi,
refugees were lined up
for receipt of food
and supplies.*

Bob Sandberg—LOOK

*The bastions
of the French in Vietnam
are forts
easily outflanked.*

janitors, clerks, secretaries—used to work for Ho Chi Minh. Now
they work for me."

The Governor, by that simple story, told me how easy it was
for Viet Minh to become Vietnam. And by implication he had indicated how easy it would be for Viet Minh to command once more
the loyalty of all the people.

CHAPTER 5

THE EMPEROR AND THE PEOPLE

I did not meet Bao Dai, as he was in France at the time of my visit. Bao Dai, forty years old, is a monarch from the Nguyen dynasty. He draws $350,000 a month from the realm; he spends little time being King and much time hunting and fishing; and he lives rather lavishly. He has a palace in Dalat about 150 miles north of Saigon, where he spends most of his time, one in Hué, and another in Hanoi. The couches in his palace at Dalat are covered with tiger skins; and those skins are all personal trophies.

Bao Dai did not need to return to Vietnam to head up the new government sponsored by the French after the massacre of December 1946. He could have lived in ease and luxury in France the rest of his life. He had interests other than being Chief of State. That office entailed responsibilities that were particularly heavy when the country was divided against itself and the jungles were filled with guerrillas. I learned from Bao Dai's close personal friends that at that juncture in his life he almost became a professional automobile racer. That was indeed his preference. Many

194

people say that Bao Dai is first and last devoted to his country. They point out that he was a patriot when he abdicated in favor of Ho Chi Minh on August 26, 1945. (Bao Dai's wife did not abdicate. So today she is still Empress, while her husband is only Chief of State.) His plea to the people on abdication was to support the new government "in order to consolidate our national independence." His plea to the new government was "to treat fraternally all the parties and groups" who fought for independence. As I will point out in the following chapter, he negotiated with the French and got a degree of independence for his nation. Only then did he agree to return to the throne. And the government which he now heads has been recognized by over thirty countries, including the United States; but the only Asian countries to give him recognition were Korea and Thailand.

I mentioned all these matters to some Vietnamese near the end of my stay in Vietnam. And they thought it was much too generous an appraisal of Bao Dai. They said he is intelligent but lacking in high character; that he detests those who recommend an energetic attitude or show themselves as more courageous than he; that he believes the cleverness and malice of the French can arrange all difficulties.

As one of them said, "Ho Chi Minh and his followers in their own interest hope that Bao Dai, servant of the French, corrupt, and incapable, should occupy first place in the Vietnam government."

He went on to say that Bao Dai lacks prestige with his people because he disdains tradition and has little of the ancient Vietnamese culture. "The sad thing," he concluded, "is that Bao Dai prefers corrupt people or people without any ideals, because by comparison he seems strong."

Whatever the truth of the charges, Bao Dai is not a forceful man; nor is he greatly respected by the Vietnamese. He is held in special low esteem by the Catholics. For not long ago he sent an emissary to the Bishop of Phat Diem requesting that a niece of the Bishop be sequestered for his amorous attentions.

He moves slowly and cautiously. He has a cabinet whose members have titles that are reminiscent of a republic—Prime Minister or President, Minister of Foreign Affairs, Minister of Education, and the like. But these men are his personal agents. Bao Dai governs by decree. There is no parliament or assembly elected by the people. There is no public forum where the people may air their grievances and enact laws to remedy them. Bao Dai is the repository of all the law and all the authority in the land.

He has had difficulty riding the storms of public opinion with his appointed cabinets. Tran Van Huu, the President whom Governor Dewey found full of promise in 1951, was gone in 1952. Bao Dai appointed Nguyen Tam in his place. Tam, whom I have already mentioned, is the "strong" man the people fear because of his record as head of the police. He came into office heralding a broad reform. He spoke proudly of a six-point program: (1) pacification of the country; (2) elimination of graft; (3) increased productivity; (4) land reform; (5) free labor unions; and (6) an elected assembly.

I sat in a large drawing room in the palace at Saigon talking with Tam. It was a room as spacious, as luxurious, as highly decorated as any Louis XIV would have wanted. The room had thick soft rugs, sparkling chandeliers, and high ornate ceilings. Tall doors opened out into a spacious and formal garden. Tam and I discussed the problem of Vietnam for nearly an hour. I opened the conversation by congratulating him on the six-point program of reform he had announced two months earlier. I was at once embarrassed because the President could not recall what the six points were. Eventually, however, he restated them, and then we discussed them.

He pointed out that until he came into power labor unions had been illegal. Now they were lawful, made so by decree of Bao Dai. (One Vietnamese hooted when I mentioned that reform. "A free labor union," he said, "is to Tam only a method of getting better police control over the working people.")

Tam emphasized how difficult the land problem was, and went on to state that it was being studied. It *is* a difficult problem. In North Vietnam where the Viet Minh is the strongest, there are not many large estates. The pre-1946 figures show that in that area (including the part held by the Viet Minh) 62 per cent of the farming families own less than .9 acre; 20 per cent less than .44 acre; 91.5 per cent less than 4.4 acres. Holdings of over 123.5 acres comprise 20 per cent in North Vietnam. In Central Vietnam 69 per cent of the peasants own less than 1.2 acres; and holdings of over 123.5 acres comprise 10 per cent of the agricultural lands. In both North and Central Vietnam, however, the legal proprietor is frequently not the beneficial owner, but a tenant making annual payments to a moneylender who allows the farmer to keep possession. That moneylender more often than not is a Chinese who has charged up to 400 per cent interest a year. Down south the holdings are not so small. Almost 72 per cent of the farmers own 12.35 acres; only about one third own less than 2.47 acres. But the large holdings—those over 123.5 acres—comprise 45 per cent of the agricultural lands. In South Vietnam the absentee-landlord problem is acute. There are some rice paddies 150,000 acres in size. There about 60 per cent of the land is leased out. The landlords act also as moneylenders and in common with the professionals charge 100, 200, 400 per cent interest a year. The landlord usually looks to usury rather than to rent for his livelihood. In South Vietnam tens of thousands of tenant families live in permanent poverty.

I had seen the Minister of Agriculture, Cung Dinh Quy, on another day and explored with him the whole land-tenancy problem of Vietnam. He is a highly cultured man, extremely able, with a highly developed social consciousness. He is one of the non-Communist nationalists who served with Ho Chi Minh in the early days. Bao Dai put him in Tam's cabinet on the threat that if he did not serve, Cung Dinh Quy would go to jail. Cung Dinh Quy spoke to me with deep feeling about the curse of absentee landlordism, the vicious practices of the moneylenders, the proclivity of landlords to take more than their lawful share of the rent, the poverty of the sharecropper in the rice paddies of Vietnam. Cung Ginh Quy was sure that the land problem lay at the heart of the social unrest that keeps Vietnam in turmoil. At the end of our talk he walked with me to my car, and his last words were, "If we have land reform, I am positive we can take away from Ho Chi Minh at least 90 per cent of his popular following."

Prime Minister Tam did not seem to think the need for land reform was so pressing. The day I saw him he had other things on his mind—punishment of dissidents and development of the Vietnam army, of which his son, General Nguyen Van Hinh (also a French citizen) is the head.

I told the Prime Minister that in my travels in his country I had heard two complaints that were louder than even the pleas for land reform. The first was the demand that the French evacuate the country. The second was the demand for an assembly elected by the people. I had heard both of these complaints over and again. At Hué a schoolteacher had summed up the popular attitude toward a parliament in the following words:

"We have tremendous problems in Vietnam—absentee landlords, extortionate interest, excessive rent, and so on. Give us a parliament and we can solve those problems. If the people have a parliament, they will have a forum for expressing their grievances and the means for getting the remedies. It's idle to talk about abolishing the landed estates by royal decree. Only the voice of the people will do that."

I mentioned these matters to Tam. He expressed the view that the people were not yet ready for a full franchise—that they were illiterate and unaccustomed to the ballot. (The fact is, however, that they have elected village mayors for decades.) Therefore, Tam thought a compromise was the best. The people of the villages would elect village notables to manage the commune; the village notables would elect delegates to a council in each of the provinces; and the provincial councils would in turn appoint a national assembly with legislative powers. Tam said Bao Dai would give the country that kind of parliament very shortly—a kind of parliament the police can more readily control.

As a step in this direction, Tam had an election in January 1953. There were local elections throughout Vietnam. Tam made out the list of the candidates in each municipality who were "qualified" to run. Their names were the only ones on the ballot. When the polls were closed, all the ballots were turned over to Tam's men, who counted the ballots and then burned them. The results showed "solid approval" of the pro-French candidates— all except the Hanoi selections. There for some reason Tam's system failed and seventeen of the eighteen winners were anti-Tam candidates.

Tam's lack of faith in the people reminded me of a conversation I had had a few days earlier with the Queen Mother at Hué.

Hué is a city of about 30,000 people in Central Vietnam. It sits on both sides of the River of Perfume, a few miles from where it empties into the China Sea. Low-lying, rounded hills, mostly devoid of trees, hem in the city on three sides. Here is the capital of the country known historically as Annam. In summer the River of Perfume is a wide purling river, reminiscent of our Mississippi. The day I saw it the river was filled with boats. Some were small sampans that would hold a few people; others were sampans forty or fifty feet long filled with freight. All had rounded roofs of woven bamboo. Some were moored at small wharves; others plied the muddy waters.

On the south side of the river are the French quarters. Bright stucco houses surrounded by white fences and spacious yards, wide streets lined with palm trees mark this section as foreign to Southeast Asia. On the north side are Vietnamese quarters. Narrow streets are lined with small bazaars that carry the marks of poverty and hard times. Block after block of squat houses with thatched roofs line the muddy streets.

A bridge connects the two sections of the city. This bridge, destroyed by the Viet Minh in 1947 and only partially rebuilt to meet military exigencies, has a single line of trolley tracks and on either side a lane laid with squeaky planks for cars, bicycles, and people. The traffic is made up mostly of women on foot. This day it was raining. There were no nylon or rubberized garments to be seen. In lieu of raincoats, the women all wore wide strips of closely woven palm leaves down their backs. Most of them had across their shoulders poles with loaded baskets. And on their heads they wore the broad-brimmed, circular bamboo hat whose crown comes to a peak. Some wore sandals made of bamboo, but the majority were barefoot. There was no laughter, no conversation, no noise whatsoever in the crowd. No one spoke to anyone. No bicycle bell, no auto horn sounded. Hundreds of people crossed the bridge as I stood watching. Each had his head down, moving on some mission that seemed to absorb his thoughts. Their movements had the ceaseless intensity the ant-hill produces. Sorrow, suffering, eagerness, passion, conspiracy, tenderness, hunger—all these walked this bridge in the few moments I stood there. Only a little girl in a tattered brown gown smiled as she escaped the picture I was about to take. But even her smile had in it the grimness of Vietnam.

The palace or citadel of Hué—copied after the walled city of Peking—sits behind high red walls and a moat on the northern side of the River of Perfume. The grounds are vast, containing gardens, offices, houses, and temples. Once the grounds may have been beautiful. But not much care and affection seem to have been bestowed on them for many years. They are ill-kept and poorly maintained. The actual residence of the King was in the Purple Forbidden City, which is the central part of this old walled town. This is still a sacred enclosure. I visited the Imperial City, another unit in the citadel, where the Queen Mother resides. The buildings of the Imperial City are mostly low stone affairs with swooping tile roofs that curl at the edges. Wide court-yards are laid with rough flagstones. The rooms of the palace, though they have many doors opening onto these courtyards, are dark. The ceilings are low and the long overhanging roofs shut out much light.

It was dark and dismal in the room where I sat having tea with the Queen Mother. There was the drip of rain from the eaves onto the flagstones. The air was heavy with water, and the heat made the day oppressive. A dankness permeated the room and added to the gloom of the conversation. Duc Doan Huy Hoang Thai Hau is a lady in her sixties. She is slight of stature with black hair slightly graying, which she combs straight back and ties in a tight knot. Her teeth are black with lacquer. Her voice is so low as to be almost inaudible, and when she speaks words come with a slow, monotonous swing. This day the Queen Mother was dressed in white silk trousers and a long yellow gown that came to her knees. She had misunderstood the message asking for an appointment and to my embarrassment had had a luncheon prepared for me. It was midafternoon when I arrived for tea; and her impatience with the aide who had given her the wrong message was still manifest. But to me she was gracious in every respect. And I sat on a couch to the right of her chair, talking with her for a half hour or more over cups of green tea.

The Queen Mother is a power in the land. The story is that she recently had one Governor discharged because he would not pay her gambling debts. Knowing that she was interested and influential in political matters, I touched on numerous aspects of the current problems of Vietnam. Finally I brought the discussion around to the question of giving the people legislative power.

"The villagers seem to want an elected assembly more than anything else," I said. "When will they get one?"

Her eyes lighted up, and for the first time in this conversation she spoke with emphasis. "This is no time to speak of elections. It will be time to consider that when we crush the Viet Minh."

This conversation with the Queen Mother came back to me as I sat in the palace talking with Tam. Tam in his conversation had implied the same distrust of the people as the Queen Mother. It was plain from the two of them that they had no faith in "We, the people." They heeded what Jefferson had decried—"the alarms of the timid" and "the croakings of wealth against the ascendancy of the people." Their political philosophy was similar to that of George III when he dealt with the American colonies. The people were an unstable, unreliable force not to be trusted. Once they earned their right to vote, they would be granted the franchise.

These rulers seemed to have no appreciation of the fact that if the people had the franchise there would be a vast improvement. Then the people would have confidence in government. Then the people would have the political, as well as the military, instrument with which to combat Communism. Once the people had a vital stake in the country, they would know new loyalties, new strength, new pride. That's what the schoolteacher at Hué thought; that was the view I encountered in the restaurants and along the highways.

The sands run fast under the feet of the Vietnam government because the franchise has been so long withheld from the people. Many Vietnamese feel that the best way to combat the Viet Minh is to let the people have their legislature. But the French do not feel that way. The French fear a people's assembly just as they fear a popular leader. Both would clamor for full and complete independence and the end of French privilege. Therefore, the French want men who are safe to manage Vietnam affairs. The French are afraid of the democratic counterrevolution—the only force that can turn back the tide of Communism. For the counter-revolution would make as its foremost slogan ridding the country of the power of the foreigner.

The demand for a legislature is insistent. As a consequence Bao Dai finally gave the people one. On September 1, 1952, Tam made the announcement. Bao Dai *appointed* a provisional council for them. By royal decree it was given advisory powers. It was handpicked by Tam and made up mostly of conservative men. These men represent not only the wealth of the country but the tradition of collaboration with the French as well. This appointed parliament, grudgingly given, is not even a symbol of what the people want. It is not a legislature in form or in substance. It can serve only to increase the bitterness among the people, to con-

202

vince them that the present government is futile. Bao Dai is off to a poor start in the contest for the hearts and minds of the Vietnamese. He offers the people no political alternative to Ho Chi Minh. Even the illiterate peasant knows that the Emperor's parliament is not his parliament.

CHAPTER 6

VIVE LA FRANCE

France has never offered Vietnam complete independence. She has never even offered Vietnam the degree of independence that a dominion such as India and Canada enjoys in the British Commonwealth, all the French propaganda to the contrary notwithstanding. France has offered Vietnam membership in the French Union. But membership in the French Union is compatible neither with independence, with federalism, nor with a dominion status. The bald truth is that the French Union is colonial in nature.

When the French broke with Ho Chi Minh in 1946, they turned to Bao Dai. Vietnamese nationalists, including Ngo Dinh Diem, met with Bao Dai in Hong Kong and asked him to call a National Convention of Vietnamese to set the terms and conditions on which Bao Dai should treat with the French. Neither Bao Dai nor the French would agree. Bao Dai went to Paris to negotiate with the French without any mandate or instructions from his people. Bao Dai was not willing to return to the throne without obtaining concessions. He obtained some. South Vietnam was united with Vietnam. Vietnam got a large degree of internal autonomy. She even got the right to diplomatic representation abroad and the right to an army. And she became a member of the French Union. But one who reads closely finds that even those rights are qualified ones, the French retaining a large measure of control. The French Union is represented in the Associated States by a High Commissioner; and the High Commissioner is represented in each of the states by a Commissioner of the Republic. These officers are free-wheeling French agents who maintain French influence and control in the three nations. French business and cultural interests are assured special prerogatives. Frenchmen are tried before mixed courts, and French law is to be applied to them. The French are preferred in appointment as foreign advisers and technicians. The French keep control of foreign relations and national defense.

The lack of independence of Vietnam in foreign affairs is apparent. "The heads of the foreign diplomatic mission to Vietnam will be accredited to the President of the French Union and to H. M. the Emperor of Vietnam." The diplomats from Vietnam will receive credentials "granted by the President of the French Union and initialed by H. M. the Emperor of Vietnam." And any agreements or treaties of Vietnam must be approved by the High Council of the French Union. As to military affairs, there is no agreement whatsoever governing the withdrawal of French troops.

Vietnam, to be sure, is represented in the French Union.

The organs of the French Union are the presidency, the High Council, and the Assembly. The President of France is the President of the French Union. The High Council—which is an administrative or executive arm of the presidency—is composed of delegates from France and from the associated states, of which Vietnam is one. The Assembly—which has consultative powers only—is composed of members representing the various countries in the Union. Of these, France has half and all the others the other half. Thus the delegates which Vietnam sends to the French

Union have a forum but no real voice. All legislative power remains in the National Assembly of France.

Vietnam, Cambodia, and Laos (the three Associated States that have replaced pre-war Indo-China) are incorporated into an economic federation, and their currency is tied to the French franc. Each of the three is a member of the French Union. All three are under the ultimate authority of France when it comes to matters diplomatic and military. Vietnam, Cambodia, and Laos can become united as one nation in a federal system or otherwise only with the approval of the Parliament of France. Paris, not Saigon, remains the center of ultimate power of Vietnam. The web of French power has been rewoven, not removed. The curse of colonialism is still upon the land.

"Under the French Union," one prominent Vietnamese told me, "the French could strangle and starve into submission any Vietnamese government that showed itself less than docile."

The French have suffered tremendous losses since 1946. The cost in dollars has exceeded the French investment in all the Associated States. It has also exceeded the amount France received from us under the Marshall Plan. The annual cost of the military program is about $1,500,000,000, of which America pays indirectly about a third. The struggle of the French has reached heroic proportions, though French law prevents a Frenchman being drafted and sent to Vietnam. The war with Ho Chi Minh to date has cost the French (Colonials and Legionnaires included) 160,000 casualties. Each year they are losing in officers almost the equivalent of the graduating class at St. Cyr.

These things, however, do not count with the Vietnamese. They remember the decades of grievances under French rule. They suspect every move of the French, every promise, every ingratiating act. French motives are suspect when the French say they will leave at the end of the war, when they say that the Vietnamese will have their independence. Even Vietnamese who can read may not be able to understand the verbiage by which

Frenchmen rule the French Union. But those who cannot read, as well as those who can, know that Jean Letourneau, the French High Commissioner, not Bao Dai, occupies the Norodom Palace at Saigon, which to the people is what the White House is to us. Bao Dai negotiated for the Norodom Palace but did not obtain it. Rather than live in the second biggest palace in Saigon, he kept face by moving to Dalat. The people know that. They also know that the High Commissioner outranks Prime Minister Tam.

These simple things mean to the common people of Vietnam that the French are there to stay. That attitude more than anything else divides the country and gives Ho Chi Minh his strength. The presence of the French dilutes the patriotism of every citizen and promotes the forces of disunity. The ideal solution would be for the French to leave the country immediately, turning over all civil and military matters to the Vietnamese. But that move would be catastrophic. There is no Vietnamese army to take over the defense. The French in their long rule never allowed one. Not until 1951 did they start developing an army. There are, of course, Vietnamese soldiers fighting with the French. They number about 130,000. But there have been no officers to lead them. By the first of 1953 there were about 800. And while a vigorous officer-training program is under way, it will take four or five years at the present rate to train enough officers to assume full responsibility for the defense of the country. Meanwhile the French must hang on. But the presence of the French gives Ho Chi Minh his most powerful platform. If the present trend continues, Vietnam will go the way of China.

The French are feeding the flames of Communism in Asia. They repeatedly proclaim, when seeking American aid, that Vietnam is as independent of France as Australia is of Britain, that they are fighting only to stem the tide of Communism in Asia. But when the Vietnamese suggest specific action to implement those pronouncements the French become indignant and threaten to withdraw their military forces. Thus the French implicitly admit that they remain in Vietnam to protect interests which they dare not confess at home or abroad.

Vietnam was saved from Communist conquest in the winter of 1950 by General de Lattre and by American military aid, as Governor Dewey shows in *Journey to the Far Pacific*. The General rallied the demoralized forces that France had in the field and America bolstered them with equipment. The fall of Vietnam today, as then, would imperil all of Southeast Asia. The prize is attractive, for Vietnam, Thailand, and Burma make up the famous rice bowl of Asia. Rice means power. China is hungry for rice. Japan imports 20 per cent of her food and is heavily dependent on rice. If the Communist forces had command of the food supplies of Asia, they would soon have the food-deficit countries at their mercy. Red China, like the China of old, seems to have imperialistic dreams. Red China in her present mood might turn to adventure in Southeast Asia, if the pressure in Korea were lifted.

At one time—perhaps even in 1946—Ho Chi Minh, though Moscow-trained, may have been more of a nationalist than a Communist. Southeast Asia thinks that if his liberation movement had been recognized at the end of World War II, Vietnam would today be passionately nationalistic and aligned with Burma in the democratic-socialist group. The answer will never be known. The vast majority of the Viet Minh probably do not know enough about Marxist doctrine to make a choice. They are caught up in a patriotic liberation movement. But, as I have said, the high command is composed of dyed-in-the-wool Communists. And they have skillfully contributed to the disintegration of the nation.

Vietnam may yet be saved. The Vietnamese are strongly suspicious of the Chinese and their foreign policies; they want their independence from all outside powers, Asian as well as European. So the growing domination of the Viet Minh by Red China will not be popular with the people. Heroic political measures can still swing public opinion behind a Vietnam government. There is no reason why Vietnam cannot outdo the Viet Minh and take the popular following from Ho Chi Minh. But it will require a genuine democratic revolution to do it.

Some Vietnamese and Americans were discussing this question one afternoon at Hanoi. We sat in the lounge of the Hotel Metropole, where Ho Chi Minh used to have lunch, drinking black tea out of heavy white cups. A Vietnamese, wise in politics and close to the pulse of the nation, leaned over and said in a whisper, "If our people so desired, they could get rid of the Viet Minh in a week."

That is the tragedy of Vietnam. If Vietnam had the zeal of the Viet Minh, Vietnam would easily win. But it will take far more than guns and francs and dollars to produce that victory.

Sweeping reforms are needed, reforms that serve to rally the people against the threat from the north. The influence of the French has always been on the side of the landlords and the other vested interests. The influence of the present Vietnam government is on the same side. The weight of the government will always be on the side of the *status quo* so long as the French colonial attitude dominates the country.

There are those who say that the military victory must be won before solutions to the political, social, and economic problems are sought. But a strong Vietnamese army is essential to such a victory. And it will be impossible to put that army in the field if the political and associated problems are not solved first. Vietnamese soldiers are not willing to die for the perpetuation of French control. They must have the hope—the firm belief—that they are fighting for a peace which has no taint of the French influence.

Whichever way the situation is analyzed, the answer is the same. The cause of free Asia demands the complete liquidation of French political control. The French cannot withdraw their troops today. But if France announced today, in words admitting no ambiguities, that Vietnam would receive a dominion status, or if the United Nations assumed in Vietnam the role

209

it served so well in Indonesia and undertook to guarantee Vietnam real and complete independence, the problems of Vietnam would begin to solve themselves. If France refuses to make that promise, no political measure, no military measure can arrest the processes of disintegration at work in the country.

PART 4

BURMA AND THE
COUNTERREVOLUTION

CHAPTER 1

"ON THE ROAD TO MANDALAY"

When I reached Mandalay I realized that Rudyard Kipling was more of a romanticist than a geographer. Perhaps a British trooper on the deck of a steamer headed east across the Bay of Bengal might think that Moulmein was on the road to Mandalay. It is, however, a port far to the south; and the only person who would go to Mandalay *via* Moulmein was one who lived there. From a troopship in the Bay of Bengal the sun might seem to come up like thunder "outer China—crost the Bay." But China is not across the bay from Moulmein or Mandalay. The sun rises over Mandalay from the mountains that mark the China border—the mountains known to Americans largely through stories and legends of Ledo and the famous Burma Road.

The road to Mandalay is normally up the Irrawaddy River from Rangoon, where, so far as I can learn, there are no "flyin-fishes." It's a trip of 400 miles that takes ten days or more, for the river boats stop at night at towns and villages along the way. That route was practically closed for two years following Burma's independence on January 4, 1948. For civil war had broken out

213

in Burma, isolating Rangoon and Mandalay. But by 1952 river travel was open not only to Mandalay but many miles beyond.

I did not have the time to make the river journey. I flew instead from Rangoon in a DC-3 owned and operated by the Union of Burma Airways (a government corporation).

Mandalay, a town of about 200,000 people, is in the broad fertile valley of central Burma that stretches on both sides of the purling, muddy Irrawaddy. To the west and to the east are low-lying hills reminiscent in contour of our Berkshires but much more thickly wooded. Rangoon, with about 100 inches of rain a year, is wet and muggy. Mandalay, with less than 40 inches and an elevation of 248 feet above sea level, is equally hot but less humid. Rangoon is the center of rich rice lands. There is rice in Mandalay, but the main crops are millet, sesame, peanuts, cotton, and beans. The August day I visited there the ancient town lay shimmering in a heat as dry as Arizona's.

The old city of Mandalay had two parts. There was the Gem City (called the Nandaw by the Burmese and Fort Dufferin by the British) which was built about a century ago by King Mindon. A great square, five miles in circumference and enclosed by red brick walls twenty-six feet high, housed the palace and the city of the elite. The wall had twelve gates, and on each of the four sides were thirteen watchtowers built of teak and decorated with gold. Outside was a moat seventy-five yards wide, crossed by five bridges, and deep enough for the royal barges. The palace, a wooden building with a silver-colored corrugated iron roof, was in the center of the square. From all accounts it was a building of splendor. Every pillar was made of the single trunk of a teak tree and lacquered red; there were mosaics of colored glass; golden doors, golden daises, golden spires. Many lesser buildings clustered around the palace; the enclosure was carefully laid out with roads and canals; and it was beautifully landscaped.

This old city (which had been taken intact by the British on November 30, 1885, at the end of the Third Anglo-Burmese War) escaped the bombings of the Japanese in 1942. It was, in fact, used to house Japanese troops during the long occupation. It therefore became a prime target for British bombers in 1945 and was totally destroyed. Today only the brick wall remains. And the moat that used to carry gilded barges for the King is now choked with red, white, and blue hyacinths.

The lesser city of old Mandalay was a shoddy and nondescript trading town. It too was mostly destroyed by the bombings. The Mandalay one sees today is newly built. The streets are dirt; there is no running water or sewerage.

Yet in spite of the desolation of the war, Mandalay is an interesting, exciting place. There is the thriving University College, headed by able U Kolay, doing particularly brilliant work in agriculture. There are farming co-operatives, irrigation projects, a land-distribution program, public health undertakings, and a host of other governmental activities going on at Mandalay. I talked with some of the participants. I saw the courts and met with the judges and lawyers. I heard from the lips of a wide variety of people the exciting story of Burma's revolution. I also visited with U Aung Myint, Commissioner of the Mandalay District, who assembled his staff to answer some of my questions. Each was neatly dressed Burmese-style—the *gaungbaung* for headdress and the *longyi* or *sarong* for trousers. We covered a wide range of topics in our conversation; and when we finished, U Sein Maung, Deputy Commissioner, said, "Come, I want to show you our pagoda."

In my travels in Burma it seemed that the whole countryside was dotted with pagodas. In Rangoon I had seen yellow-robed monks climbing hundreds of steps to reach remote shrines. I had seen at dawn through a leaden sky the haunting beauty of the golden dome of the Shwedagon. The Shwedagon (which was built long before the British captured Rangoon in 1824) stands on a low mound about two miles from the center of Rangoon. It rises about 370 feet and is about a quarter mile in circumference. The spire, whose top is inlaid with diamonds, is solid gold.

In shape it is an inverted lotus flower. On the murky morning when I first saw it, Shwedagon pointed like a tongue of fire into the sky. At noon on a clear day it was peaceful and sublime. On a moonlight night it had a mystic cast. The Shwedagon can be seen from any point of the compass. Its moods are the moods of man; and yet its dignity, its plain beauty, its purity make it the symbol of the noblest things for which man has strived. I have seen sunsets and storms, glaciers and peaks, flowers and faces that have moved me more. But of all the things that man has created by his hands, the Shwedagon is the loveliest I have known. It made my heart leap when I first saw it; and its beauty keeps coming back to me no matter how distant I am.

In Mandalay I had been surfeited with views of pagodas. Mandalay Hill, which rises about 500 feet above the city, has a temple on top and numerous pagodas and resthouses on all of its slopes. It is a place of pilgrimage, a retreat for laymen and clergy alike. At its foot on the southeast side are three groups of pagodas. Kuthodaw is a golden pagoda surrounded by 729 other pagodas, packed close together. Each of the 729 is pure white; and each contains a stone on which Buddhist scriptures are engraved. Beyond this group is another. The Sundamuni pagoda is in the center of 758 smaller ones which contain 1,775 scriptural slabs. Here also is the Kyanktawgyi pagoda, containing a large alabaster Buddha and surrounded by 28 smaller pagodas.

In the vicinity there is also the Shwe Kyaung or Golden Monastery. And on the opposite side of the town is the most famous pagoda of all—Arakan Pagoda (Maha Myat Mu Ni).

Arakan has a twelve-foot brass image of the Buddha, covered with gold leaf now four inches deep. This Buddha was captured by an ancient king in 1784 and brought to Mandalay from Akyab on the Bay of Bengal. We took off our shoes outside the pagoda beside a large pool where sacred turtles are kept. Inside the pagoda are long colonnades supported by over 250 pillars. These colonnades lead up to the Buddha. The pillars are gilt; the ceiling, frescoed. Shopkeepers with small stalls along the colonnades and attendants of the pagoda are busy selling candles, gold leaf, and incense sticks.

There are courtyards off the main pagoda where bells are hung which the faithful ring after they have said their prayers. A few brass statues are there which are thought to have special powers. Two are of a man and woman standing in an alcove. A person who has a stomach-ache rubs one of their navels; one who has a headache rubs one of their foreheads. So many thousand fingers have rubbed these spots they have made sizable holes.

When I visited the shrine, the Buddha was wearing a removable coat made of gold mail. Three men were gaining merit by pasting gold leaf on the image. Most of the worshipers were women. Women in Burma have full political and social equality. They have, indeed, a rare degree of independence. Before my visit to Arakan I had talked with U Kolay of University College about it over a luncheon of fried chicken and rice. He had explained that in Burma there are no family names, that a child seldom takes his father's or mother's name, that he had acquired the name Kolay quite by accident. His sister had called him that from boyhood days. It means Younger Brother. When he reached maturity, he decided to retain the name. And so he became U Kolay, Mr. Younger Brother.

"And is your wife's name Mrs. Kolay?" I asked.

"My wife take my name?" he said, his eyes warm with the memories of a loved one. "Certainly not. Burmese women are too independent for that."

But Burmese women worshiping in a pagoda do not have full equality with the men. The women at Arakan were on their knees fifty feet from the Buddha. They could get no closer. A woman, under the Buddhist theology, may on her reincarnation become a man. But until she does she can only aspire to be reborn a male and must worship the Buddha from a distance.

Those had been my experiences with Burmese pagodas. And so when U Sein Maung asked me to see his pagoda, I thought

217

that I would see the commonplace. Instead I learned a new lesson in devotion.

U Sein Maung took me across from the square of government buildings to a small wooden pagoda perhaps thirty feet wide and seventy feet long. This pagoda, open on both sides, is a plain, unadorned structure with none of the startling beauty of the Shwedagon, none of the richness of the Arakan. At the far end is the figure of Buddha. U Sein Maung and I took off our shoes and entered. Then he turned to me and in a hushed voice said:

"This is where we pray."

"Whom do you mean by 'we'?"

"Those of us who run the government—judges, clerks, assessors, tax collectors—about forty-five in all."

"When do you pray?"

"Each day when we finish work at five o'clock."

"And what do you ask in your prayers?"

"That we will administer the laws faithfully, showing no discrimination against any person or race—that we will be true to Buddha's teachings."

I thought of Washington, D.C., and the hurry of our officials at day's end to get to teas and cocktail parties. I thought of the callous and corrupt men I had seen on my journeys in Asia. I had been puzzled by what I had seen in Burma. Much of it had been blurred and confused. I had heard of corruption in Burma too—corruption and inefficiency. I had, however, met the top men—the important men—and I knew U Nu, the Prime Minister, Ba U, the President, and others in the Cabinet were honest and devoted. As I stood in stocking feet in the little pagoda in Mandalay, the pieces began to come together. I suddenly realized that it was a great religious force that was uniting Burma in a mighty revolution and keeping it clear of Communist taint.

As I stood there an after-dinner conversation in Rangoon at the home of the Foreign Minister, Sao Khun Khio, came back to me. He and his colleagues were reviewing the early days of Burmese independence, the economic, political, social, and military problems that confronted the new nation, the stresses and strains that threatened to tear the country apart. Rangoon and Mandalay were shambles. Buildings were gutted by fire. Dock facilities were destroyed. Communications were disrupted. Mines were flooded. Oil refineries were blasted; oil wells were in ruins. The streets were filled with rubble. Sewage systems were not working. Unemployment piled high. The British, on their return, had demonetized the Japanese yen. That had ruined everyone, for when the Japanese arrived they appropriated all the Burmese rupees, making their possession a capital offense. Thus when the Japanese yen that the people received in exchange was declared valueless, no one had any money. Poverty, disease, and Communist guerrillas walked the land. Rangoon was cut off from the rest of the country. Terror and death stalked the highways.

Moreover, Burma had little trained leadership to deal with these violent internal problems. During the long British rule, very few Burmese had been educated for or admitted to the public service.

Few Burmese had held senior administrative posts under the British. Of twenty major department heads, there had been only two Burmese. In the lower echelons the percentage of Burmese was no greater and often much less. The posts from top to bottom were filled largely by Britishers or by Indians. The absence of a Burma civil service was the reason why many Britishers thought that the best policy was to promise Burma her independence and to take twenty years to train men and women for government service, as had been done in India. But that plea was as idle as an effort to stop a roaring express train with a raised hand. If England had held on longer, she would, in my view, have succeeded only in consolidating the country under Communist auspices. Yet the bald truth is that when the British withdrew, the task confronting Burma was almost an impossible one for the political amateurs who came to power. The government, however, achieved the impossible. Against overwhelming odds it kept the nation on the democratic front, controlled the virus of

219

Communism that had reached epidemic proportions, and restored law and order.

That night at Sao Khun Khio's home I pointed out that world opinion during that period had given Burma only a slight chance to survive. And I asked what the secret of the victory had been. After a long silence U Chan Htoon, the able Attorney General and lay head of the Buddhist Church in Burma, answered, "It was a miracle." And after a pause he added, "A miracle due to prayer and grit."

As I stood in the little pagoda at Mandalay where government officials pray at day's end, the full meaning of those words came home to me.

CHAPTER 2

THE COMMUNISTS LAY SIEGE

The Communists gained the ascendancy in Burma
during the Japanese occupation in World War II.
The Japanese at first had been welcomed. The hatred for the
British was so great that the Japanese were looked upon as liberators. The anti-British feeling was so strong that the late General Aung San and his irregular troops met the Japanese land
forces beyond the Thailand border and served as their scouts on
the march to Rangoon. The Japanese at the beginning acted with
propriety. They did not molest the pagodas or the priests. In fact,
they tried to exploit Buddhism as a bond between the two nations. But soon the surly nature of the Japanese Army appeared.
Burmese became despicable people to the occupying force. They
were treated cruelly and insolently. Some of the temples and
monasteries were used to house troops. The Japanese yen that
was forcibly exchanged for the British rupee became a cheap in-
flated thing. The Japs killed and ate over two million carabao,
the faithful work animal of Southeast Asia. The grievances
mounted and dislike of the Japanese grew.

This dislike for the Japanese turned into hatred and caused a vast resistance movement. General Aung San, who had led the Japanese into Burma in 1942, surreptitiously organized the Burmese Army against the Japanese during the occupation. His example of courage and character was followed by thousands. An effective "underground" grew up. Five hundred thousand Burmese flocked to it. The People's Voluntary Organization (PVO) became a powerful political as well as military organization. Some PVOs were Communists; most were not.

When the war was over, the PVO was used by the Communists as a divisive force within the nation. Burma received her independence from England on January 4, 1948. Shortly afterward the Communist Conference was held in Calcutta; and at its command the Communists in Burma, like those in Malaya, undertook a campaign of terror. Some remained under the PVO standard; some became White guerrillas (Stalinists), some Red (Trotskyites). These armed terrorists ruled large areas of Burma. Only the larger cities retained their freedom.

The trouble did not end with the Communist guerrillas. Down south the Karens revolted, demanding a separate state. There are a million and a quarter Karens in Burma. They are a racial minority, squat in stature, and with flat faces that are less Mongol than those of the Burmese. About a fifth of them are Christians (Baptists), the rest Buddhists. They were the ones around whom the British built their Army when they ruled Burma; and the Karens did glorious work for the Allies in World War II. The Karens seized a large area in the south, including the port of Moulmein at the mouth of the Salween River. They joined forces with the Communists and held the fertile delta built around the eight mouths of the Irrawaddy.

That was not all. Up in the northeast about ten thousand Chinese Nationalist troops came in from China and occupied a large part of Kengtung Province. They always tried to indicate that they had American backing. They even went so far as to pay

---

for commandeered supplies by offering Shan villagers I O U's reading "America will pay." They do that today.

In 1948, 1949, and 1950 even the suburbs of Rangoon were not safe for travel by day or night. Communist guerrillas infested the outlying villages, laid ambushes on the highways, and lived off the country. Every night the residents of Rangoon heard gunfire on the edges of the city and saw searcher bullets streak the sky. Rangoon, Heho, and Mandalay were remote islands in bandit land. In those days it was often said that there was a stalemate between the guerrillas and the government; that if either were only a bit more efficient, the other would be overwhelmed.

Today the guerrillas are more and more in the eclipse. The back of the Communist resistance movement was definitely broken by 1952. The Karens have not yet agreed to the boundaries of the new Karen state; but progress has been made. Troops of Nationalist China are still in northeast Burma and are supplied regularly by two planes a week from Formosa. The Burmese Army was much too busy with other insurgents to move against these troops of Chiang Kai-shek. But by early 1953 these Nationalist forces were a serious threat. They were raiding and burning villages. Some turned south to assist the Karens. Burma, knowing they operate in violation of international law, turned to the Security Council for relief. There is cause for alarm. The presence of these troops may be an excuse for Red China to intervene.

In 1952 there were marauding bands of Communist guerrillas at large in the country, and they still held sections of the delta. The night of August 20, 1952, when I was in Rangoon, they struck fifteen miles outside the city and cut the water line that supplies the 500,000 people of that metropolis. Up at Mandalay townsfolk were still uneasy about traveling the country roads at night. And the inland town of Heho was still beset.

Heho is a small town in a valley set among rolling hills, thick with brush and trees. Its airport has a gravel runway surrounded by barbed wire and guarded at several points by sentries protected by sand bags. There is a small one-room building apparently designed as an airport office but devoid of chairs, ticket counter, and attendant. When the plane taxied to a stop and the passengers disembarked, I talked with the pilot, a tall lean Englishman in his thirties. As we talked an Army truck pulled up and a dozen soldiers got out. This truck had the marks of ambush on it. There were bullet holes on the sides and one neat one through the windshield. I asked him the reason for the guards at this nondescript airport.

He smiled dryly and said, "Communist guerrillas." Then after drawing deeply on his cigarette he added, "A few weeks ago I put down here, and as the passengers started to disembark, some guerrillas started shooting. They hit two of my passengers and almost hit me. I got the wounded back in the plane, slammed the door, and got the plane out. It had a few bullet holes, nothing serious."

Thus in the summer of 1952 inland travel in Burma was fraught with some dangers. There were pockets of Communist guerrillas in many regions. There were also armed gangs (*dacoits*) preying both on the guerrillas and on other travelers. But the main arteries of travel were becoming fairly safe for the average man.

In 1952 travel in Burma was fraught with some dangers.

In Mandalay I had been surfeited with views of pagodas.

U Sein Maung said,
"This is where
we pray."

Bob Sandberg—LOOK

CHAPTER 3

BURMA'S GUERRILLAS

As I have said, it was touch-and-go during 1948, 1949, and 1950 whether Burma would survive. The armed terrorists under Communist leadership swept to victory after victory. The Communists infiltrated the ranks of labor and almost paralyzed the country. But the government of Prime Minister U Nu stood firm. The Prime Minister, a devout Buddhist whose party in recent elections got 85 per cent of the seats in Parliament, repudiated "the cult of the gun." He proclaimed over and again that anyone in Burma could have any political ideology he chose; that the people could adopt Communism as their form of government if they set about it constitutionally; but that no group would be allowed to deprive the people of their constitutional rights at the point of a gun.

"If the government becomes vicious and you want to remove it," he proclaimed, "go to the people and ask for power by means of the democratic method." That was the democratic philosophy in which U Nu tried to educate the people during the turbulent days of the civil war.

The government used force to break the Communist strikes that threatened to paralyze the nation. Ne Win, General of the Army, conducted a vigorous campaign against the insurgents. The tide began to turn in 1950.

Today there are more guerrillas in rehabilitation centers than there are in the jungles. There are four of these centers that in 1952 housed some 15,000 men. I visited the one at Aung San, about twelve miles north of Rangoon—one named for Burma's George Washington, General Aung San, who at the age of thirty-two was assassinated while head of the provisional government. That was in July 1947, before independence had actually been achieved. But since Aung San's efforts had brought it within reach, he more than any other of the revolutionaries is honored in Burma.

The camp named for him has the outward appearance of a military area—broad streets, parade grounds, and barracks. The barracks are built of split bamboo sidings and thatched roofs. Some central buildings are made of brick with concrete floors. There were over 3,000 men in camp the day I visited it. They were between eighteen and thirty-five and drawn from applicants screened for their past deeds and potential worth. Guerrillas who have not committed rape, robbery, or murder are accepted for rehabilitation without punishment. U Win Maury, the educational director, said that 75 per cent of them were ex-guerrillas. But whatever their past may be, it is difficult to find any one of them who will admit to having been a Communist.

These camps, though run on military lines, are somewhat comparable to our CCCs during the thirties. The enlistment is for two years. While in camp the trainees get instruction for four hours a day and then do camp work for four hours. Instruction is in reading and writing, personal hygiene, public health, well-drilling, construction of latrines, protection of water supplies against contamination, woodwork, carpentry, masonry, brick-laying, and numerous other manual arts. The trainees do military drill under the supervision of Bo Min Lwin, brigade commander, but they have no arms and receive no military training. They have playgrounds for soccer and assembly halls for lectures and movies.

The camp reminded me of a large manual-training shop such as we have in our junior and senior high schools. There were planing machines, band saws, electric drills, and lathes. There were tools and machines that these men had never seen before. They were fascinated with them, like boys seeing an electric train for the first time. Chin hillmen with long hair were working in a planing mill with long teak planks. As they pushed the planks through the machine, they grinned and chattered gaily, like any high school boys caught up in fine adventure.

The training schools in manual arts are being expanded to include auto mechanics, leather tanning, plumbing, electrical work, radio, and sheet-metal work. The rehabilitation camps are evolving as schools in adult education for men who had no education and who in the turmoil and privations of war learned that terrorism and robbery were easy ways to earn a living. As I stood at Aung San I thought how wonderful it was that with a few simple tools a poor and illiterate peasant could be transformed into an enterprising and successful artisan—how he could in a few months bring the industrial revolution to the humblest village of feudal Asia.

At Aung San I caught something of the enthusiasm at the grass roots of Burma. These men had a bustling energy and a bristling eagerness. They were not disheartened, listless men raking leaves or shoveling dirt as if each exertion were unpleasant and each movement perhaps the last one. These men had the enthusiasm of crusaders. It was as if they were in a close competition. There were no loafers in camp. Those sawing wood were doing it in an all-out effort; those pounding out bolt heads from red-hot metal had the determination of the village blacksmith; those who for practice were laying bricks in sand instead of in mortar were completely absorbed in the problem. Adult education in the manual arts was being received by ex-guerrillas not as a chore, not as a discipline, but as an exciting, exhilarating experience.

"How many of these men have been truly reformed?" I kept asking. No one knew the answer. The officials did not know whether some of them could be trusted in the Army. But the supervisors were sure that a transformation was under way, that these men, intensely proud of their race and of their leaders, were beginning at long last to realize that they too had a stake in their country, that they too could share the good things of life.

This feeling of belonging to their community, of making a contribution to their country, comes about partly by the field work which these ex-guerrillas undertake. They stay in camp for six months of basic training, then go to the field for six months, then back to camp for six months of advanced instruction, then to the field again. The field work to date has been largely under Army auspices, but it is of a public nature. For example, when I was at Aung San one of the battalions was at Hmawbi, thirty-five miles north of Rangoon, where it was building Army barracks and constructing highways. At Prome, a badly bombed city 150 miles north of Rangoon, other trainees were repairing streets. In some centers they work on government housing projects. They move throughout the country working on public projects of various kinds. The aim of the government is to make these rehabilitation battalions a permanent institution. Many trainees will be released, but over the years enough will be recruited to keep one rehabilitation battalion at work in each of Burma's thirty-six districts.

There is no difficulty to date in getting recruits. The spirit and morale of the men are so high that most of them want to stay on. Thus the enlistment of the men at Aung San was for the two years ending May 1952. When that date arrived, 90 per cent of them re-enlisted for another two years.

The aim, however, is to send as many of these men as possible back to their villages. There are large plans for them which Dr. Ba Nyun, district health officer at Aung San, explained to me.

Next door to the Aung San rehabilitation camp is a health center. It administers mostly to maternity cases—pre-natal and post-natal care of mother and child, the training of midwives and practical nurses, the vaccination of children, and the dispensing of medicines. Dr. Ba Nyun has used the proximity of the rehabilitation camp to further some public health measures. Through the help of ECA he has a village water-supply project under way. Wells in Burma are apt to be shallow and contaminated. The government, as part of its public health program, is promoting drilled wells. Large supplies of drills have been obtained, and American-Burmese teams are at work finding new water supplies. Simple hand pumps are installed in the new wells. And instruction is given in the construction of latrines, the drainage of waste water, and other measures to protect the new water supplies from contamination.

Dr. Ba Nyun proudly explained to me how the ex-guerrillas at Aung San were being trained in this project. He said an ex-guerrilla returning to his village would be more than an artisan setting up his own shop, more than a carpenter or mason coming home with new-found skills. He would also be a community leader who would know about such things as water supplies and latrines and the repairing of pumps. There was fire in this missionary's eyes as he said, "We will make good public health officers out of most of these ex-guerrillas. Won't that be wonderful for our people?"

I had to see Aung San to understand how deep down Burma's revolution had reached. This was no concentration camp where men with dangerous thoughts and a record of dangerous proclivities were isolated. These men had had dangerous thoughts and they had been ready instruments for exploitation by clever Communist intriguers. But they also were potential apostles of a different faith—a faith in the dignity of man, a faith in a society where the mind of man is free, a faith in a nation that offers a worthy place even to the humblest of the people. The men at Aung San were revolutionaries in the best American sense—they were learning self-reliance, pride in their country, confidence in their fellow man, and the mysterious power of individual enterprise. At Aung San I knew that a nation that was committed to those policies would never exchange its God for the mechanical robot designed by Marx and Stalin.

CHAPTER 4

VILLAGE REHABILITATION

The grass roots of Burma are receiving major attention from the government. And the main agency through which it is acting is the Mass Education Council, authorized by Parliament shortly after Burma received her independence in 1948. The father of the movement is U Aung Min, an educator of distinction. U Aung Min knows not only conventional education; he is also well versed in adult education and community welfare problems.

His principal aim was to restore the traditional Burmese conception of community life and to develop the villages in the democratic framework. The village had been an important governmental unit in Burma's history. Community life in Burma, which had suffered under the British rule, was practically destroyed by the Japanese. By 1945 the idea of villagers co-operating with each other on community projects had been largely dissipated; the idea of every man for himself became prevalent. The restoration of responsible local government was one of the chief aims of the revolutionaries who took over the reins of government in 1948.

Civil war delayed the mass education program until 1949, when training classes for Mass Education Officers (MEOs) were started. The first group was sent into the villages in May 1950. By the fall of 1952, 260 MEOs were functioning in 150 centers. Some of these centers were small—one MEO to a little village or group of small villages in a five-mile radius; two or more MEOs to more densely populated places.

These MEOs are men and women between twenty and thirty-five who have finished high school and who have the capacity and interests necessary for social service and community leadership. They receive about six months' training in public health, sanitary engineering, sports, handicrafts, agriculture, and community relations. U Ba Lwin, a Buddhist monk with a shaved head and yellow robe, is U Aung Min's Deputy Chairman of the movement. He told me how they had borrowed a leaf from Dr. James Yen's book—the pioneer in mass education who started in China thirty years or more ago a four-point program at the village level designed to eliminate illiteracy, to introduce modern methods of agriculture, to improve public health, and to train villagers for citizenship. The Burma program has emblems illustrating the same four-point program—an *open book* for literacy, a *plow* for improved agriculture, a *red cross* for health, and *three links* of a chain for community relations. Nationalist China, which is now using the program on Formosa, could have made it the counter-revolutionary force against Communism on the mainland. Where Nationalist China failed, Burma is succeeding.

The first emphasis of the movement is on health and sanitation. The second is on the development of community life—the organization of discussion groups, the encouragement of community projects such as schools, libraries, and the like. The third is the introduction of improved techniques in farming. The fourth is the elimination of illiteracy.

A MEO assigned to a village lives like any other villager. He (or she) too has a simple *basha*—a split-bamboo hut. But he aims to make that *basha* the model one. He builds a model latrine (and always uses it), puts in drainage ditches to eliminate breeding grounds for mosquitoes, drills a model well, keeps his house and yard clean, and prepares meals that give a balanced diet. His *basha* is soon the cleanest, brightest one in the village and his example attractive.

He tries to develop his *basha* as a community meeting place. In Burmese villages there are no movies, snack bars, or bridge clubs. The women usually squat in small groups in the morning (and the men at night), discussing problems of the day—the price of rice, the recent guerrilla raid, their complaints against the government. There are no newspapers for these people and seldom a radio. News passes by word of mouth. The MEO tries to make his *basha* the place for these meetings. He subscribes to a newspaper and reads it to the assembled group. He has picture books showing how flies carry disease, how mosquitoes bring malaria, how tuberculosis is communicated, how model latrines are constructed. He tries to make his *basha* the community headquarters for discussion of all projects, all ideas. The MEO is not the aggressive reformer. His role is a quiet, unobtrusive one.

As U Aung Min said, the aim is to make the movement one of "the people themselves, not something imposed from above." The MEO is to teach by example and to stir in the villagers a desire to improve their own lot.

He has a simple first-aid kit and runs a medical clinic. When the initial supply of drugs is exhausted, he collects a few *pyas* (cents) from each villager for the purchase of more. He brings with him to the village one soccer ball. The game, which is fast developing into a national sport, is very hard on the ball when the playing field is dirt and gravel. A ball is soon worn out. The MEO then takes a collection for a new one. He does the same for thread and needles, for weaving yarn, for library books.

The MEO tries to organize village projects in which each family participates—digging drains, repairing roads, disposing of garbage.

The MEO also serves as the liaison between the village and the government. If livestock are infected, if irrigation projects are needed, if wells run dry, the MEO is the one who contacts district headquarters for advice or assistance. Government has been a power of which the people over the years have become suspicious. The MEO educates them on the value and importance of government. He prepares the ground for vaccinations and health inspections. He explains in simple terms what the problem is and he dispels fears of the new and mysterious methods. If the MEO is a successful leader of public opinion, the visiting health officers will find the villagers waiting for them, their sleeves rolled up, or the people assembled in the clinic in readiness for trachoma treatments.

The MEOs by the fall of 1952 had induced 136 villages to build their own schools and equip them. Volunteers served as teachers until the government could send trained teachers. Some of the volunteers were monks from nearby Buddhist monasteries. The government has supplied 5,000 monasteries with slates and books for that purpose.

The MEOs try to get the villagers to build community centers where they can stage plays, listen to visiting lecturers, maintain a library, play dominoes, or have community meetings.

Experience has shown that it takes an MEO almost eighteen months to complete the rehabilitation work in a single village. At Htauk Kyan, twenty-one miles north of Rangoon, U Ye Hmee, a thirty-five-year-old schoolteacher from the delta, is the MEO. In this village eighty-four huts had grown like Topsy. There were no central streets, only little winding paths. Pigs, dogs, and chickens were everywhere. There was not a single decent latrine, the paths and yards being used instead. Today this village is a model one. In less than a year after U Ye Hmee arrived, such a strong community consciousness developed that all eighty-four houses were torn down and rebuilt on wide clean streets. The village now has latrines, the animals are corralled, a school flourishes, and there is a new pride in the faces of the people.

By late 1952 the MEOs were in 150 centers. The aim is to locate them in 1,000 centers.

Some of the centers where the MEOs are located are in Communist areas. So far the MEOs have not been disturbed by the Communists in their persons or in their work. That has not always been the fate of community projects.

For example, in some of the areas occupied by the Communists during 1948–50 there were co-operative rice mills and co-operative fisheries that were run for the benefit of the peasants. These co-ops were taken over and run by the Communists. The profits from the operations were not returned to the farmers; they were siphoned off and placed in the treasury of the Communist Party. The ineptitude of the Communists in their public relations could be illustrated over and again. A recent example was the cutting of the water line into Rangoon on August 20, 1952, to which I have already referred. Even the lowliest of the city folks resented this. The Burmese are a clean people, bathing several times a day. In order to bathe on August 21, 1952, they had to buy water— and, thanks to the Communists, it cost them five cents a gallon from the carts of the water vendors. Similar acts of terror, destruction, and appropriation have brought the Burmese Communists much discredit.

The Communists in Burma are known as the "everything-is-free boys." They promise the peasants freedom from taxation, freedom from rent, freedom from usury. But even these promises boomerang. Not all Burmese peasants are miserable sharecroppers. Many have their own plots of farmland that they rent out on shares. When the promise of the abolition of all rent is made in a village, the small owners as well as the large ones shudder.

Perhaps even the Communists are learning a political lesson. The fact that they have left the MEOs strangely alone is an indication. The MEOs are very popular in the villages; they have won the support and admiration of the peasants. Any interference with them would antagonize the villagers.

At least that is the view in the higher circles at Rangoon. And it is evidenced in numerous ways.

I talked with the Minister for Housing and Labor, M. A. Raschid, who, with the advice of American and European experts, has conceived what promises to be the brightest low-cost housing project anywhere in the world. Raschid has started it in seven cities and in one village in each of ten districts. The village projects are designed to create model modern villages, including schools. Some of the villages are in areas where the Communists are still active.

"Do you expect the Communists to interfere?" I asked.

Raschid, a tall man with a serious face and deep-set eyes, replied with feeling, "Let the Communists destroy these model villages if they will. If they do, they will only incur the wrath of the people." And after a pause he added, "We are sure the Communists will not *dare* molest our new villages."

What Raschid said about the new housing projects others said about the MEOs. The villagers know that their new government is kindly, tolerant, and generous. They know that the MEOs are their friends and that through the MEOs they can attain a better life. They know that from the Communists they have never received anything of good—only terror, destruction, and appropriation of their property. Therefore, if the issue is drawn between the Communists and the MEOs there is no doubt that the villagers will be on the side of the MEOs. The Communists, therefore, dare not attack either the MEOs or their work.

The plight of the Communists was highlighted in the talk I had with U Ba Lwin, Deputy Chairman of the Mass Education Council, and two of his assistants, U Tint and U Bo. We had tea together, discussing the mass education program and the role of the MEO in the new democracy of Burma. Finally Lwin, a devout Buddhist, said in a rather matter-of-fact way, "The MEOs are a powerful anti-Communist influence; they are indeed anti-Communist cells. Once our program is established on a nationwide basis, we will have voices in all the villages to educate the people against Communism and to reveal to them the tactics of the Communist organizers."

Already the MEOs are the greatest enemy of Communism in Burma. But the irony of it is that the MEOs are so popular the Communists are unable to move against them. For once in Asia, the counterrevolution has acquired and held the initiative.

CHAPTER 5

THE WELFARE STATE

Burma has one advantage in the contest against Communism that other Asian countries have not enjoyed—she has no overwhelming population problem. Burma, with a population of eighteen million, could easily support five times that many people without any major industrialization program. Burma is rich in land and has a food surplus. Burma indeed exported before the war over three million tons of rice a year. Burma is also rich in oil, timber, tungsten, lead, tin, zinc, and other minerals, and many precious gems. They would be indeed a prize for any foreign nation. Those resources could also be a great boon to her own people if that wealth were exploited for *their* benefit. And that is precisely what this young government undertook to do.

Burma started with a constitution that permits development in that direction. It accepts in the main two great principles of the American Constitution—the sovereignty of the people and the separation of powers. It guarantees freedom of expression, of worship, and of assembly, and the equality of citizens regardless of race or sex. It recognizes the right of each citizen to work, to maintenance in old age and in sickness, to leisure, and to education.

It guarantees a degree of civil liberties to persons not citizens. (There are about 800,000 Indians and 250,000 Chinese in Burma. To be a citizen, an Indian or Chinese has to have at least one grandparent who belonged to a race indigenous to Burma.) It gives women the right to the same pay as men for similar work; it abolishes forced labor or involuntary servitude; it guarantees every person freedom of worship; it outlaws discrimination against any person in regard to admission to public schools on the ground of race, religion, or language. It incorporates into the Union various indigenous groups along the frontiers. The Shans, the Kachins, the Chins, the Nagas, the Was, and the Karens are minority racial groups with differing languages and cultures. The British (perhaps with an eye to keeping their own approaches to India, China, and Thailand open) wanted these frontier minorities to have their separate states. But the Burmese nationalists stood firm against the idea; and those groups agreed to enter the Union. Their states are recognized by the Constitution and tied closely to the Burmese Union in a semi-federal system; and several of these states are represented in the government.

Sao Khun Khio, the Foreign Minister, is a Shan; Sither Mrs. Ba Maung Chain, Minister for Karen Affairs, is a Karenni; and the ministers for the other frontier states are nationals of their respective minorities.

Though the Constitution is permeated with a Jeffersonian philosophy, it also has a socialist tinge. Burma, somewhat like England, has married the two and launched in feudal Asia a challenging experiment that is proudly referred to as the Welfare State.

Industry. The chief complaint of the Burmese over the years has been the exploitation of the resources of the nation for the benefit of the British, the Indians, the Chinese. It was in that order that the wealth of the nation was enjoyed. At the bottom were the Burmese. Any trade not pre-empted by the British and the Indians was almost entirely in Chinese hands. It was, for example, very rare for a Burmese to be awarded any license to import goods; and the Burmese industrialist was almost non-existent. The exploitation was real and earnest. British capital returned 20 per cent, 50 per cent, and even 100 per cent a year.

As a result there were in Burma no native industrialists like Tata or Berla in India. There were no Burmese industrial and financial interests to entwine with British power. There was in Burma hardly any middle class at all. Thus both the quality and the pace of Burma's nationalism were set from the beginning by the radical intelligentsia. These young rebels were aroused at the exploitation of Burma's resources for the benefit of foreign capital. They inveighed against the "economic fascism of monopolists and capitalists" as well as the political fascism of dictators. Not only had these young rebels seen how the British, the Indians, and the Chinese had exploited Burma for their own benefit; they were steeped in revolutionary literature. The revolutions they knew most about were the Russian and the Chinese. The Communists were ready with literature to explain how to go about it. The Communist literature that the young Burmese read most avidly was not Russian but that of Mao Tse-tung. They had a long saturation in it during their student years.

The socialist philosophy of the new government does not outlaw private property or private enterprise. The new Constitution sanctions private enterprise, outlawing merely cartels, syndicates and trusts formed to dictate prices, monopolize markets, or injure the national economy. Provision is made for the nationalization of an industry "if the public interest so requires." The policy is that "all public utility undertakings" be operated by the state or by "local bodies or by people's co-operative organizations." The Constitution also provides that the state shall direct its policy "toward giving material assistance to economic organizations not working for private profit"; toward giving preference to "co-operative and similar economic organizations"; and toward the "exploitation of all natural resources" by the state, by local bodies, or by co-operatives.

The present government, however, has left most private enterprise alone. Railroads, inland waters, and air lines have become state monopolies. The export of rice and lumber has also been taken over by the state. In the case of rice the government fixes a minimum price for the farmer. If the retail price falls below the minimum, the government steps in and buys until the price rises above that minimum. All millers (private operators) must pay the farmer that price. The profit from the export of rice (and timber) now accrues to the government. In the case of timber the state monopoly is not complete. Licenses for export can be obtained by private interests. In 1952 nearly a third of the government's revenues came from the export of rice (on a volume one half of normal) and .3 per cent from timber exports.

The Rural Economy. Before the British took over Burma, money was lent only against a farmer's crop, for his land was inalienable and could not be sold on a mortgage foreclosure. The British introduced property laws that allowed mortgages to be foreclosed and tenants to be dispossessed. Then the Indian moneylenders from Madras (chettyars) descended on the country with their fat purses. They took mortgages from the peasants and charged interest as high as 180 per cent a year. The Indian moneylenders grew richer and richer. They got their original loans back many times over, foreclosed on vast acreages, and reduced thousands of former owners to the tenant class. By 1941, 60 per cent of all the agricultural land in Burma was owned by landlords, their largest holdings being in the delta. In the delta, 50 per cent or more of the land was indeed in the hands of absentee landlords; and in some areas of the delta the percentage owned by absentee landlords was as high as 80 per cent.

This meant a wholesale liquidation of the stable Burmese farming class. Moreover, the Burmese farm tenants were under new pressure from Indian immigrants, who with their lower standard of living were willing to pay higher rents for agricultural land

241

than the Burmese. Rents rose, evictions for defaults increased, the number of migrating tenants grew. Burma became more and more a nation of landless laborers who had no roots; the village community that had been a stabilizing force grew weaker and weaker; crimes increased; and agrarian dissatisfaction and revolt mounted.

It was against this background that the new Constitution declared that "the State is the ultimate owner of all lands" and has the "right to regulate, alter or abolish land tenures or resume possession of any land and distribute the same for collective or co-operative farming or to agricultural tenants." And the Constitution grants the Parliament the right to fix the maximum holdings by private parties. The Land Law of 1948 cuts down old holdings to 50 acres, limits new holdings to about 12 acres, and restricts the annual rent to about 8 per cent of the crop.

To date there have not been many redistributions of land under the new law. The government has been retarded by the fact that the Communists possessed many of the important areas where reforms were sorely needed. Moreover, most of the Indian moneylenders left the country, leaving their landed estates behind. Squatters took over many of these holdings and lessened the pressure on the government for immediate action. The government is proceeding carefully and cautiously. It wants co-operative farming and collective farming to develop, if the farmers prefer those methods. It wants large-scale mechanized farming where that proves to be the most productive method. It wants to be sure that the units of land distributed to private operators are economical and efficient units. It is therefore making extensive surveys, training and establishing local agencies to administer the program, and developing, in connection with land distribution, projects for rural housing, rural electrification, rural education, and all the other aspects of a healthy farming community.

The herds of carabao (depleted by the Japs) are being built up. Research into diseases of livestock, the manufacture of vaccines (especially for hogs and chickens), development of new types of rice, the building of demonstration centers—these are part of an attempt to bring modern science to Burmese farms. Veterinarians are being trained in government schools, and when they graduate they will work exclusively for the government.

The reign of the avaricious moneylender is nearing a close. A central land bank is being formed. Meanwhile the local governments are advancing agricultural credit. Thus in Mandalay, loans are made to farmers' co-operatives at the rate of 6¼ per cent a year—and to date 90 per cent of the loans have been repaid on time.

Housing. The Constitution of Burma pledges the state to the promotion of schemes "for housing" for the benefit of workers. There has been little building construction in Burma since 1941. Many houses were indeed destroyed during the war years, and the civil war that followed brought a halt to construction. The flocking of refugees to cities produced slums as bad as any in Asia.

The Burmese have gone about the housing problem in a thorough way, sending representatives to Europe and to America to study plans. Burma now has a more promising housing program than any I have seen. Rangoon, a city of 500,000, has been swelled by refugees to a city of 750,000. I saw at New Kanbe on the outskirts of Rangoon a project for the resettlement of 20,000 of these families now piled up in miserable huts in Rangoon. George L. Reed of our TCA is advising on it. It has two-room brick houses adequate for five people. They have high ceilings and good yard space. In the alley are faucets and toilets for each house, with a modern sewerage system. These houses are being built by the government and will be sold at cost—on a convenient installment basis—for about $1,000 each.

Similar projects will be launched in other large cities. And one model village will be built in each of Burma's thirty-six districts. These model villages will include a mass education school, a health center, some cottage industries, and an agricultural institute.

The housing plans include the manufacture of building materials from products available in Burma and the training of skilled labor for the construction. The state does not propose to do all of the construction work. Arrangements are being made for co-operative building associations under private auspices.

Labor. The Constitution makes it the duty of the state to secure to workers "the right of association," to limit "their hours of work," and to insure them "annual holidays" and an improvement in their "working conditions." The Constitution provides that the state "shall direct its policy" toward securing to each citizen "the right to work," "the right to maintenance in old age and during sickness or loss of capacity to work," and "the right to rest and leisure." But the Constitution also authorizes the state to impose "compulsory service for public purposes without any discrimination on grounds of birth, race, religion or class."

About 30 per cent of Burmese labor is unionized, mostly in transport, docks, shops, rice mills, and government agencies. There are Communist and non-Communist unions. But the Communist unions are in the minority. Of 70,000 union members in Burma, the Communist unions claim only 2,000.

There is compulsory arbitration of labor disputes before an industrial court, whose decree is binding on both parties.

There is a minimum-wage law (which is beginning to be enforced) and a maximum-hours-of-work law (44 hours a week with double pay for overtime) which is generally obeyed.

Working days are limited to six a week and working time to eight hours in any one day within the period from 5 A.M. to 9 P.M. Annual leave for workers includes ten days' earned leave, fourteen days' leave for religious and national holidays, six days' casual leave, and thirty days' sick leave. There are also regulations of health, safety, and welfare conditions in the factories.

Public Health. The Constitution makes "the raising of the standard of living" of the people and "the improvement of public health" a primary duty of the state. It directs the organizing of health services, hospitals, dispensaries, sanitoria, nursing and convalescent homes, children's homes, day nurseries, and maternity and infant welfare centers.

Public health in some of its aspects is an appalling problem in Burma. Accurate vital statistics are impossible to get. But it is estimated that the death rate is from 28 to 30 per thousand, the infant mortality rate between 200 and 300 per thousand live births, the death rate under ten years of age about 500 per thousand, the life expectancy at birth between thirty and thirty-eight years. About 50,000 people die each year from malaria. The tuberculosis mortality rate is around 200 per 100,000 population. Smallpox claims 5,000 a year. Leprosy is common. Environmental sanitation is so poor that the enteric or fecal-borne diseases are a constant threat. The climate and geography make Burma conducive to the propagation of rodents and ectoparasites that serve as hosts and vectors of disease.

A national malaria program has been drawn up by a joint group of the Burmese Government, our TCA, and the United Nations WHO. It essentially is a program of DDT spraying. In 1952, 500,000 people were made immune from malaria.

Water-borne infections have been attacked by the institution of a national environmental sanitation program. Here, too, TCA has helped. The program includes the drilling of wells and the proper disposition of excreta through modern latrines and otherwise.

In all of Burma there are only 1,200 trained doctors to care for 18,000,000 people, and there are no dentists as we know them (with the exception of five in Rangoon). Even so, medical practice is not completely socialized. A doctor need not work for the government; and hospital doctors on the government pay roll may have private practices on the side. Burma has 8,000 hospital beds (about 50 per cent of which need renovation). They are free to those who cannot afford to pay, as are medical care and medicines.

More doctors are being trained and additional doctors are being imported from India. Paramedical personnel are badly needed.

The government is trying to meet these requirements by expanding training facilities.

Vaccinations for tuberculosis are under way as part of a vast educational program in preventive medicine. Infant mortality is due mainly to dysentery. Preventive medicine and first-aid centers are the main reliance both as respects infants and adults.

Health centers handle maternity cases, vaccinations, and first aid. They train nurses and midwives. They teach sanitary engineering—the construction of latrines and the protection of wells.

The government has also established a Health Institute (similar to ours) that will manufacture vaccines and pharmaceuticals and do research on nutrition. And it has a Department of Health and Medical Services that has launched, with the help of TCA, an extensive public health educational program.

Education. The Constitution directs the state to undertake to secure to each citizen "the right to education," to make education compulsory, and to furnish it free. It especially emphasizes the duty of the state to provide education for the young.

Education is a special concern to Burmese because they were long discriminated against by the British. Their intelligentsia were freely admitted to schools in England and to the university at Rangoon. But the British did little to satisfy the needs of the masses. Today one hears more in Burma about education than perhaps any other subject. Free education is provided everyone from primary schools through the university. It is not as yet compulsory, for there are not enough schools or teachers to go around. But it will be made compulsory for the primary and secondary schools as soon as teachers and facilities are available. And the school-construction and teacher-training programs are going ahead full blast. The Burmese language is taught in the first four grades; after that, English. The problem in Burma, as in other Asian countries, has been to get students who go to Mandalay or Rangoon for university training to return to the villages to live. More and more teachers are now returning to the villages, owing in part to the Mass Education Movement.

These are the highlights of Burma's domestic program—measures which are the product of a leftist philosophy. In the words of U Nu, "In a Leftist country there will be no such thing as a handful of people holding the monopoly over the inexhaustible wealth of the land while the poor and the starving grow more and more numerous . . . in such a country the aim of production is not profit for the few but comfort and happiness of a full life for the many . . . in the Leftist country there will be no distinction between the employer class and the employed class . . . the governing class and the governed class."

One who looks at Burma casually may see little evidence of change or improvement. The slums still overshadow the new housing projects; most of the villages do not yet have first-aid stations; even the large landholdings are as yet largely undistributed; hungry moneylenders still practice their profession. But each of the social ills is being remedied. There is progress on every front.

Exploitation of the resources of Burma, whether for the masses or for shareholders of private companies, requires capital. It is estimated that at least half a billion dollars will be needed for the development of Burma's mineral resources. The over-all demand for capital certainly will be great. The Burmese expect to obtain some of it from the profits of state enterprises such as the export of rice, some of it from reserves from foreign exchange, some of it from private foreign sources. Burma so far has taken a few steps toward industrial development. She joined the Colombo Plan in December 1951. She has entered some joint agreements with private companies—one with the Burma Oil Company for the production and refining of oil, one with the Burma Corporation in the field of mining. She has opened a textile mill, and plans to build a modern sawmill, steel mill, paper factory, and chemical plants. How socialist Burma will manage its capital development remains to be seen. But the Burmese are not so slavish to political dogma that they are likely to become impractical or visionary planners.

247

Tremendous problems remain—in finance, in industry, in the practical and efficient administration of the program for the Welfare State. For example, oil production that used to be a million tons a year is only a tenth of that today. But there is growing intelligence in Rangoon and an increasing awareness of the need to be practical to win Burma's crusade against the inveterate enemies of man—ignorance, poverty, disease, and misgovernment.

The burden of the domestic program is carried by Burmese. But the United States—and the United Nations—both supply technical assistance; and the United States has provided some capital funds for rehabilitation. The United States, through TCA and ECA, is tied into eighty-six different projects in Burma, on which we have been spending about eight million dollars a year. The Americans in charge of these projects have caught the spirit of the powerful revolution that sweeps Burma. They are making as fine a contribution as any nation could hope to make in a foreign land.

What we are doing in Burma is illustrative of Point Four at its very best. Point Four in Burma is not an adjunct of a feudal government seeking popular support. It is an instrument of the counterrevolution against Communism. It is putting the weight of American influence and prestige behind an Asian grass-roots rebellion against both Communism and the form of capitalism that bled Asia white for the benefit of foreign powers.

Though many of the things that the Burmese Government is doing have a socialistic tinge, she is devoted to the democratic cause.

The land taken from the landlords is not confiscated. Nor is the Soviet principle of expropriation applied to nationalized industries. Owners are compensated for what the government takes. In the case of land the compensation is equal (approximately) to one year's crop. Though that might not satisfy Anglo-American standards, it is a basic departure from Soviet philosophy.

Habeas corpus during the days of chaos was suspended in a few regions. But today it is not. Any person detained can test before the courts the legality of his detention. Subversive elements are detained. But so far as I could learn, protective custody is not employed to crush political opposition even as respects members of the Burma Workers and Peasant Party (a Communist-front organization).

The civil courts are open, and even guerrillas are tried there rather than before military tribunals. In all trials due process of law in the Anglo-American tradition is faithfully applied. All confessions are carefully scrutinized for the influence of fear and coercion. In some respects the Burmese courts, like the British courts whose example they follow, are ahead of our own. Thus statements of the accused to the police are excluded from evidence.

Prime Minister U Nu and Attorney General U Chan Htoon were responsible for setting up a powerful anti-Communist organization known as the Sasana Council. Its executive committee of twenty-seven is evenly divided among the Buddhist monasteries, the government, and the people. Burmese leaders know that the Buddhist way of life would be threatened by the highly disciplined ideology of Communism.

Buddhism of the southern school (Hinayana) has had no central organization—no Dalai Lama who ties the various units of the northern school (Mahayan) together. It has had no Pope to unite the church against Communist ideology. Consequently the Communist propaganda in Asia frequently tries to twist Buddha's teachings to support Communist principles. The Sasana Council will combat the highly organized and disciplined ideology of Communism. It has under way large programs for anti-Communist propaganda and for educating the people in the evils of Communism. Buddhism is so much a part of the Burmese way of life that the defense of it is basic to the public policy of Burma. When the creation of the Sasana Council was presented to the Parliament in 1950, the Communists were very much opposed to it. Once in a while the Communists publicly inveigh against the church. In 1946 they placed placards in the sacred Shwedagon Pagoda that expressed irreverence for Buddha. But that is unusual. So strong is the Buddhist influence among the people that not a single Communist in Parliament voted against the bill creating the Sasana Council or the appropriations to maintain it.

The Council has already announced the Sixth Great Buddhist Council on World Peace to be held in Rangoon in 1954. Its aim is to promote a revival of Buddhism in Asia, a revival that will help bring peace to the world. The Council is called the Sixth Great Council (Chattha Sangayana) because it will be the sixth of its kind held since the death of Buddha. The twenty-five hundredth anniversary of Buddha's death will be in 1956, the year that the two-year Council ends. On that anniversary the Burmese believe there will be a great revival of the faith that will spread peace across the world.

Peace is a slogan heard often in democratic Burma. There is a graceful World Peace Pagoda newly erected on the outskirts of Rangoon. Facilities for 5,000 people to eat and sleep are being erected there. The Burmese have beaten the Communists in enlisting PEACE on *their* side.

Burma, the first Asian country to recognize Red China, is stoutly independent of Communist influence both inside and outside the country.

The Communist Party was vociferous in Burma beginning in 1948. It called for the confiscation of all British property and its nationalization. It declaimed against landlordism and promised its abolition. The Communists ruled over large areas of Burma during the civil war. In fourteen districts they actually undertook to redistribute the land, instituted their own courts, reduced interest rates, and annulled debts owed landlords and moneylenders.

Now that the government has the upper hand and the main power of the Communist guerrillas is broken, the Communist Party, although not declared unlawful by the government, has gone underground. The political party that serves as its front is the Burma Workers and Peasant Party, which in the 1951 election won less than 4 per cent of the seats. Its main complaints against the government are (1) the slowness in realizing land reform,

(2) acceptance of economic and technical aid from the United States, and (3) the presence of a British military mission (which in 1952 amounted to 20 men).

The Chinese Communists have assumed a different role in Burma. The Chinese are an honored group in the Burmese community, though they have had no political rights and have been debarred from owning land. They are mostly in the mercantile, trading, and financial fields. Though the Chinese community in Burma is a fairly wealthy one, it was inclined to be sympathetic to Mao Tse-tung and his regime when Nationalist China fell. Red China today, however, has lost much of its support among Burma's Chinese as a result of the stories of atrocities and liquidations coming out of China. At the same time, the Chinese in Burma have not swung over to Chiang Kai-shek. They are mostly fence-sitters who do not openly criticize Red China for fear of retaliation and yet have the political realism to know that Chiang Kai-shek holds no hope for Asia's future. There are not many Chinese Communists in Burma, and those who are there never attack the government on any of its policies. They work quietly and unobtrusively, never giving offense. Their main strategy has been to obtain control of the Chinese schools—private institutions that perpetuate Chinese history, Chinese culture, Chinese language. The Chinese Communists took over 80 per cent of them by infiltrating the boards of trustees and the teaching staffs. They even succeeded in getting textbooks from Red China introduced into the schools. When the conservative Chinese community awakened to what had happened, measures were taken to oust the Communists. But in 1953 about a third of these vernacular schools are still Communist-dominated.

Burma tolerates the Communists because its standard of civil liberties teaches that an ideology driven underground develops into a more virulent form than it would if it is allowed to press for acceptance in the market place of ideas. Buddhists, however, know that Communism is incompatible with their religion. Even the humble peasant can quickly realize it. Buddhism teaches that

251

a man's present condition is due in large measure to his actions in his previous lives and that if he is good in this life and behaves himself, his lot will improve when he is reincarnated. Communism collides head on with that gentle philosophy. It teaches that man's misery is due to the capitalists; and it tenders bloody revolution and terror as the solution. This realization of the incompatibility of Buddhism and Communism conditions every domestic move of the Burmese Government, every policy it adopts respecting its internal affairs.

In her foreign relations Burma does not flout the Communist nations. She has an 800-mile border with Red China that so far has produced no incidents. Moreover, the Burmese see in the Chinese revolution an emancipation of the Chinese peasant from the old feudal regime that cruelly exploited him. Perhaps the new regime is better, perhaps not. But the Burmese, bent on liberation themselves, are not quick to condemn those who likewise are escaping. They do not want for themselves what Red China has imposed on her people; but they will not inveigh against Red China because of it.

On issues such as the admission of Red China to the United Nations, Burma votes in the affirmative. But Burma is no tool of Chinese interests, no satellite. U Myint Thein, presently Justice of the Supreme Court, was the first Burmese Ambassador to Red China. When he arrived in Peking and tried to arrange to present his credentials to Mao Tse-tung, he was advised that since Mao Tse-tung was very busy and a bit under the weather, a deputy would receive the credentials. U Myint Thein refused, saying he brought credentials from one sovereign nation to another and could not present them to one of lesser dignity than the head of the nation. The Russian Ambassador intervened, advising U Myint Thein that the satellite countries of Eastern Europe had presented their credentials to the deputy and that Burma should follow suit. U Myint Thein, still adamant, cabled Rangoon for instructions. The Cabinet met and unanimously resolved that if U Myint Thein could not present Burma's credentials to the head of Red China, he should return home. When that news was transmitted through the protocol channels of Peking, Mao Tse-tung suddenly got well and received the Burmese Ambassador.

It is clear, however one views the Welfare State of Burma, that it offers a democratic, not a Communist, answer to the problems of feudal Asia.

CHAPTER 6

"WE MUST DO IT OUR WAY"

It was a rainy day in Rangoon, not a day of driving
rain but an overcast day of intermittent low black
clouds that sprayed the city with a soft warm rain. A small group
of us sat with U Chan Htoon on the porch of a club near the
outskirts of Rangoon, discussing Burma and her problems. A lake
of perhaps ten acres was below us. A fisherman in a small skiff
withstood all the squalls, intent on his line. Across the lake in a
thin grove of trees was a camp of several hundred Karen troops.
They had surrendered in the battles down south and were brought
here as prisoners. But the honor system was imposed; and the
Karens came and went freely through the unguarded gate. The
trees that rimmed the lake were mostly wide and spreading. At
times a curtain of fog would roll in, making them dim and indis-
tinct. Then the fog would lift, a shaft of light break through, and
for a second I would see in the distance the golden spire of
Shwedagon.

The quiet of the place, the peace of the scene, the softness of
the rain were so relaxing that they seemed even to lower the

voices of those who spoke. U Chan Htoon had talked of the ancient Burmese kings, the rule of the British, the occupation under the Japanese, the operations of the Communist guerrillas, the ethical standards for public office, the position of the Buddhist Church in the secular affairs of Burma, and the struggle of India and Burma for release from British rule.

"Why did you not become a British dominion like India?" I asked.

It seemed that Burma might well have become one but for an inept move by the British. At the end of the war the Burmese intellectuals were demanding independence. This group, partly underground during the Japanese occupation, was steeped in nationalism. As I have said, the literature of revolution that was spread before Asian students during the previous twenty years was Communist literature. The Burmese students, though not converted to Marxism, had been fired by Communist theories of emancipation.

During the occupation practically all Burmese nationalist factions had joined together in the AFPFL (Anti-Fascist People's Freedom League), the organization whose initial leader was the late Aung San, the organization that today holds the great majority of seats in the Parliament.

When the British returned in 1945, they issued the British White Paper on Burma. The British became at once the symbol of opposition to nationalist ambitions. The White Paper spoke of eventual self-government for Burma within the British Commonwealth. But the promises were vague and it seemed from the reading of the document that the British would be in command during the indefinite future.

The Governor whom the British sent to Burma—Sir R. H. Dorman-Smith—was imperialistic in the full Churchillian sense. His measures produced mostly disorders, political disaffection, and defiance of authority. He proposed to bring back the hated Indian moneylenders who had fled when the Japanese invaded. But the one act which stung the young nationalists worse than any other was his refusal to accept Aung San and the rest of his group as representatives of the people, and his appointment to government posts of Anglophile Burmese instead. The latter were Burmese who during the Japanese occupation had formed somewhat of a government in exile in India. They were men of character, but they had not been through the crucible of the occupation; they had not led the underground; they had not suffered humiliation, torture, and suffering at the hands of the Japanese. They were not the symbols of the new nationalism. When the British insisted that those men rather than the patriots who had remained in Burma head the new government, the die was cast. The young Burmese rebels decided to a man that they would be rid of Britain once and for all, that they would keep no ties to her, that even a dominion status would be unacceptable.

It was Sir Hubert Rance, a comrade-in-arms and an admirer of Aung San and successor to Dorman-Smith, who did in Burma what Lord Louis Mountbatten did in India. He sensed how deep the nationalist feeling ran and, with Attlee, shaped British policy to grant Burma her independence quickly.

U Chan Htoon recited this history. Whether the Burmese were logical or not, unfair or not, was beside the point. Burmese nationalism was a powerful, leaping force that nothing could turn back.

"It was our independence that was at stake," he said. "We dreamed about it, talked about it, planned it for years. We had to have it our way. Our way meant no British strings attached."

There is passion behind the nationalist sentiment in Burma, as there has been behind every great crusade in history. Back in the 1920's and the 1930's Burmese students at the university in Rangoon were striking against British rules and regulations. In retrospect the offending measures do not seem important even to the Burmese who were involved. But it was their undemocratic character, their imposition from above, that hurt. And the strikes closed the university. The same spirit of resistance still pervades the country—resistance to dictation from anyone. It relates to all

*In Rangoon I had seen yellow-robed monks
climbing hundreds of steps to reach remote shrines.*

The houses at New Kanbe, Burma, are being built by the government and sold at cost.

Burma's health program trains nurses and midwives.

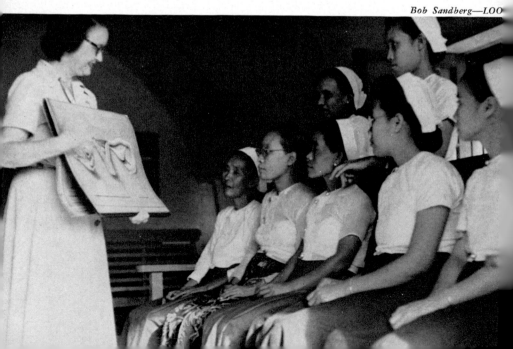

matters—to questions of military missions, financial agreements, industrial projects, and foreign aid of all kinds. We Americans have often heard critics say that no loans should be made to socialist countries because socialism is anathema to our system. U Chan Htoon touched on these things. He said rather subtly (and most courteously) that some people thought America was trying to remake the world in her own image, that American aid meant subservience to American influence and power.

He raised his voice as he said, "Burma wants to be a warm friend of America. America has helped us much, and we are most appreciative of what she has done. But our friends in your country must remember that out here we come at a problem from a different history, a different background, a different experience." He made clear Burma's desire for additional American help; and he defended the Prime Minister against the Communists' denunciation for accepting it. "America, more than any other nation, has the materials and the expert advice we need," he exclaimed. "But there never must be strings attached."

Now his eyes were flashing with the intensity of his feelings and there was such fervor in his voice that it seemed he was trying to speak for all Burmese.

"We need American help and American experience to work out the solution of our problems. But please remember this—we must do it our way."

The same testimonial to Burmese independence is repeated over and over again as one travels the country and moves among the people. A most revealing incident happened in Rangoon on August 4, 1952. The government convened a conference of some twelve hundred government officials to discuss and explain Burma's program for the Welfare State. The Prime Minister spoke for an hour and a half. It was an earnest, moving speech telling of Burma's past and her plans for the future. The Prime Minister was interrupted by applause only once, and that was when he raised his voice to say, "We abhor the very idea of acting as a disciple to any Big Power or as a satellite of any political bloc. We do not like to lift our fingers or nod our heads at a signal from anyone."

At that point the crowd broke loose in a deafening applause that was more eloquent than any speech. They were registering a warning to Russia, to China, to the United States. They were expressing the spirit of a people who are bent on having their revolution their own way. And thanks to the influence of Buddhism, that revolution is in the democratic—not the Communist—pattern.

PART 5

FORMOSA, KOREA,
AND THE FIFTH FRONT

1

THE GODDESS OF MERCY MOUNTAIN

Formosa was called the Island Beautiful (Ilha Formosa) by Portuguese sailors in the sixteenth century. The Chinese named it Terraced Bay (Taiwan). It deserves a name of beauty, for it is one of the prettiest places I have seen in all of Asia.

It is about 240 miles long and 90 miles at its widest point. Three mountain ranges run the length of the island. They occupy indeed about two thirds of it and reach as high as 12,960 feet. On the east coast the mountains rise almost straight from the ocean 1,500 to 7,000 feet. On the west coast and in the north are fertile plains. There are oak, bamboo, teak, camphor, black ebony, sandalwood, and acacia in the lower reaches of the mountains. Above 5,000 feet are pine, spruce, fir, hemlock, and cypress. These mountains have peaks that lift the heart, sheer walls hundreds of feet high, and harsh hogback ridges. The swift water from their slopes runs numerous hydroelectric plants. The forests feed many lumber mills and serve as the haunt of bear, panther, wild boar, monkeys, apes, deer, and armadillo.

261

The valley bottoms are filled with rice paddies, fields of sugar cane, orchards of bananas and pineapple. Every square foot is tilled. The draws are also planted with rice; their terraces march as far up the canyons as the ingenuity of man can provide water for irrigation. The foothills are dense with hardwoods and brush. They have ferns as big as trees and ginger flowers that have the scent of gardenias. There are lilies, azaleas, and orchids, lush and thick. Clear cold water pours mysteriously off a cliff, drops a hundred feet or more, and then is swallowed in dense brush as it works its way to the ocean, leaving behind only the roar of the falls and a cool spray.

These lower reaches are filled with the music of birds. One can walk for hours thinking he is deep in the forest, only to come out on a shoulder that has been cleared, where tea plants stand in neat rows and often streak in terraces across a whole mountainside. This is tea America has long known—the famous oolong (half-fermented) tea. It grows both in fields high on the sides of these foothills and in terraces that step gracefully down their sides.

From a distance these slopes present as colorful an effect as I have known. The monotony of the dark green of the hardwoods is broken by clumps of bamboo. Bamboo is slim, tall, and graceful; bamboo is useful; bamboo is durable. It is somehow a symbol of the survival value of the Chinese, of their ability to endure the severest tests which nature provides, of their capacity to suffer all adversity and live for the promise of another day. The leaves of bamboo are feathery. Their green is light and gay. They give to a stand of hardwoods the zest and life that our tamarack, alder, or willow give in the fall to slopes of pine and fir. And when the breeze comes up on an afternoon and the sun catches the bamboo, the light green leaves make a whole hillside shimmer.

Formosa's climate is subtropical. The Tropic of Cancer crosses Formosa just below its center. South of there the climate ranges from warm to hot. North of there the climate is hot and moist in the summer and cool in the winter. Rainfall averages 100 inches a year. Earthquakes average 330 a year. The summers—which run from May to September and bring the typhoons—are hot and humid in the plains. But the foothills are always cool at night. The winters are short—December to February—and also mild. The climate is so favorable that two or three crops of rice can be grown each year, plus another crop of turnips or cabbage. Sugar cane, which takes twelve months to grow in Java, takes eighteen months in Formosa. Thus the sugar industry is at some disadvantage. But the island is so rich in soil, the fruits and vegetables so numerous, the industry of the people so great that Formosa is a neat garden. The garden is gay with flowers, lush with produce, closely manicured, and very tidy. And above this garden rise towering heights of crags and cliffs that give fleeting impressions of our Bitterroots and Cascades. One of the lower peaks out of Taipei is Grass Mountain, about which Patricia Meissner has written:

They call you Grass Mountain because you are green.
Your clothes are made of mossy emerald velvet.
You are standing there, silently, and yet I can hear you whisper.
For your whisper is the breeze I feel now.
I live with you, Grass Mountain, up high near the sky
So that I feel you very near, and know your every mood.
You are always proud of course, and yet you unbend at will.
Sometimes I can hear you laughing, or gently sighing.
I know when you are happy or sad, and I feel the same.
On days when the rain has drenched the cherry blossoms,
When the streams are overflowing with tears,
I can see your shoulders droop in despair.
Then when the sun comes out once more, you stand up straight,
And wear your hibiscus like a flaming sword or medal pinned
And the camellias and lotus flowers as torches.
I shall always remember you, Grass Mountain.
Tsau Shan—Grass Mountain, I toast you!

Never has a countryside given me such a sensation of peace and serenity as I experienced in Formosa. Perhaps it was because

263

the jungles and ambushes of Malaya, the road mines and hand grenades of Vietnam were behind me. Whatever the reason, the mood was deep and lasting. I remember especially one late afternoon when I drove out of Taipei perhaps twenty miles to the foothills to see Ch'en Ch'eng, the Prime Minister, who was recuperating from a severe stomach disorder. It had been hot and humid in Taipei all day. A storm seemed to be making up toward the west, but it never gathered with the force needed to cool the plains. In twenty minutes we were above the town, perhaps a thousand feet, and a cool breeze was sweeping down the draws. As we rounded a bend on the climbing road I saw to the north, perhaps ten miles as the crow flies, a mountain that had the profile of a woman in sitting position.

"What is that?" I asked my host, Howard P. Jones, Counselor of the Embassy of the United States in Formosa.

"The Goddess of Mercy Mountain," he replied.

The Goddess of Mercy is an intimate, friendly mountain, known in Chinese as Kuan-yin Shan. It is about two thousand feet high and dominates miles of rice paddies and tobacco fields that lie on both sides of the Tan Shui River. This first glimpse I had of it was quick and fleeting. The mountain was gone from sight in a few seconds as we made the turn to the Prime Minister's house. His house, like most Formosan homes, is Japanese-style with low ceilings and furniture made for floor-sitting. China lost Formosa to Japan in 1895 at the close of the first Sino-Japanese War and regained it only in 1945. During the fifty-year interim Formosa became saturated with Japanese culture as part of the price of being a Japanese colony. So it was that the Prime Minister, Mr. Jones, and I sat on low cushions in a circle as we sipped green tea and talked of the disaster on the Chinese mainland and of the hope that millions had in Formosa.

The Prime Minister is a slight, short man in his middle fifties, with dignity on his face and a piercing light in his eyes. He wore sandals of rattan, loose gray trousers, and a blue tunic buttoned at the neck. Though he was once a professor of English in a

Chinese university, we talked through an interpreter. The Prime Minister spoke of his gratitude to America for the material and technical aid which we had sent Free China. These were important, he said. But more important than any material aid was America's moral support. Would America help sustain Free China in her struggle to escape Communist conquest? America and Nationalist China were basically allies in a common cause. Allies in the cause of freedom were not numerous in Asia these days. Friends should stick together. These were in the main the ideas expressed by the Prime Minister over the teacups.

I felt perhaps I had stayed too long because the Prime Minister had been ill for weeks and only this day had been up and about. His face was drawn, his cheeks thin, his voice weak. But there were warmth and eagerness in his eyes, and there was never a break in the conversation.

When at last I had departed and returned by car to the paved highway leading up to the foothills, the sun was down. But there was a minute or two of afterglow in a clear opening of storm clouds. Between me and the afterglow was the Goddess of Mercy Mountain. Now the features were clear and precise—a rather noble brow, the eye and cheekbone perfectly formed, the nose beautifully proportioned, the chin round and precise, the lips full and round. The silhouette was short and fleeting. But to me it was as moving and dramatic as any phenomenon nature has produced. There was a second when the lips were so soft and warm with expectancy that it seemed they might speak.

The Goddess of Mercy in Asia, where brother is pitted against brother, class against class! The Goddess of Mercy in a continent where conspiracy, hate, and cruelty have long ruled! The Goddess of Mercy competing with the Kremlin's creed of terror! What would Mercy say if she could speak?

Then she was gone as quickly as the afterglow of the sunset. Only a formless hulk of a mountain lay against the western sky. Formosa was now swallowed by darkness, a darkness that this night seemed to be deep and eternal.

CHAPTER 2

THE BELATED REVOLUTION

My visit to Formosa brought back memories of the winter of 1947–48 in Washington, D.C. The China Aid Act was before committees of the Congress. The conditions on the mainland of China were desperate. The United States was making frantic efforts to help the Nationalists stem the Communist tide. Dr. James Yen was in Washington, D.C., working to get at least a part of the proposed American aid earmarked for a program of rural reconstruction. Dr. Yen had started the mass education movement in China a quarter century earlier, as related by Pearl Buck in *Tell the People*. It was a movement designed to rid the villages of poverty, disease, and the oppressive business and governmental practices that kept the peasants in perpetual serfdom. Sun Yat-sen had written the first slogans of reform. Chiang Kai-shek had made some gestures. But for one reason or another little or nothing was done. It might now be too late to save the mainland by political measures. But Dr. Yen pleaded for the chance.

He talked with everyone in Washington, D.C., who would lend

266

an ear. Congressman Charles A. Eaton of New Jersey, Congressman Walter H. Judd of Minnesota, and Congresswoman Helen Gahagan Douglas of California gave him support. As a result of their efforts some of the funds appropriated by the China Aid Act of 1948 (62 Stat. 158) were allocated to rural reconstruction in China under a part known in the legislative history as "the Jimmy Yen provision." Under this provision a five-man commission, the Joint Commission on Rural Reconstruction (JCRR), was established and manned by three members appointed by the Chinese Government and two by our government. Dr. Yen was a member of the first JCRR and was instrumental in getting rural reconstruction projects started in Hunan, Kwangsi, Kwangtung, Szechwan, and Fukien provinces on the mainland and in Formosa. On the mainland JCRR operated only from October 1948 to September 1950, when its operations were closed out because of the Communist conquest.

In Kwangsi and Szechwan on the mainland JCRR was responsible for getting land rents reduced by 25 per cent. It organized many farmers' co-operatives on the mainland for the obtaining of farm credit, for the purchasing of farm supplies, for the marketing of farm produce. It organized health centers for villagers and programs for the control of prevalent animal diseases. It promoted irrigation projects and the selection of new varieties of rice, wheat, sweet potatoes, and cotton.

I did not see the work of JCRR on the mainland. But I talked with those who saw it, as well as those who partook in it; and I have read most of the accounts concerning it. As a result, I was convinced that if it had been started a decade or even five years earlier, it might easily have become the counterrevolution that would have swept Communism aside.

JCRR had the technical competence to deal with China's rural problems. It was a grass-roots operation, raising the standard of living of the man at the bottom of Asia's fuedal system. It struck at the evils of that feudalism—the monopoly which the few elite had over the wealth and resources of the country and over its

267

political institutions as well. Its aim was to create for the Chinese coolie a stake in his country.

The program of JCRR had another virtue as well. It was Chinese in origin. It had political appeal, the kind of practical common sense that could be understood in every village. It was therefore something for men to look to for escape from their awful misery. It seemed indeed to be the only *political* program capable of stopping Communism on the mainland. This program of rural reconstruction basically is the one that Burma is using to roll back her Communist tide. The final adoption of JCRR's rural reconstruction program for China in the fall of 1948, when that nation was all but lost, is the saddest application of "too little, too late." The program that held the brightest promise for keeping China in the free world ended as a valiant rear-guard action.

Today JCRR flourishes on Formosa. The Chairman is Dr. Chiang Monlin. The other two Chinese members are Dr. T. H. Shen and T. H. Chien; the American members, W. H. Fippin and R. H. Davis. I sat with the group and listened to their discussions. I went with them to the country and saw some of their projects. And what I saw and heard emphasized over and again that this program was what feudal Asia needed most. It is not an idea imported from abroad, but indigenous to the Asian continent—conceived and developed by the Chinese themselves. Moreover, Dr. Chiang Monlin, like Dr. James Yen before him, does not impose the program from above. It is daily redesigned to meet the needs of particular villages. The villagers are not told what their problems are. They draw their own complaints; they write their own declaration of independence. Then JCRR helps them achieve their goal or overcome their problem—whether it be saving pigs and cows from disease, getting medicine for the sick, constructing a school, or getting a landlord or moneylender off their backs.

The program of JCRR for Formosa covers six main subjects.

Agricultural Improvement. There is an extensive program for the development of improved varieties of rice, wheat, sugar cane, potatoes, and other vegetables. Seed farms, seed granaries, seed curing houses have been built and maintained; and educational work has been carried onto the farms. By the use of pure Horai rice seeds JCRR has increased production per hectare 50 per cent or more. Elaborate control projects have been launched against pests in rice, fruit, vegetables, and tobacco. Research in pesticides has been undertaken and extension services established. Chemical fertilizers have been introduced. Green manure (peas, soybeans, lupine, and other leguminous plants) has been demonstrated. Liming for acid paddy soil has been introduced. Fertilizer mixing plants and farmers' compost houses have been demonstrated and built. Reforestation projects have been launched and windbreakers have been erected. Sericulture has been promoted, with the result that silkworm production has become established and the development of a series of rural industries has been started. A jute program has resulted in a substantial increase (about 50 per cent) in production. Rehabilitation of the tea industry, which suffered greatly in World War II, has been undertaken. Propagation of fresh-water fish has been started. And improved pineapple varieties have been introduced.

Farmers' Organization. An extensive program for the organization (and reorganization) of farmers' associations has been launched. Many associations, organized by the Japanese, had become political agencies. JCRR has made them more truly co-operatives and under the control of bona fide farmers. Elections have been reformed. Uniform and simple accounting and book-keeping systems have been introduced. Equitable fees to be charged the co-operatives for their services have been established. Technical assistance to the co-operatives has been rendered. Financial assistance has been given some co-operatives in repairing or constructing warehouses and other physical facilities. Extension services, in-service training programs, training institutes, and short courses have been given the staff members of these co-ops.

Animal Industry. Animal disease-control work—rinderpest, cholera, and erysipelas particularly—has been extensive. Isolation quarters for livestock being imported or exported have been built. The manufacture of veterinary biologics has been put on a sound basis. New breeds have been introduced, especially Berkshire boars.

Irrigation Engineering. Loans and technical assistance have been given twenty-three irrigation and reclamation projects. The loans when repaid will go into a revolving fund to finance other rural projects.

Rural Health. The aim of JCRR is to have a health center or station in each village and in each important district of every city. It has established to date 378. These health centers are first-aid stations and drug dispensaries. They administer care in maternity cases. They have traveling clinics—nurses on bicycles who attend to as many as 100 families a week. These centers are also responsible for school health programs, public lectures, and the vaccination of young and old. JCRR also gives financial assistance to three malaria-control centers. And it has arranged for a short intensive course in health education to be given to at least one teacher in each of Formosa's 1,200 primary schools.

Rural Economics. Reorganization of the hog and fish wholesale markets has been accomplished. Loans for the rehabilitation of banana packing houses have been advanced. Studies of rice prices and the cost of tea production have been made. What the farmers pay for their daily necessities for subsistence often exceeds what they receive for their farm products. Ways and means of putting floors under agricultural commodities have been recommended.

Land Reform. The Formosan Government in 1949 reduced farm rentals from an average of 50 per cent to 37.5 per cent. JCRR has been helping the government police operations under that law. It has trained villagers in each of the districts in the operation of the law and the manner in which disputes under it should be handled. It has also helped survey the agricultural lands of the island for the purpose of aiding the government in formulating the last phase of the reform program—distribution of the land to the tenants.

I caught the spirit of JCRR when I visited some of its projects. At the Provincial Teachers College in Taipei I saw a hundred or more men from the villages of Formosa attending seminars on the new land program and learning how to handle the varied disputes that may arise.

Outside of Taipei I visited the Hsinchuang Farmers' Association, a co-operative that has numerous activities. It owns a warehouse where rice is stored and a mill where rice is polished. It buys fertilizers for its members and sells them at slightly above cost. It has a dozen or more Berkshire boars who are bred to Formosa sows. The Formosa pig is a long, lean sway-back whose belly almost touches the ground. It never would be able to negotiate a log. Crossed with Berkshire, it makes a respectable hog, well shaped with increased poundage. And it is carried to market proudly in a woven rattan cage. The co-op, for a service charge, loans the boars to its members.

I visited the Kwei San Hsiang Health Center about thirty miles southeast of Taipei. It is under the supervision of Dr. Hsu Shih Chu, head of the Rural Health Division of JCRR. Dr. Chu was once a student of Dr. Yen and caught from him the vision of rural reconstruction as a revolutionary measure against the feudal system that held the peasants in servitude. At Kwei San Hsiang he told me of his experiences, of the spiritual uplift Dr. Yen had given him, of the missionary effort which every educated Chinese owed his people.

Dr. Chu showed me eagerly through the health clinic. Two young first-aid attendants and three young nurses (neat and prim in their blue dresses and white collars) were there to greet us. This clinic gives pre-natal and post-natal care to women. It has a children's center; and it ministers to the needs of all the people with a first-aid clinic. Here I saw chloromycetin, aureomycin, penicillin, and terramycin—all American products bought with MSA funds. Here I also saw Epsom salts, iodine, Band-Aids, gauze, tape, and all the other supplies of a model first-aid station. The nurses of this station travel each week a long circuit on bicycles to take care of the outlying villagers. But to those who can walk, the station is no more than two hours distant.

As the inspection of Kwei San Hsiang ended and we strolled back to the car, an American attached to JCRR cast a shadow across my enthusiastic response. He pointed out that Formosa already had a population of about eight million people, which is double that of Wisconsin. But the area of Formosa is only one fourth that of Wisconsin, and two thirds of Formosa's land is mountainous. Formosa's population is now three times what it was at the turn of the century. Families of seventeen or eighteen are not uncommon. Marriages occur at an early age. The death rate is already down to 12 per thousand. If the health program of JCRR succeeds in reducing the death rate further, an average couple can expect to live to eighty and have a thousand descendants during their lifetime.

"The birth rate is forty-two per thousand," he said. "And with a death rate of twelve, the gain is thirty, which is 3 per cent. Applying the compound interest table to 3 per cent, it means that the population doubles every twenty-five years."

"How about the food problem?" I asked.

"We cannot hope to increase the production of food by more than 25 per cent every twenty-five years."

"What are the practical consequences?"

"A gradually lowered standard of living, until on this bountiful Island of Formosa there will be starvation similar to that on the mainland of Asia."

"What is the answer?"

"Birth control."

"Is there any chance of that?"

"Not much. The militarists are in control here. They believe that human cannon fodder is a necessity. Those who don't believe that believe that Sun Yat-sen knew what he was talking about when he published that the population of China was decreasing."

"Is there moral objection to birth control in Formosa?"

"Certainly. In Formosa, just as in America, there are those who believe that planned parenthood is an interference with God's laws. But they disregard the parallel fact that every time an irrigation project is built, every time an injection of vaccine is given, there is a like interference with the workings of raw nature."

"What about the Communists on the mainland?"

"Oh, they don't go in for birth control either. But they have publicized over and over that they intend to reduce the population of China by anywhere from twenty-five to one hundred million."

"And what have they done to date?"

"Liquidated about sixteen million. But I submit that birth control is more humane than genocide."

These ideas of overpopulation and death were whirling in my head when we stopped to visit Liu Lau-Sheh, a peasant who owns a small farm planted to a new species of high-producing rice developed by JCRR. He is a middle-aged man with a wife, half a dozen children, and a father with a silky gray beard and a benign countenance that makes him look like a professor of philosophy. JCRR had shown him how to lay concrete threshing floors so that none of the rice would be lost in the dirt. It taught him how and when to plant the new rice seed which JCRR had developed. It proved to him the advantages of the co-operative. This man, after two years of JCRR tutelage, was happy and prosperous. He had saved out of his 1¼ hectares $2,000 (U.S.) and with it bought bricks and tile for a new house. The house had been finished just prior to my visit. It has two rooms, and the walls are hung with a family picture, some ancient Confucian symbols, and a calendar from a Taipei oil company.

In the total mounting population of Formosa there may well be sheer disaster for the common man. But Liu Lau-Sheh, happy in his new prosperity, was wholly oblivious of it. He was Mr. Contented Farmer who at long last had inherited his piece of the earth.

Liu Lau-Sheh owns his land. But in 1952 most of the farmers of Formosa were still tenants. Land reform, promised since the days of Sun Yat-sen, had never reached the farmers on the mainland, except in a few areas, and then only in the last frantic days of the debacle. By the time Chiang Kai-shek and his entourage reached Formosa in 1949 their political default was plain. The failure to carry out land reform on the mainland, the attempt to keep the ancient feudal system intact—these were some of the reasons that Communism flourished on the mainland and swept the country even faster than its protagonists had dreamed.

Chiang Kai-shek left the mainland for Formosa in April 1949. On December 8, 1949, Taipei was made the temporary capital of China. Even before that happened land reform was launched in Formosa. By a 1949 act, rent reduction was decreed. But after that nothing was done; the government temporized. Of Formosa's total arable land, 56.3 per cent was cultivated by tenants and much of it in small uneconomic units. Seventy per cent of all the farmers were tenants. The power of the landlords in government remained strong. Nothing was done to break up their holdings. In 1951 and 1952 some *public lands* were sold to farmers. But it was not until 1953 that the landed estates were distributed. Some 500,000 acres were then ordered distributed, the government buying from the landlords and selling to the tenants, who pay in twenty installments over a ten-year period with interest at 4 per cent a year. About 250,000 tenant families (which is over 39 per cent of the present farm families) have received or are in the process of receiving land as owners. As a rule, landlords are cut down to 7.4 acres of medium grade paddy land and to 14.8 acres of medium grade dry land. The landlords receive cash, land bonds, or stocks in corporations which the government took over when Japan lost World War II and ceded Formosa back to China. Formosa's land-reform program, as finally evolved, will rank along with Japan's as a cure for some of the evils of feudalism that have cursed Asia.

Although agrarian reform, which JCRR has managed so effectively on Formosa, goes to the root of the disaffection on which Communism has thrived, more than agrarian reform is needed if there is to be social and political stability in Asia. Formosa's long-range problem is industrial rather than agricultural. For the island can never keep food production apace with an uncontrolled increase in population.

When Japan held Formosa, she used it at first as a source for essential foodstuff—principally rice and sugar. After the outbreak of the Sino-Japanese War, Japan began to develop Formosa as an important industrial link in her "Greater East Asia Co-prosperity Sphere." During the latter period Japan built factories, constructed hydroelectric projects, and knit the several parts of the island together with railroads and a fine system of paved highways. She built fertilizer plants, textile mills, an oil refinery, paper mills, and other processing plants. Her hydroelectric development of Formosa (drawing most heavily on Sun Moon Lake) was so advanced that many straw-thatched huts in the villages had electric lights!

The industrial plant which Japan built in Formosa was greatly damaged during the war. Its rehabilitation was the first requirement. MSA has helped the Chinese substantially to complete it. The industrial future of Formosa depends more on the supply of power than on any other factor. Hydroelectric power, installed by the Japanese, has been greatly expanded and hitched to vital industries—some new, some rehabilitated: a steelworks where tin cans necessary for Formosa's processed foods are made, a creosoting plant for the treatment of railway crossties, oil-processing plants, textile factories, copper mines, coal mines, sulphur mines, calcium cyanamide plants, caustic soda plants, sugar factories. Most of the projects were aided by MSA with dollars or with the genius of American engineering.

During her rule Japan allowed a small trade-union movement

to develop. Some thirty trade unions with a total of 6,000 members were affiliated in the Taiwan Federation of Labor. These unions, suppressed during the war, have been encouraged by the government in recent years. The government has also favored labor in other ways. In 1950 it provided accident, disability, birth, death, and old-age insurance for all public and private employees. Three per cent of the worker's monthly wage is put into a fund for the purpose. The worker supplies 60 per cent of the amount, the employer 20 per cent, and the government 20 per cent. There are close to 200,000 workers presently covered by the plan.

Formosa has a long way to go. Military costs absorb about two thirds of the budget. She has a population of nearly eight million, which excludes the large military establishment. (All of the Japanese, about 478,000, were deported.) She has survived to date solely because of United States aid. In 1949 Formosa was not only crippled by war damage; a wild inflation had made her currency practically worthless. The influx of over two million people drained her economic resources. There were not enough goods to go around, and there was no foreign exchange with which to buy them. It seemed for a while that Formosa would descend into economic chaos.

Political chaos was close at hand too. Many of the two million refugees were Communists or employed by the Communists to wreak havoc in Formosa. Chiang Kai-shek's government was indeed in peril the moment it set foot on Formosa. There was not only the threat of the Communist Army 100 miles away on the mainland; there were Communists right in Chiang Kai-shek's government. The Deputy Minister of Defense had a secret two-way radio in his office by which he communicated with the Red government every day. He was quietly arrested and the radio taken over by the police. For several months the police exchanged messages with the Reds and slowly compiled a list of collaborators. The list was long and important and included the heads of all the public utilities on Formosa. The plan for seizing the island was well laid.

One day, when the secret radio had served its need, all collaborators (including ninety high-ranking civilian and military leaders) were arrested.

"What happened to them?" I inquired of an American attaché.

"Most of them were shot," he said. And then he quickly added, "Without due process of law."

Today there is law and order in Formosa. Today Formosa is doing a valiant job in social reconstruction. Formosa today is experiencing the beginnings of the revolution which Asia has long expected and wanted. It comes belatedly and under the compulsion of dire circumstances. It therefore does not carry the inspiration and force expectant in the promises of the leaders when the Kuomintang was a revolutionary party. But the revolution is real to Formosans. They are beginning to see the end of the feudalism that has cursed the politics and the economics of Asia from time out of mind.

JCRR and MSA—the two American agencies that have been active in Formosa on social and industrial problems—were greatly responsible for the revolution. Many agencies, many people cooperated. The Prime Minister Ch'en Ch'eng led the fight for land reform. K. C. Wu, the present Governor, threw his weight behind liberal reform measures. But it was the quiet voice of JCRR and MSA that gave direction to the movement. Those agencies furnished much of the vision, much of the drive. They were on hand to counsel and to encourage when defaults seemed likely.

CHAPTER 3

THE TRAPPINGS OF DEMOCRACY

I do not propose an inquest on the loss of the mainland to the Chinese Reds. I will only say that I think
the American White Paper of 1949 was too critical of the Nationalists. I do not think Chiang Kai-shek and his followers were the
rascals they have been made out. There were crooks among them;
but there were good men too—as fine, as decent, as idealistic as
one will find anywhere. America's fault was in a lack of understanding of the nature of the revolution that was sweeping Asia.
We subscribed for a while to the idea that the Chinese Communists were only "agrarian reformers." We had the rather naïve
belief that somehow the conservative, reactionary Kuomintang
could manage the situation. We had no conception of the nature
of the counterrevolution necessary to save an Asian country from
Communism. If foreign aid alone could have saved Chiang Kai-
shek, he would today control the mainland.

Many of the men on Formosa are Christians. Many were educated in America or in England. Most of them have insight into
and knowledge of the causes and tactics of Communism. The sin

of many of them was not corruption but political ineptitude—the failure to see the force and power of the Communist creed and the nature of Communist tactics. Some were compromisers; some lacked courage; some had in mind more the interests of their class than the interests of the peasants; many were petty politicians rather than statesmen. Today they are mostly chastened men.

Today the Formosan regime is one of austerity. Salaries of government employees are at a pitifully low level. The Formosan Government is largely free from corruption.

But this does not mean that these men, their slogans, banners, and their armies can lead the counterrevolution in Asia.

Formosa, in spite of her belated revolution, still nourishes repressive practices. There is in the first place the Secret Police.

Chiang Ching-kuo, the eldest son of the Generalissimo, is in charge of the police. He has spies and counterspies. Everyone is watched. Russian-style, Chiang Ching-kuo has political commissars attached to the Army. They are responsible to him, not to the Commanding General, Sun Li-jen. There are two political commissars to each platoon. They have an "Overcoming Difficulties Movement" which is an attempt to induce the soldiers to grow vegetables and to raise livestock to supplement their rice diet. And these political commissars also have a "Thought Control" project aimed at keeping "dangerous ideas" out of the heads of the troops.

One can walk the streets of Taipei or travel the highways of Formosa in safety, night and day. One does not need to hide his wallet at night or fear for the loss of cameras from a car. But the atmosphere of peace is somewhat superficial. There are strictures on newspapers and other publications. There is no censorship; one can print what he pleases. But if his articles engender "defeatism," he can be punished. For the encouragement of "defeatism" is a crime. An author or publisher can be tried *in secret* by a military court. (The actual instances have been rare.) Anyone deemed "subversive" can be arrested, tried by a military court in secret, hustled out to the race track at Taipei, tied to a post, and shot through the back of the head by the Secret Police. (These instances have been quite common.) There are also detention camps ("rehabilitation centers") where suspects and political prisoners are kept.

As Ravenholt, in "Formosa Today," 30 *Foreign Affairs,* 612, 620, says, "For the great majority of Chinese on Formosa the fearful feature of this situation is the lack of legal protection for the ordinary citizen. He can be arrested at night by a squad of military police, tried by a military court-martial, and sentenced with little opportunity to appeal. Once taken into custody, the ordinary Chinese is in effect at the mercy of the garrison headquarters. A person may be arrested because he actually is a subversive. He can also be picked up because someone who wants his job or property has denounced him as a Communist to the authorities."

There is an effort being made to limit the jurisdiction of military tribunals over offenses committed by civilians. But in 1953 the military are still supreme.

Formosa lives, of course, on the edge of danger. The Communists on the mainland are well organized; and they have perfected the tactics of political infiltration. Severe, not soft, measures are necessary. Yet China, even in its heyday under Chiang Kai-shek, never knew due process of law in the Western sense, nor freedom of the press, nor free speech. So Formosa is not the case of a people who live so close to the brink of disaster and oblivion that they have forsaken their traditions of civil liberties. Rather, they apply in Formosa the same traditions they knew on the mainland and justify it on the grounds that reasons of security permit no more. But the fact remains that though Formosa professes the democratic faith and is far more tolerant of minority views than Red China, she has many earmarks of a police state. The crushing of a "large Red underground" may be no more than front for the execution of the Generalissimo's political enemies.

Chiang Kai-shek's rule is by clique. All power centers in him, all lines of authority run to him both in civilian and in military matters. His party, the Kuomintang, has now been reorganized to control all the patronage, to determine the policies. It reaches into every school, into every village.

When Formosa was returned to China, the Kuomintang laid a bloody hand on the people. Its agents in Formosa were no better than "carpetbaggers" bent on loot, pillage, and exploitation. Chen Yi was appointed Governor of the island. He used a cruel plot to kill the outspoken, intelligent Formosans who had led an independence movement against the Japanese. He even murdered young high school students who protested his reduction of school budgets. This was in 1947, and the episodes are still fresh in Formosans' minds. Chen Yi was later executed for going over to the Communists. And K. C. Wu, the present Governor, has done much to regain the confidence of the Formosans by appointing them to government posts. But Formosans (who are Chinese speaking the Fukienese dialect) still tremble at the power and tactics of the Kuomintang.

Formosa has a legislature—the Legislative Yuan—which has representatives from all the provinces of China. Those seats are hold-over seats, dating back to the time when the Kuomintang ruled China. The Legislative Yuan is the symbol of China as she was before the debacle. The Legislative Yuan therefore could not be an elected group like our Congress. For, with the exception of Formosa, the Communists control all of the provinces represented in this legislative body. The terms of the members expired in May 1951 but were extended by Chiang Kai-shek. The Kuomintang holds two thirds of the seats in this legislature and controls more than that.

The Legislative Yuan elects the President and Vice-President. It granted Chiang wide powers of government by decree for the duration. The President appoints the Executive Yuan (the Cabinet) and the Judicial Yuan (the judges). Thus the power of the Kuomintang is complete.

There is a beginning of self-government on Formosa. In 1950

and 1951 there were elections for district commissioners, for mayors, and for district and municipal councils. Then the district and municipal councils named the members of the Provisional Provincial Council of Formosa. This is a council of fifty-five members, five of whom must be women. The Council is purely advisory. It has been quite active in reviewing the budget and accounts of the province and in voicing its opinion on matters of public interest.

But those elections do not have the significance that is claimed for them.

First, the local officials who are elected do not have full authority in local affairs. They exercise only those powers delegated by the central government. And they share those powers with officials appointed from on high.

Second, the elections in 1951 were not honest ones. They started in the southern part of the island; and it soon became apparent that the Formosans were going to win the great majority of the offices. The Kuomintang stepped in at once and "controlled" the remaining elections so that their men won. Where their candidate did not win, they made up for the defeat by putting one of their men in the office alongside the winner.

The Generalissimo and the Kuomintang do not trust the peasant with the ballot. Formosans are quite literate; by mainland standards they are indeed well educated. The Japanese gave Formosa a good public school system, providing primary schools for over 70 per cent of the children. The people of Formosa are well equipped to exercise the franchise. Men like K. C. Wu want them to have it. But the weight of the government is opposed. The government plans to delay giving the people the vote until the mainland is reconquered. Universal suffrage is the goal; but the Kuomintang thinks the people are not ready for it. The Kuomintang says that the effects of Communist indoctrination must be done away with before the people can be allowed to vote.

Meanwhile the Kuomintang is reorganizing itself into a more efficient, a better-disciplined party. In 1950 it announced that it had adopted the system of "democratic centralism." That permits wide and open discussion in party meetings but requires blind and complete obedience once a decision is reached. Democratic centralism—a working instrument of the Communists—is now a working tool of the Kuomintang.

The Kuomintang is not influenced by traditions of civil liberties. It believes in neither economic nor political democracy. The reforms it belatedly made were in large measure thrust upon it. Land reform was long delayed because of the opposition of the landlords who dominate the Kuomintang. I related in the Philippine part of the book how I inquired in Taipei concerning the reasons for the long delay in getting land reform through the Legislative Yuan and the reply I received from an old, wise Chinese. "Negotiating with the tiger for his fur—that's the reason," he said.

The Kuomintang is the tiger. The Kuomintang is still the vested interest, the status quo in Asia. There are revolutions in Asia—Burma, India, Pakistan, Malaya, Vietnam, the Philippines. Some are Communist-dominated; others are not. But the Kuomintang would label them all "subversive." The Kuomintang has trappings of democracy; but at heart it represents the opposition to change. What Asia wants is leadership for her revolutions. Formosa does not supply it—actually or symbolically. For the Kuomintang represents the past—some of it decent, much of it reactionary, most of it full of despair.

CHAPTER 4

THE ISLAND AIRPORT

I saw Chiang Kai-shek's Army in training. I went with a fine American officer, General William C. Chase of MAAG, and General Liu of the Chinese Army to Shulinkon one bright afternoon. This is a valley in the foothills about a three-quarter-hour drive out of Taipei where about three thousand men were in various stages of training.

The Chinese soldier is an individualist to start with and has never been taught the rudiments of team play. He therefore does not understand the co-ordination of infantry and artillery, of artillery and air. He can be taught, for he is as bright and able as anyone of any race. But it takes time and patience. And it is more difficult the older he gets. The average age of Chiang Kai-shek's Army is close to twenty-eight years. That is late in life to learn teamwork and co-ordination. But the troops at Shulinkon were hard at it.

Some stood eight in line with a huge log alongside. They were lifting the log and shifting it in unison from one shoulder to another, holding it high, letting it down, turning and twisting it.

Some stood in groups of three. One would be hoisted to the shoulders of two men, and then the three of them would charge another set, trying to knock or drag the opponent off the shoulders of his teammates.

Some ran relay races. Others were organized as teams which competed in climbing a pole and then sliding down a rope.

There were groups on the target range. Others were doing bayonet drills. And there was of course the long obstacle course such as our Marines have at Quantico—ditches to jump, fences to hurdle, holes to crawl through, pits to traverse on narrow planks, high walls to scramble over, barbed wire to crawl under.

There were platoons receiving instruction in range finding, machine guns, hand grenades, the art of concealment, the use of the terrain for protection, enfilading, mortar fire, and the like. One subject was taught at each station; and at regular intervals each platoon would shift to another station until the entire seminar had been given every platoon.

The grenade instructor divided the platoon into two groups. The first group tossed a hand grenade at the second group and then ran for cover. Before the grenade exploded, the second group was supposed to toss it back. There were close calls, but the soldiers were adept at it and never missed.

One platoon was on a target range, shooting at about five hundred yards. There was an earthen wall thrown up from a trench behind which men were controlling the targets. They would expose for fractional seconds the figures of men in various positions. The firing was more or less constant. To one edge of this earthen wall and behind it perhaps fifty yards, was a peasant's cottage. An old lady came out of the front door, not to run or dodge but to watch. Though bullets were ricocheting every which way, the old lady sat nonchalantly in her front-row seat on the firing range. The fact that she was behind the targets did not seem to bother her.

"The Asian's disdain for life," someone commented. Whether the old lady was brave, stupid, or reckless, I never knew. A few

285

minutes later, bullets and shrapnel were whining around General Chase and me as we saw a fine piece of field maneuvers.

Soldiers dashed a mile across broken ground under fire to take a low-lying ridge. Mortar fire was hitting perilously close both in the rear and in the front. There was devastating machine-gun fire so managed as to place a ceiling of hot lead over the troops. They crawled and squirmed their way forward, barely missing mortar hits and crouching low to avoid the singing bullets above them. There were no casualties. The timing, precision, courage, and endurance were excellent.

Chiang Kai-shek's Army numbers about 600,000. It's an inexpensive army as armies go. It costs about $600 a year to maintain a Nationalist soldier as compared with $5,000 for an American. Less than half of the Nationalist soldiers are well trained. The Nationalist Navy and Air Force are of little consequence. Five hundred pilots, however, have been trained to fly jets. But up to the spring of 1953 they had none.

In Taipei one hears Chinese generals (of whom there are 1,700) talk of military operations against the mainland. There are these days numerous commando raids against the islands near the mainland. Chinese officers think Chiang Kai-shek can seize a portion of the mainland, hold it while disaffected elements join him, gradually extend his beachhead until a strategic province is taken, and then start the reconquest of the mainland.

Perhaps he can. But I left Asia convinced that he could not do it without the United States Navy and the United States Air Force in support. And even then I am not sure he could do it without the United States Army. But if the United States joined Chiang Kai-shek in such an adventure, we would be in all-out war with China. *And in my view war with China for that purpose would be the most disastrous course we could conceive.*

Chiang Kai-shek's war would be our war. If he won, it would be due to American equipment and American lives. America's self-interest demands that we not undertake that commitment nor be maneuvered into it. If he lost, it would in Asian eyes be an

American defeat. Moreover, the appearance of American forces on the Chinese mainland in aid of Chiang Kai-shek would be the rallying cry to unite all Asia against the West. It is one thing to go to Korea in defense of the principle of the independence of nations. It is another to underwrite with American lives and American resources the political fortunes of a Chinese politician. It is disastrous to do so in any case. It is a tragedy when his cause is a lost one.

As good as the achievements of Chiang Kai-shek on Formosa have been, they do not rally the peoples of Asia. The Formosan regime represents the past that failed, not the hope of the future. The rich Chinese who have made their fortunes in Southeast Asia and sit on their moneybags in the Philippines, Malaya, Burma, and Siam do not, by and large, look to Formosa for salvation from the ills that beset Asia. Many of them are afraid to visit Formosa for fear the Kuomintang will arrest them for old grievances and lead them to execution or cause them to be swallowed up in a detention camp. To the masses of Southeast Asia, Formosa does not represent the people's movement, the rallying point for revolution, the way to escape the serfdom which both the Communists and the landlords hold for them. Once Chiang Kai-shek was the young revolutionary who could turn fighting phrases and rally men to a cause. He still is a gallant figure; but his charm, his appeal, his popularity have passed.

To the peoples of Asia the good things that have happened on Formosa with American aid and with American technical assistance are not the heroic deeds of men who have long struggled for the welfare of the peasants. On the contrary. They represent the belated concessions of men who long stood in the path of change and progress. They represent what was forced on an old leadership, not what was won by an eager one. Asia is not turning back to feudal overlords, to conservative politicians, even to fine old men for leadership. Asia is explosive, turbulent, impatient. It will follow only the banners that have promise and hope.

That is why Asia repudiates Chiang Kai-shek. That is why

America would be championing a lost cause if it underwrote Chiang Kai-shek and his invasion of the mainland. In Asian politics Chiang Kai-shek is politically bankrupt.

There is much written, much discussed about the practical realities of an invasion of the mainland by Chiang Kai-shek. Some say there is great disaffection under Mao Tse-tung, that Chiang Kai-shek on the mainland would rally vast forces. I was not on the mainland, so I do not know. But from Indians who have been to Peking recently and from the listening post at Hong Kong I learned that Mao Tse-tung has a hold on the people— especially the group between eighteen and thirty years of age. And the techniques by which he has achieved it are authoritatively related by Liu Shaw-Tong in *Out of Red China*. I cannot believe that the Kuomintang—discredited on the mainland and not appreciably different now from what it was—could win that group away from the Communists. There may be a force inside China that can do so, as Carson Chang in *The Third Force in China* maintains. But the force symbolized by Chiang Kai-shek is not it.

Red China may be as great a menace as her worst critics have claimed. But to most Asians she is not. Asians today are escaping a feudal system that has enslaved them. Some feudal overlords were foreigners with a white skin, some were colored and of the same race as the exploited. But whatever their race or color, the overlords are on their way out. To Asians, any nation that gets rid of her overlords is to be acclaimed. Many Asians who do not respect Communism (and most of them do not) give Mao Tse-tung some credit. Certain it is that he has cruelly liquidated tens of thousands of people. Certain it is that he has large concentration camps and millions of slave laborers. But those who have visited Red China also say that he has raised the standard of living of the peasants and largely eliminated graft from the government. By their lights he has served his country well, even though he has used cruel and bloody tactics. The fact that he is a Communist is less important to Asians than that he is Chinese.

*We visited several
observation bunkers
at the Korean front.*

*We put down
at several places
along the base
of the Iron Triangle.*

*I saw
Chiang Kai-shek's army
in training.*

*In Formosa I met Mr. Contented Farmer,
who at long last had inherited his piece of the earth.*

Those who do not want Communism for their own nation often support and defend Mao Tse-tung for accomplishing the Chinese revolution. Perhaps that is not rational; perhaps it is shortsighted. But that is an Asian point of view.

Asia wants peace, not war. Yet as one prominent Indian told me, "Chiang Kai-shek is the one man in the world who really *wants* war." War is essential to him, lest his claims to the mainland become worthless and forgotten. The prospect of war is necessary if he is to hold Formosa together, if he is to keep the morale of his government and his Army high. If the future were known to offer peace, not war, Formosa would no longer be a staging ground. It would be reduced in size to a small Asian power of little consequence in the politics of that continent.

What, then, is the value of Formosa to America?

Formosa lies athwart any sea route south to the Philippines. It is a short bomber run from Bataan. The Japanese attacks on Bataan took off from Formosa. Formosa is only several hours by bomber from Japan. It is not far from Manchuria.

Formosa would of course be invaluable in case we had all-out war with China. But the real importance of Formosa is in a defense against Russia—the line of defense that runs from Alaska down through the Aleutians and Japan and on to Formosa, Okinawa, and the Philippines.

Formosa, then, is only a bomber base. If Formosa is conceived in larger terms, our future is dark. The great risk is that, owing to the Korean adventure, Formosa will be conceived in larger terms.

CHAPTER 5

KOREAN INDEPENDENCE

One of the objectives of World War II was to free
Korea from Japanese control and grant her independence. That was the solemn declaration at Cairo on December 1, 1943, and at Moscow on December 27, 1945. The 38th
parallel was not designed to partition Korea; it was merely a line
above which the Russian Army and below which the American
Army were to accept the Japanese surrender. Russia broke faith
and used the occupation for another purpose. She occupied North
Korea until December 25, 1948; and when she withdrew her
troops, she left behind a well-trained Communist government
with a blueprint for unifying Korea Soviet-style.

Korean independence is neither an easy problem nor a short-
term one. If Korea today were freed of hostile armies, it would
take years for her to become strong and self-reliant. I had seen
the war-battered cities of Europe; but I had not seen devastation
until I saw Korea. Cities like Seoul are badly mangled; but a
host of towns and villages, like Chorwon on the base of the Iron
Triangle, are completely obliterated. Bridges, railroads, dams are

290

blasted. Farms have been wiped out and trampled over, schools and hospitals destroyed. Over a million refugees have been piled up in Pusan, living in mud in the rainy season and in dust and filth the rest of the time. Pusan, a pleasant seaport town of 400,000, has indeed become a gigantic slum. Misery, disease, pain and suffering, starvation—these are all compounded beyond comprehension. Beneath it all the human spirit, the will to live, somehow survives. But it will take much capital, astute management, and wise therapy to heal the deep wounds of this war.

Yet that phase of the reconstruction is not the most serious one. Far more difficult is the task of developing a democratic government in Korea.

Korea had been under the rule of the Japanese since 1910. The Japanese did much to develop the country industrially. They installed hydroelectric dams, built a railroad to Manchuria, and developed a few light metal industries. Korea, however, was a nation to exploit. The new wealth was not used to raise the standard of living of the Koreans; it was appropriated by the Japanese. The Japanese even went so far as to export from Korea about one million tons of rice a year, leaving practically none for the Koreans. To feed the Koreans, the Japanese imported millet and barley from Manchuria—grains that are inferior by Asian standards. That practice has a profound effect even today. Today the Koreans eat more rice than they should. They spurn barley and millet, thinking those grains not fit for people. They follow with interest the market price of rice. One can ask the taxi driver about the price of rice and get the morning's quotations. But ask him the price of barley and he will reply sullenly, "I never eat barley."

The Japanese always considered the Koreans an inferior people, and they reduced them to virtual peons or slaves. Most avenues of activity were closed to them. They could not even aspire to be locomotive engineers or firemen, for those jobs were reserved exclusively for the Japanese. The economic pinch on the Koreans was so severe that one million of them moved to Siberia and Manchuria in search of a living.

Koreans have talents and abilities as great as any other people. Yet during the Japanese rule education in elementary and secondary schools was made available for not more than one third of the children. The Japanese maintained twice as many police stations as elementary schools, more than twice as many policemen as teachers. The colleges and universities were open only to those who could speak Japanese. In some institutions the number of Koreans was therefore negligible. Few Koreans were able to receive professional training—few in law, few even in medicine, and practically none in government. Some were employed in the lower echelons of the national government; quite a few in the provincial governments; none in any posts of responsibility in the national government. I mentioned the tragedy of this history to an American who is expert in the Far East. He did not minimize the tragedy but said, "The Japanese discriminated against the Koreans. But their discrimination was not in that respect as serious as our own discrimination against the Negro." However that may be, the Japanese policy was tragic. There are in South Korea today only a few hundred men and women out of twenty-three million people who have any training for the responsibilities of government.

Those few, though talented, are neophytes when it comes to administration. It will take years to develop a civil service skilled in public administration, trained in the concepts of democracy, imbued with the ideals of civil liberties, educated to civilized standards for the police.

Syngman Rhee, Korea's President, is a short, slight man with white hair that is thinning, dark oblique eyes, and large ears. He speaks English fluently and by nature is very talkative. Rhee is a great patriot—the George Washington who worked for Korean independence for a quarter century. His name is the one name known to all Koreans. To the peasants he is a great national hero. When a young man, Rhee published a newspaper in Korea. He was kept in jail for seven years by the Korean King, who preceded the Japanese rule, for demanding democratic reforms. On the eve of the seizure of Korea by the Japanese, Rhee came to America, where he got an A.B. degree at George Washington University, an M.A. at Harvard, and a Ph.D. in political science and international law at Princeton under Woodrow Wilson. In 1919 Koreans, fired by Wilson's doctrine of "self-determination" for all people, organized a great independence demonstration in Korea. Rhee, in the United States, managed the affair. It was put on at 2 P.M. March 1, 1919. The demonstration was bloodily suppressed by the Japanese. But the event was used to organize a Republic of Korea in Exile, of which Rhee became the President. For a quarter of a century Rhee kept up an appeal for Korea's independence. He worked through diplomatic channels. He organized operations in China. His men raided Korea from across the Yalu River; they planted bombs; they plotted the assassination of Japanese. Rhee became the symbol of independence, important to every Korean household.

Rhee has stood for good things in Korea, apart from independence. As President of the new republic he put his weight behind land reform; and today when it is mentioned, his eyes light up.

In the spring of 1950 there were in South Korea about 300,000 landlord families who rented out all or part of their land to tenant farmers. The Korean Government listed those holdings as follows:

Owning less than 2.45 acres . . . . 213,453 families
Owning from 2.50 to 4.9 acres . . . 45,692 "
"   " 5 to 7.45 acres . . . . 19,058 "
"   " 7.5 to 9.9 acres . . . . 44,413 "
"   " 10 to 12.45 acres . . . 2,676 "
"   " 12.5 to 24.45 acres . . . 5,488 "
"   " 24.5 to 49 acres . . . . 2,892 "
"   " 49 to 122.5 acres . . . 1,292 "
"   " 122.5 to 245 acres . . . 469 "
"   more than 245 acres . . . . 272 "

By the end of World War II over 50 per cent of all Korean farmers were tenants. The tenants paid half or more of their crops as rent.

293

North from Malaya

The American Military Government (AMG) took over all the land owned by Japanese and sold it to the tenants for 3.75 times the value of a year's crop, payable at the rate of 25 per cent of each crop for fifteen years. Nearly 25 per cent of all South Korean farm families became owners in this way. When the Republic of Korea was established on August 15, 1948, Rhee took up the cudgels for further land reform and drew heavily on American experts for advice. The Assembly, which contained many landlords, objected to the idea. Rhee put the pressure on. He sent back inadequate bills until he got a real land-reform law. The new law went into effect March 25, 1950—shortly before the Communist attack. But in spite of war, invasion, and all of the attendant dislocations of civil strife, the old estates were broken up and distributed by the end of the summer of 1951. The former owners were paid in government certificates which can be cashed in or used to buy industrial properties taken over from the Japanese and, since 1948, operated by the Korean Government. The tenants pay for the land. Payment is generally about 150 per cent of the average production of the main crop of the particular farm, as determined by a local committee. This amount was payable in five years; but in 1952 the term was extended to ten years.

Land reform, according to Rhee, was the most wonderful thing that ever happened in Korea. "Now we have a firm basis for a true democracy," he told me when I saw him in Pusan on September 8, 1952.

Rhee was a man of vision in other respects too. When Korea was liberated in 1945 and Rhee returned after his long exile, the Communist underground loudly proclaimed him as the President of the People's Republic. Rhee at once made a speech, denying it. He said he would have no traffic with the Communists. He explained Communism to his people, saying that those who followed that creed owed their allegiance to Russia. He denounced their creed and their tactics. During the hour I spent with Rhee in Pusan, he vividly recounted the episode to me. And I am convinced that his heroic denunciation of Communism in 1945 saved

South Koreans from being swept along by its powerful tide. To-day, of course, his neck is at stake. But in 1945, when he had the opportunity to be called to power by the entire population, Communists included, he refused.

Today Rhee insists that there be a united Korea. He told me about the high mountains in North Korea along the Yalu-Tumen line. "Once the Communists are driven beyond that line, we can keep them from returning," he told me. "That is our natural line of defense."

Rhee today is still a patriot, one who will not compromise his principles with Communism.

So there is much to Rhee's credit. But today he is old. He claims seventy-eight, but the records show more years than that. He is feeble these days. He has never had administrative or executive experience. He seems to have little conception of the tasks and functions of modern government. During my hour's talk with him he seemed lost when it came to such mundane questions as inflation, price control, rationing of food.

Inflation is serious in Korea. There are first the bank loans that are almost unrestricted. Over half are unsecured. The banks are merely lending agencies of the government. Loans are made for any project that is politically expedient. Loans to anti-Rhee men are hard to obtain. Then there is the printing press and the currency it spawns. Rhee admitted to me that the inflation was awful and that the government was making it worse by printing 100,000,000 *won* a day. He seemed to overlook that *he* was the government. He said that control of prices was impossible, that clever profiteers were operating in Korea, that no one obeyed the law against profiteering, that it was a law that could not be enforced. I inquired about the possibility of a new law. He only shrugged his shoulders.

I asked him about the food problem. Previously I had talked with the Prime Minister, Chang Tang-sang (until recently a professor of English), who had impressed on me the acuteness of the food problem. At Pusan the food shortage was so great in September 1952 that children were getting only one meager meal a day and were becoming bloated and deformed from starvation. Yet rice was being hoarded and a black market flourished. I mentioned these matters to Rhee and asked why a food-rationing program was not adopted. His reply was instant, "There is not enough food to ration."

On these matters Rhee did not seem lucid. He was lucid, however, in demanding $300,000,000 to stabilize his currency, many million dollars to rebuild Seoul, admission along with Japan to the Pacific Pact, and an increase in the South Korean Army.

I left his office rather depressed. The head of the South Korean Government, patriotic and courageous as he was, seemed oblivious of the fact that *he* was the government, that *he* had the power, that it was *his* task to put the house in order. Rather he seemed to think that some outside force would have to straighten things out.

Rhee, the executive, may be inefficient; but Rhee, the politician, is smart. From the very beginning of the republic he and the Assembly have been opposed. Rhee has been very jealous of legislative power, very suspicious of all opposition. Rhee has wanted to pull all power unto himself. The Assembly has looked with mounting suspicion on any dilution of their authority, on the concentration of authority in the Executive. In 1949 the Assembly undertook an investigation of the Executive branch. It rendered a scathing report in January 1950, denouncing police methods, illegal arrests, judicial delays, and corruption. The Assembly demanded a constitutional amendment making the Cabinet accountable to it. That effort failed in 1950; but the bitterness between the Executive and the Assembly grew.

Rhee insisted there be no appeal from military commissions imposing the death sentence. The Assembly was for an appeal. The Assembly won out. Rhee arrested fourteen members of the Assembly on charges equivalent to our crime of sedition. Rhee was criticized on the ground that this was his way of killing the independent, critical spirit that was developing in the Assembly. (Thirteen were convicted and sentenced up to ten years.)

In 1951 the Assembly kept a close watch on the Executive branch, summoned Cabinet officers before it for questioning, and put a curb on the use of emergency powers. It got martial law lifted from most of South Korea, limited the right of military tribunals to try civilians, and exposed corruption. There was free and vigorous criticism of all policies. From 1948 to 1951 Korea was developing a healthy parliamentary system. Then came the bitter year, 1952.

Under the Korean Constitution, as originally written, the President was named by the Assembly (presently composed of a House of Councilors whose members are elected for a term of six years and a House of Representatives whose members are elected for a term of four years). Rhee, who was designated as President in 1948, had a four-year term ending in 1952. In the 1950 elections his opposition won a majority of the seats in the Assembly. In the spring of 1952 it therefore seemed that the Assembly would not reappoint him as President when his term was up that summer.

Rhee demanded a constitutional amendment making the choice of the President depend on the popular vote and making the Assembly bicameral. The Assembly refused. Rhee denounced the members as "Communists," though there was no evidence his opponents were subversive, and as "landlords." He also started a program for their recall. When the Assembly still refused to agree to the constitutional amendments, Rhee declared martial law and immediately put in protective custody over fifty deputies without preferring charges against them. He had twelve others arrested on charges of being "subversive." Rhee later released five of the deputies who had been arrested, as well as those held in protective custody. Seven were tried; and according to British and American observers, the trial was a farce. There was no evidence of any substance that these men were "subversives." Their worst offense was that they were political opponents of Rhee. These suits were not in the civil courts but before a military commission. An effort was made to refer the question of the jurisdiction of the military commission to the Korean Supreme Court. But Rhee as President and Commander-in-Chief prevented that. In the midst of the trial the Assembly met to vote on the constitutional amendments. Rhee released the seven deputies so that they could vote; and when they had properly voted, the suits against them were dismissed. Under that pressure the Assembly capitulated and agreed to the constitutional amendments, including two additional ones—confirmation by the Assembly of the appointment of the Prime Minister and dissolution of the Cabinet by the Assembly on a vote of no confidence. Rhee, by coercion, forced the constitutional amendments on the country.

There are other episodes that have helped alienate from Rhee many liberal elements in South Korea. In the midst of the crisis with the Assembly, Rhee invited into the Cabinet a younger man by the name of Lee Bum Suck and made him Minister of Defense. It was understood that Rhee would support Suck for the vice-presidency in the 1952 election. Suck indeed ran on Rhee's ticket. Rhee sent word down to the tongs—the political wards— to vote for Suck. The tongs are controlled by the police and by youth groups that Rhee organized. The election was to be held on August 5, 1952. Only ten days were reserved for the campaigning. A few days before the election Rhee got scared of the growing popularity of Lee Bum Suck. Lee Bum Suck had resigned as Minister of Defense to run for Vice-President. Therefore, he lost control of the police. Rhee appointed a new minister who would do his tidings. Word was again sent down to the police and the youth organizations, this time to withdraw support from Suck and to give support to Ham Tai Yong, an octogenarian who was no potential competitor of Rhee. The youth groups and the police rounded up the votes in the tongs. The election was calm and peaceful. Rhee was overwhelmingly elected. Ham Tai Yong defeated Lee Bum Suck by a comfortable margin.

Rhee's opposition is considerable. The young liberal forces are allied against him. But his passion for power is so great, his jealousy so sharp, that some of the loyal opposition has either fled the country or is in jail.

Rhee plans other constitutional amendments which will put the legislature under his thumb. One amendment would in effect give Rhee the right to arrest a deputy and ask for an election of someone to take his place. Another would take the power of impeachment away from the Assembly and give it to the people. Another would give Rhee the power to take some public measures away from the Assembly and refer them to the people. These would tend to destroy the Legislative branch of government and shift the power to the Executive. Rhee, the President in control of the police and the youth groups, could then write the laws his own way and reduce his opposition.

South Korea has her independence—protected today by United Nations' armed forces. But if peace suddenly came to Korea, if all the armies left, if war and threat of war ended, Korea would be a long, long way from being able to enjoy her independence. It may take a generation to produce young leaders devoted to the democratic ideal and able to manage a government in the democratic tradition. Syngman Rhee, patriot that he is, has set some poor examples. Yet over-all, Korean independence has had a sturdy start. There are fight and spirit in the Assembly. There is the beginning of a good Supreme Court under Chief Justice Kim Byung Ro. The system of checks and balances has seen tumultuous days; but it has survived. The government has been sturdy enough to escape a cataclysm. Though 1,200 villages have been completely wiped out, though millions of people have been uprooted, the farmers have produced near-normal crops. In sum, Korea impressed me with having survival values, whether it be viewed from the country or from the capital.

CHAPTER 6

THE BASE OF THE IRON TRIANGLE

It was September 6, 1952, a bleak overcast day, and I was at an outpost on the central western sector of the Korean front. General Yu of the Second ROK (Republic of Korea) Corps was talking. "My men did not run. They stayed and died. The ROKs never run; they die first." His broken English came in clipped fashion. His dark face was without expression; but his eyes showed the fire of determination that was in him.

General Yu was reporting to General James A. Van Fleet on the now famous battle for Capitol Hill. We were standing between two low hills in a narrow draw that emptied north into a small plain. Beyond it was a tumbled mass of mountains through which the Pukhan River wound its way. In the plain about a thousand yards from where we stood were three low hills, the rounded one on the right (or east) being Capitol Hill. The night before (September 5, 1952) the Chinese had dropped 20,000 rounds of artillery shells and mortars on those three hills in one of the most intense bombardments the front had ever seen. Two platoons of ROKs on Capitol Hill were wiped out, and now that outpost was held by the enemy. General Yu was telling General Van Fleet his plans for retaking Capitol Hill.

I had flown to the front from Seoul with General Van Fleet. We traveled in the L-19 plane, the two-seater that can land and take off in any pasture. General Van Fleet's plane led the way; mine followed. The day was overcast; and though the clouds were breaking after long rains, they still hung low over most of the peaks. This was close to the end of the rainy season. The opposing armies had been dug in for several months; rain and fog had made air reconnaissance difficult; mud had hampered the movement of tanks and artillery; nightly patrols had been about the only activity along the front.

Now that the skies were lifting, the tempo of events was increasing. The dirt roads that streaked north from Seoul were thick with trucks and tanks rolling toward the front. The fields and valleys were drying quickly after the long rain. The ground was so firm that the heavy guns could now be moved with ease. Until last night the Red Chinese had none near the front. But under the cover of darkness coolies had pulled by hand artillery and mortars for five miles or more and brought them within range of Capitol Hill. The Chinese Army had blazed away all night. Before dawn the guns had been moved again, this time far to the rear, and concealed there. This mobility of heavy weapons marked the beginning of new offensives. The lull in the Korean War was over.

Out of Seoul we followed the railroad the Japanese built during their long occupation, the line that under more peaceful conditions used to run through twisting valleys to Manchuria. At the beginning of the flight the valleys pouring down to Seoul were wide and lush. But as we went north we came into harsh, rough country where mountain peaks dominated the scene and the valleys became narrow and winding. This country reminded me of the breaks of some of our Western mountains. The tops are not high by our standards, running usually between four and eight thousand feet. But the slopes are steep, the peaks often sharp, the trees and underbrush thick. There are deer high up and pheasant in the valleys. But these days the hunt is different. Tessie, Big Nori, Little Nori—peaks made famous by the armies of the United Nations—were on our left. Their tops were half concealed by fog, and billows of smoke rolled against their eastern slopes.

"Artillery fire," the pilot told me.

He went on to say that we were flying low so as to be under the barrage being laid down by American batteries. These batteries were concealed in pockets to the east, camouflaged positions which we occasionally located by the fire from the guns. At this point we were following the front line that ran almost due north. At Old Baldy, whose southern face has been heavily scarred by artillery shells, the line turned east along the base of the Iron Triangle. This is a line that in the main follows a narrow meandering valley. At one end in more peaceful days was the thriving town of Chorwon; near the other end, a place called Kumhwa, and beyond it Kumsong. Today those towns have nothing standing—no tree, no piece of broken wall, no remnants of a roof. Only the dark outlines of old foundations are left. War has leveled everything.

We put down at several places along the base of the Iron Triangle. We visited field units near White Horse, the Arrowhead Hills, Triangle Hill, Papasan, Sniper Hill, and Finger Hill. I saw Ethiopians, Colombians, ROKs, and Americans. There were artillery placements behind us lobbing shells into Chinese positions. Engineers who had received enemy fire while repairing a bridge threw out a vast smoke screen for protection. Helicopters with wounded men in stretchers on each side whirled in from outlying positions to field hospitals. Reconnaissance planes darted in and out of foggy valleys looking for openings in the clouds. At field headquarters we scanned maps for the latest accounts of operations. We sat in tents and had sandwiches and coffee with officers and got a measure of the spirit that pervades the front. I talked with GIs freshly in from patrols and learned about the tactics of "Joe Chink." Finally in late afternoon we came to Capitol Hill, where I met General Yu.

General Yu spoke feelingly of the ROKs. It is an army that has been widely criticized for its conduct at the beginning of the Korean War. At first it did not hold together under pressure. But its retreats were always for lack of discipline or of equipment, not for lack of courage. Today discipline has been instilled and, as General Yu told me, the ROKs will be wiped out to the last man rather than retreat.

A few hours after I spoke to him General Yu launched an attack designed to retake Capitol Hill. That night—September 6, 1952—500 ROKs were killed or wounded; and the next morning Capitol Hill still remained in the hands of the Chinese. But General Yu renewed the assaults. The ROKs finally recaptured Capitol Hill on September 11, 1952, hundreds dying in the process. Capitol Hill to them was a matter of honor and prestige, though it is an insignificant military objective in the totality of the Korean War.

The same story of valor can be written about all the units on the Korean front. The Ethiopians deserve a special word. Up to the time this is written the Ethiopians have never yielded a position, never yielded a prisoner, and never had a man "missing in action." They have standing orders never to be taken prisoner. And they would rather fight with bayonets than with guns.

In the winter of 1952 there were approximately 590,000 troops on the United Nations' side of the struggle in Korea, 490,000 being ground forces. Nineteen nations contributed 40,000 troops to the ground forces, South Korea 200,000, the United States 250,000. And the United States has contributed, in addition, 50,000 through the Air Force and 50,000 through the Navy.

General Van Fleet pushed hard a training program for ROKs. From the beginning of his command he tried to get more and more ROKs in the front lines. At the turn of the new year, 1953, two new ROK divisions were ready to take their place alongside the ten ROK divisions then in the line, leaving 100,000 in training.

Korean men between the ages of seventeen and thirty-one number about 1,400,000. The draft of men in that group has been increased from 700 daily to 1,100 daily (about 40 per cent are rejected for poor health and other deficiencies). The ROKs have now advanced so far that they can handle most of their own training.

The cost of equipping and maintaining a ROK army is low, relatively speaking. About twenty-eight ROKs can be kept on the front line for the cost of just one American GI. ROK privates get 3,000 *won* (25 cents U.S.) a month; a lieutenant general, 372,000 *won* ($31 U.S.). The ROK soldier eats about the same as the Japanese soldier—boiled rice, bean-curd soup, and an occasional fish. The ROKs, in order to supplement their income and send money home, have commercial sidelines—selling foodstuffs, charcoal, and wood; operating fishing fleets; maintaining farms in rear areas.

So far as I could learn, the ROKs are a first-class army for ground warfare. They could not today take over the entire defense of South Korea. They lack the necessary officers; they do not have an air force or navy; they have only the beginnings of a tank corps; they are still deficient in field artillery; and they lack experienced leadership. It will take years to develop the ROKs to the point where they can perform all the functions which the United Nations now perform. It will even take several years before the ROKs alone can man the front lines; and perhaps the best they can ever do is to relieve three quarters of the United Nations divisions at the front. But everyone in South Korea was unanimous in thinking that the sooner the ROKs take over the defense the better.

The Korean War does not suffer for lack of military leadership. General Van Fleet—whom I have seen in action both in Greece and in Korea—was an outstanding military leader. And the same was true of the officers under him. Korea has not suffered for lack of military equipment. It has the best—the latest improvements on jet fighters, warming tents for thawing out, helicopters to bring the wounded from the front lines to an advance hospital in a few minutes, heated latrines, prefabricated bunkers, and facilities that give every GI, no matter how far front he may be, ice cream three times a week.

The Korean War does not suffer for lack of morale. I saw troops of several different nations and heard reports about many others. In my journeys in Southeast Asia I had seen soldiers just back from a tour of duty in Korea. Without exception the spirits of the men were high.

At the front I had a deeply moving experience. This effort of the United Nations to stop aggression has brought together in a real crusade men and organizations of many nations. I got this message from the lips of Ethiopians and Colombians. I heard it from Greeks and Filipinos. This fight for freedom has welded people of different races and cultures behind one cause. At the Korean front I felt the real fraternity, the warm community, of the United Nations. The harmony and devotion I saw at those far-flung outposts were far more eloquent than the speeches at Lake Success.

As Homer Bigart of the New York *Herald Tribune* has reported, "American morale out here is better than it is back home. The weariness and whining to be observed in the United States, the clamor for withdrawal of American troops from front-line fighting have no echo here." As near as I could tell, the same high morale obtains in all the units of the United Nations Army.

All aspects of the military situation in Korea are sound. The Korean problem has suffered from only one thing—the absence of a clear-cut political decision.

CHAPTER 7

DECISION IN KOREA

Some think that President Truman's decision of June 27, 1950, and the vote of the Security Council of the United Nations to defend Korea against the invasion of the North Korean Army were mistakes. In their view it was a commitment to action in an area beyond the bounds of our national interests. Others think the Korean venture was one cleverly conceived by General Douglas MacArthur and others to start a drive toward the heart of Red China in furtherance of the cause of the Chinese Nationalists. A few follow the outright Moscow line that the Korean venture was a demonstration of American imperialism.

In my view the President's decision and the action of the Security Council were sound *political* measures. I felt that way at the time, and my conviction has grown the more I have seen of Asia. The decision to defend Korea was sound as a matter of principle. The alternative was to let force and terror become political instruments in international relations. The decision was also sound in terms of the practical politics of Asia.

One who travels the long borders of Russia and China, stretching from the Black Sea to the Pacific, realizes that the Korean decision was not merely to be preferred, but was vitally necessary. The reason is a simple one, at least for those not caught up in the fanaticism of Communism nor blind to its real purposes. Asia and the Middle East have long been feudal—that is to say, their nations have been owned and controlled by a few. Sometimes those few were foreigners, sometimes not. But the wealth and the political power have for centuries been closely held. That feudal system is breaking up. Its passing is as inevitable as the movement of the tides. The only question is, how will it be changed?

The Communists propose to change it by force and then to tie the new regime into the empire of Soviet Russia.

Men like Nehru in India, Soekarno in Indonesia, U Nu in Burma propose to change it by peaceful, democratic means. But the peaceful route takes time; and people the world around get impatient. If the technique of the North Koreans were a success, it would be an inspiration to every adventurer in the Communist cause. Had the North Koreans been victorious, there is no doubt in my mind but that Asia would have seen a series of violent eruptions which by now might have extended the Communist power over vital areas. Nothing succeeds like success; and once Asia learned that force and terror went unchallenged, Soviet power would have a quick and easy expansion.

The *political* decision to defend Korea was not a decision to launch an all-out war. The 38th parallel was the line that had been violated; and it was to resist that violation that the United Nations came to Korea's defense. The second major *political* question was whether to pursue the enemy beyond that line once he had been driven back across it. The ROKs crossed that line in pursuit of the North Koreans on October 1, 1950, and the main American forces followed on October 10, 1950. That *political* decision was even more vital than the earlier one, for as events turned out it brought Red China into the war.

I personally think the conflict with Red China in Korea might

have been avoided. I was in Asia in September 1950. I had seen
Nehru and most of his Cabinet in New Delhi. I had talked with
Indians back from Peking. The consensus of Indian opinion was
that Red China was anxious to make a political settlement with
the United States and that if one was not made and if we crossed
the 38th parallel Red China would enter the war. The pact that
Red China and North Korea had signed in Moscow supported
that view.

Up in Hong Kong on September 27, 1950, I met three Chinese
businessmen (non-Communists) who had come down from
Peking especially to see me. They were sent by my old friend Lu
Tso-fu, at that time head of the Ming Sung Shipping Company,
which operated a vast fleet of coastwise shipping vessels in the
China Sea. I had last seen Lu in Washington, D.C., shortly after
the loss of the mainland to Mao Tse-tung. That night Lu—millionaire and public-spirited citizen, long associated with Dr.
James Yen in the Mass Education Movement—told me that he
would return to the mainland, not to Formosa. He thought there
was a chance of survival under Mao Tse-tung. He said there was
a group in Mao Tse-tung's camp who were anti-Russian and pro-
West, that he thought the latter group could win out if the situation was carefully managed. That gamble cost Lu his life, for he
either was killed by the Communists or driven to suicide in the
spring of 1951. But in the summer and fall of 1950 Lu was still
hopeful. The three men he sent from Peking had messages for me.

1. The anti-Russian element in the Mao Tse-tung government
was still strong and might prevent China from going over to
Russia and thus save the day for both China and the West.

2. That element in China wanted increasing dependency on
the West, decreasing dependency on Russia. What was needed
was a resumption of trade between America and Red China that
would start rebuilding the relations between the two countries.

3. Red China was concerned over America's intentions in
Korea. Was it merely to repel aggression or was it part of a plan
aimed at Red China? The United States had backed Chiang Kai-

shek on the mainland, and it was still backing him on Formosa. On June 27, 1950, President Truman had ordered the United States Navy to "neutralize" Formosa (the order changed by President Eisenhower on February 2, 1953) and the Seventh Fleet was now patrolling the Formosa Strait. Were these acts part of an over-all arrangement between the United States and Chiang Kai-shek for the reconquest of the mainland? Were the defense of Korea, the rearming of Formosa, and the arrival of the Seventh Fleet in China waters all part and parcel of an offensive against Red China?

4. Did General Douglas MacArthur reflect the American attitude? General MacArthur had visited Formosa on July 31, 1950. Had MacArthur and Chiang Kai-shek made a pact aimed at Red China?

These were the four main topics that Lu's emissaries from Peking discussed with me. They insisted that this was the time for America to sit down with Red China and explore the possibilities of a settlement of their differences. Time was of the essence, they thought. "If America does not halt at the 38th parallel and talk with Mao Tse-tung, China will enter the war," they said.

Washington, D.C., was adamant. Red China would not enter the Korean War. Moreover, the Chinese Communists were nothing but murderers and Washington would not think of making overtures to them. The die apparently had long been cast. There was no stopping the United Nations at the 38th parallel. We crossed the 38th parallel, and in a few weeks Red China entered the war.

We will never know whether conflict with Red China could have been avoided. But we do know that today Red China is firmly entrenched in Korea. Her Army is good, if not first-class. It has been well trained under Soviet auspices; it has almost unlimited man power; it has a fanatical zeal and a dogged determination; and it is well clothed and well equipped. Since the armistice negotiations started in July 1951, the Red Chinese have dug themselves in for a depth of thirty miles. The "front line" is no line in any conventional sense. There are no trenches, no string of fortifications. There is in fact a great dispersion of enemy troops. They are in small scattered groups twenty feet underground. The Communist tactical theory apparently is that armies are safe underground, even though the whole of the territory they occupy is seared with atomic bombs. During the armistice talks the Chinese-North Korean force of 500,000 men was almost doubled. And the armies of the enemy were echeloned in depth through North Korea into Manchuria.

The cold political fact, the cold military fact, is that Red China is deep in Korea. She can be dislodged; but unless all-out war is waged along the lines urged by General Douglas MacArthur, with heavy bombings deep in Manchuria, Red China cannot be driven from Korea without enormous sacrifices.

Asia has patience we do not know. Red China in her present mood is, I believe, ready to sit it out in Korea indefinitely. The Chinese Communists have used the war as an excuse to tighten their hold on their people. There are rumors along the Chinese border that the war is not popular with the Chinese people. However that may be, it is saddled on them; and the government has used it as a means of rallying the younger generation in a crusade against America. And Red China—now a junior partner with Russia in the exploitation of Communism—manages the situation to fit Sino-Soviet ends.

What, then, should American policy be? There are, it seems to me, five possible courses of action.

First. Maintenance of the present limited warfare. This is plainly undesirable. Even though there is no offensive under way, even though patrolling is the only activity at the front, the United Nations' casualties average sixty a day. Moreover, the present stalemate resolves no controversy and does little to advance the cause of Korean independence.

Second. Withdrawal from Korea. If we withdrew from Korea without more, that country would be condemned to Communist conquest. Moreover, we would lose face, not in the superficial sense but in the deep sense of honor and integrity. Our word in Asia would be forever debased.

Third. An armistice with Red China. An armistice as a prelude to a political settlement with Red China would be hopeful. An armistice without a prospect of any political settlement is more than useless. Red China indeed used the armistice talks of 1951 and 1952 merely to entrench herself more deeply in Korea. If there were only an armistice, Red China, deep in Korean territory, would probably stay there. If she withdrew, she probably would leave behind a Communist puppet government of her own creation that would set the stage for another invasion from the north. If the stalemate following an armistice were indefinitely prolonged, it is doubtful that we could match the patience of the Chinese in waiting out the situation.

As Syngman Rhee said to me, "Truce talks are nonsensical if they are to leave Chinese troops in Korea."

Fourth. A political settlement with Red China. Red China, though controlled by the Communists lock, stock, and barrel, is a political reality and the only power on the mainland. Red China is a real power in Asia, potentially the greatest perhaps.

Ernest T. Weir of the National Steel Corporation on January 5, 1951, put in sober words the basic issue between the United States and China.

> . . . we cannot *assume* that we know the opinion of 400 million Chinese people. We must think seriously as to what this opinion actually is, and then we certainly must be influenced by it once we have some real idea as to their beliefs. We say they are communists. We, of course, do not like communism, but we cannot eliminate communism in the world by war. Certainly, we cannot ignore the fact that there are many people in the world today who believe, so far as we know, that communism is of value to them.
>
> If we refuse to recognize and deal with the present Chinese Government because it is communistic, we assume

the dangerous position of trying to tell the people of other important nations what kind of government they must have. As a matter of fact, we have done this very thing in the case of Spain through our refusal until very recently to have dealings with a Spanish Government that has been in existence for 13 years, solely on the ground that it is a fascist government and, therefore, not to our liking. Such positions make us intruders in the internal affairs of other nations.

Communist China is a political reality, not a mere paper claim to a region. Mao Tse-tung controls the mainland. His hold on the people becomes stronger with each passing day. His program of indoctrination is making the present generation fervent apostles of the Communist creed. Non-Communist Asians who have visited Red China insist that the Communist regime is there to stay and that an attempt to dislodge it by military means would be disastrous.

The important question of the age is how to live with Red China. It may be that a political settlement with her would be impossible. A settlement would of necessity include Vietnam and Formosa as well as Korea. Certainly a political settlement and "recognition" of Red China (which Britain accorded her January 5, 1950) would not mean "approval" of the Red regime. "Recognition" and "approval" are not synonymous. We "recognize" Soviet Russia but we do not "approve" her Communist regime. We "recognize" various types of dictatorships that we do not "approve." President Franklin Pierce, in a message to Congress in 1856, summed up the historic attitude of the United States in these words, "It is the established policy of the United States to recognize all governments without question of their source, or organization, or of the means by which the governing persons attain their power, provided there be a government *de facto* accepted by the people of the country. . . ."

Before and since that time American policy has been variously worded. But it has been substantially uniform through the years.

The test has been whether the new government represents the will of the people of that country, substantially declared. (Hyde, *International Law* [1945 2d ed.], pp. 158 *et seq.*, Vol. I.)

Secretary of State John Foster Dulles summed the matter up succinctly in 1950 when he said in his book, *War or Peace:*

"If the Communist government of China in fact proves its ability to govern China without serious domestic resistance, then it, too, should be admitted to the United Nations. However, a regime that claims to have become the government of a country through civil war should not be recognized until it has been tested over a reasonable period of time.

"If the United Nations membership were made substantially universal, that might end a preponderant voting superiority of the United States and its friends which, while pleasant, is somewhat fictitious. Communist governments today dominate more than 30 per cent of the population of the world. We may not like that fact; indeed, we do not like it at all. But if we want to have a world organization, then it should be representative of the world as it is."

"Recognition" of Red China would start a new chapter in American-Sino relations. It would enable America to work within China at the diplomatic level. That would hold some promise of prying China loose from Russia, of making her less and less a Soviet tool, of orienting her more and more to the West.

Theodore Roosevelt with rare prescience saw the great danger that would come to America and to Europe the day Russia got the Mongols to fight her battles for her. That day has arrived. It is to Russia's interest that we continue to fight China. Then we deplete our own strength and make China more and more dependent on Russia. Then we help unite China and Russia in a common cause. Then we become heavily embroiled in Chinese affairs while Russia expands elsewhere.

Today Red China may be in no mood to make a political settlement with the West. Or if she is, Russia may be in no mood to let her do so. Moreover, Red China might set too high a price for a settlement. In my view the price would be too high if Formosa were to be surrendered to the Communists. Formosa has earned her right to an independent regime. China today is not one country. Formosa is one sovereignty and the mainland another. The integrity of Formosa should be maintained and her seat in the United Nations preserved, even if Red China were recognized. A division of China is not without reason. The mainland of China itself is not a unit. Even Tibet, Mongolia, and Manchuria on the mainland are vastly different from the region of which Peking is the center.

No one knows whether a political settlement with Red China is possible. No one will know unless the matter is canvassed. The burden of war in Korea indicates that it should be tried. A political settlement with Red China is the only *peaceful* way of getting the Chinese Army out of Korea and of unifying that nation.

Fifth. All-out war with China. If Red China were approached on good faith for a political settlement and she refused, only one real alternative would be left—all-out war. Or perhaps Red China would need a taste of all-out war—a hard knock, as they say at the front—in order to be willing to make a political settlement. However an all-out war came, it would have as its aim the unification of Korea and the fulfillment of the promises made at the Cairo and Moscow conferences.

It is an easy temptation to send Chinese troops from Formosa to Korea. At first blush the reasons may seem compelling. But that decision, simple as it may seem, would change the entire character of the Korean War. Then the Korean campaign would become more than a war to free Korea; it would become a war to free the mainland.

As I have said, that is a war in which no American blood should ever be dedicated. That war would in Asian eyes be proof of the return of the white man for purposes of conquest. Asia would unite against the West. American influence and prestige would greatly suffer. Soviet influence would be given impetus. A military commitment of America to help Chiang Kai-shek free the mainland of China would be the most reckless venture in international politics we have ever known.

These alternatives must be viewed full-face if a Korean decision is to be reached. That decision is more difficult today than it was in September 1950. But the need for a clear-cut, final decision has never been more important.

It is time we restated in simple terms the issues at stake in Korea.

The fight in Korea is symbolic of the struggle going on all over Asia and Africa. It is the struggle for the independence of nations, for the equality of people regardless of race or color, for the right of every people to their own culture, their own religion, their own way of life. That issue is the foremost political issue in the world today. It is vital to world peace. Its recognition and maintenance are essential if the beginnings of democracy and independence in the Philippines, in Indonesia, in India and Pakistan, in Burma, are to flourish. If the heavy hand of Soviet Communism can be laid on Korea, it can be laid on any other free Asian nation. If the Koreans can be deprived of the right to choose whatever government they want, if the Koreans can be regimented by force and terror, so can the Indians and the Burmese. So can the Indonesians and the Vietnamese. So can the Filipinos and the Siamese.

The independence of nations, the right to self-determination, is today the outstanding issue in international affairs. If at any time we desert that cause, we are unworthy of our traditions. If we ever do desert it, we will concede Communist imperialism the formula for engulfing the earth.

The active fighting fronts in Asia today are Russia's fronts. Of these, Korea is the most dangerous of them all. It is the most dangerous because in Korea the issues are more likely to become confused. In Korea we are apt to believe what Formosan propaganda continuously chants, that the real enemy of the West is Red China. Someday Red China may fill that role. But today the real enemy is Russia, who uses Communism to build the most ambitious empire, the most oppressive one, the world has known. *If there must be a fighting war against Communism, Russia is the only nation to fight.* Without the inspiration, direction, and support of Russia all five fronts would be reduced to local affairs, easily managed.

SUMMARY

Our Ignorance of Asia

Whenever I return from Asia I have a disquieting experience. My own country with its high mountains, free press, and flourishing public schools seems more precious than ever. But the gulf between America and Asia seems so vast, so unfathomable as to be startling. There is of course the obvious difference between electric lights and tallow light for reading, automobiles and carabao for transportation and power, tiled bathrooms and muddy ditches for bathing, air conditioning and a palm leaf for relief from the heat. But those differences are minor. The important differences relate to attitudes and points of view. There often seems to be no nexus of understanding between the two continents.

Both sides are doubtless to blame. American intentions are often suspect even when our heart is right. We are frequently credited with designs and schemes which are imaginary. Yet all of them—imaginary or not—are resurrected against us when our policy does not fit Asia's needs or when we really get out of bounds.

317

On our side there is also exaggeration and misunderstanding. Our press is often blatant and arrogant. We shake our fist at Asia in threatening ways. Our views seem pretty well set, and many minds are closed. Bombs often seem to take the place of political inventiveness. It sometimes almost seems that we have become as dogmatic as the Soviets.

I exaggerate a bit, for there are bright spots. Conversation with people in America's small towns is more encouraging than conversation in sophisticated circles. The lower echelons in the State Department have had men of vision who, knowing Asia, despaired of our actions and our words. And the example of some of America's outstanding representatives in Asia—Bowles in India, Sebald in Burma, Spruance in the Philippines—has made an impression in widening circles. But the exceptions are not many. By and large we have treated Asia with disdain and disrespect.

America's attitude toward Asia is due not to perverseness but to ignorance. Our contacts with Asia have been extremely limited. It was only a century ago that we made our first treaty with an Asian power. We have long had warm cultural ties with Europe, and a community of interest, growing out of a common origin. This has also been true of our relations with South America. But as respects Asia the ties of race, history, and culture have been few. Prior to World War I we had hardly any schools specializing in Asian history, Asian politics, Asian literature. Even today we specialize in them at only a few centers. Asia has been a region little known, little understood, little appreciated. Mr. Dooley summed it up pretty well in 1898:

". . . Suppose ye was standin' at th' corner iv State Sthreet an' Archey R-Road, wud ye know what car to take to get to th' Ph'lippeens? If yer son Packy was to ask ye where th' Ph'lippeens is, cud ye give him anny good idea whether they was in Rooshia or jus' west iv th' thracks?"

Until recently Asia did not loom large in American interests. There was of course commerce. We also had strong emotional attachments. Learned Chinese, Japanese, and Indians made their imprint here. We saw paintings, jewelry, tapestries, and other works of art that were products of civilizations which we knew were great. But they were distant and remote, like the pyramids of Egypt and the Persepolis of Persia, with no relation to the present. We sent missionaries to Asia to convert the "heathens," oblivious of the fact that these teeming millions had spiritual heritages as rich as any we ever knew.

Our attitudes toward Asia have been largely sentimental. We have reached Asia through the heart, not through understanding. The humanities of Asia have been largely closed to us—the novel, poetry, religion, philosophy, history, law. We have read of Gandhi, Aung San, Sun Yat-sen; but we have had little understanding of the forces behind them. We have known Kipling. But Kipling's Asia was probably not the Asia of his time, and it certainly is not the Asia of today. We formulated high-sounding policies about Asia, yet never became students of Asia. We assumed that Asia's problems were like our own, that what was good for us was good for Asians. We were sensitive to political forces at home, but largely unaware of the political forces sweeping Asia. As a consequence, American policy in Asia has been witness to a half century of woe and wreckage. The Boxer Rebellion of 1900, the Manchurian debacle of 1931, the disaster at Pearl Harbor in 1941, the Communist conquest of China in 1948–49, the Korean episode in 1950 were all major calamities. They might have come on the West anyway. But they were long in making; and at least we Americans never comprehended the forces behind. There has been tragedy in our ignorance. Lenin said long ago that "the road to Europe runs through Peking and Calcutta." If Lenin was right, that highway has already been half completed.

Recent American Policy in Asia

Since the surrender of Japan the United States has done many good things in Asia. We have sometimes served on the side of freedom and independence. We have supplied financial and technical support to democratic movements aimed at demolishing the

319

political and economic feudalism that has long ruled Asia. But our good deeds have been somewhat diluted. We have emphasized the *military* rather than the *political* approach to the problems of Asia. We have been more *against* Communism than we have been *for* the revolutions through which Asians are striving to obtain their independence. We have emphasized *guns* more than *ideas of freedom.* As a result, not many Asians have come to know the warm heart of America and the enduring principles of individual freedom for which we stand. This emphasis upon military values has hurt us in Asia. We have also suffered by reason of our insistence that Asia align with us against Russia.

It is perhaps good politics for a candidate to act on the premise, "You are either for me or against me." Choosing up sides is deep in the wards and precincts of this country. But it was a mistake to approach Asia in that manner. We have asked Asia to choose sides—either for us or for Russia. We have assumed that if a nation is not for us it must be against us. Communism is an evil that all can see. A nation that temporizes on that issue, a country that fails to join our crusade against it must be on the other side, covertly if not openly. That has been our attitude, and it has done great damage to us in Asia.

Asia's Isolationism

Asia has wanted to escape the mounting conflict between Russia and America. The Asian countries have felt toward it what we for years felt about European politics and European conflicts. Since the late nineteenth century we thought that aloofness from the affairs of the Old World was the basis of our security. Our driving desire was to remain free from them. We saw no necessity to get involved abroad. We long maintained that Europe's rows were not ours and that we had no business intervening in them. That is, indeed, the deep taproot of isolationism that is still alive in America. Asia has the same feeling, the same attitude. She has a strong resistance against involvement in the American-

Soviet conflict. Asia did not originate the conflict, and she hopes to avoid participating in it.

Moreover, every Asian country knows that, in case she is allied with the United States when war comes, she will feel the force of it. Her airports will be bases for American bombers. Her cities will be targets for Russian bombs. Asia has a proximity to Russia that we do not feel. Russia has a bomber base only 650 miles from New Delhi, India. And Russia, now that she has the run of China, has innumerable points from which she can strike almost any Asian target. Asia knows these things; and, knowing them, she wants to keep World War III from her. If it must be fought (she says), let Russia and the United States fight it.

This attitude may be unreasonable and illogical. It may be the product of wishful thinking and have no relation to reality. But sound or unsound, it is the Asian attitude. Time and circumstances may change it. But the people of Asia who hold this isolationist view cannot be easily changed by argument any more than the isolationists in America.

That is why Asia has rebelled so violently against the American policy. "You are either for us or against us" has alienated Asians. The sensitiveness of Asia on this score is illustrated by the fall of the Sukiman Cabinet in Indonesia in 1952. The Foreign Minister, Subardjo, signed a Mutual Security Agreement with the United States in which Indonesia agreed to contribute "to the defensive strength of the free world." Indonesia was rocked by that single phrase. Indonesian opinion was that the country had been drawn into "the American orbit" and its "policy of independence" violated. President Soekarno later announced that Indonesia was resolved to occupy "the No Man's Land" between the United States and Russia, reserving to herself "the right to associate with this or that country, irrespective of membership in a bloc, on specific issues." He said that, while Indonesia did not want to take sides by tying herself to a bloc, she did not intend to keep aloof from the controversies "between the opposed blocs." He proclaimed that Indonesia's role was "not only one of passive neutrality, but of active independence." Lest we be too critical of Indonesia, we should remember that the United States after the American Revolution was so apprehensive of new European efforts to colonize this hemisphere that the historic Monroe Doctrine was promulgated.

What Soekarno said in 1952 represents the dominant attitude in Asia today. That point of view is behind the desire of Asians for a Pacific Union (Asian League)—an alliance of nations free both of Russia and of the United States and dedicated to preserving their independence. This in turn has led to suspicions in official and unofficial circles in this country that Asia's Third Force is merely a device to divide the free world and so to play into Russia's hands.

One may think that Asia's isolationism *is* foolhardy. It is apparent how the Communists use it to promote a situation of weakness. But Asia's ideas of independence are not Communist in origin nor aimed to serve a Communist end. Nor is Asia's isolationism an attitude of neutralism toward Communism. *A nation (like a person) who is neutral on the issue of Communism forfeits its moral position, sacrifices its moral strength.* Asia, whose roots are deep in religion and philosophy, has no purpose to repudiate that inheritance. Asia's isolationism is the product of a long historic process.

Asia and Independence

Most Asian countries have long been under the domination of some great power. The British, French, Dutch, Japanese, and now the Soviets are the most conspicuous. But they are newcomers. The control of Asia by conquerors and invaders goes far back in history. For centuries Asia accepted that condition with the fatalism that has governed many of her attitudes. Asia became wedded to the view that she was born to the servant class. She accepted her servile condition and her poverty and fashioned out of them the religion of the renunciation of life. The influence of renunciation is strong in the East today. But Asia, awakened, is ridding herself of the notion that she was predestined to be exploited by the West.

The Russian Revolution was one influence that gave encouragement to the idea that men could cast off their yokes. Woodrow Wilson's Fourteen Points was another. The teachings and example of Gandhi made a powerful contribution. So did the Atlantic Charter. And the Communist victory in China gave tremendous impetus to the idea of revolution. It made the colored people of Asia realize that no matter the depth of their misery and poverty, no matter the strength of the chains that held them, they too could escape. Fast communication facilities, the increased movements of peoples, the intensified tempo of propaganda, all played a part. The causes were many; and they varied from country to country. In each nation they built up into a demand for independence. A wide variety of political programs followed. Color-consciousness became an active force in public affairs. Land reforms were a rallying point. Medical care was promoted as a public cause. Socialism was embraced, primarily as a revolt against the sweatshops of private capital and as an assurance that the people rather than some promoter would get the dividends from the new wealth.

These causes went under various banners, some of them Communist. And they created such turbulence and unrest that it often seemed Asia was in a vortex from which she could not escape. One reason was the political immaturity of Asia. There are few Asian countries that have political parties as we know them. Political power in Asia tends to gravitate to strong personalities. In India the Congress Party is an amalgamation of many groups, designed to protect the nation against a host of factional political units.

The paucity of political parties in Asia is of course due to the long lack of opportunity for the people to develop political traditions. From time out of mind the peoples of Asia were subservient in the political as well as in the economic sense. Political traditions are the product of experience. The powers that long ruled

Asia developed none of them. The sudden necessity to be an independent nation thrust political responsibility on a people who never had political experience. To the outside world these new political forces often seemed irresponsible and inefficient. In actual performance—notably Burma, India, and the Philippines—they proved to have survival values that confounded even the Communist opposition. They demonstrated, I think, that even politically inexperienced people, united by a burning cause, can do heroic things. The cause that united them in Asia was independence.

Squandering American Prestige

At the end of World War II the people of Southeast Asia looked to the United States as the champion of their independence. Leaders of the nationalist movements counted on the United States for moral backing. The words of Franklin D. Roosevelt had indeed stirred their hopes. In 1945 the prestige of America was great. It overshadowed the prestige of every other power, including Soviet Russia. But what we did in the years that followed dissipated much of our influence. When Indonesia was clamoring for her independence from the Dutch, we sat on the sidelines and let her clamor. Nehru summoned an Asian conference at New Delhi to consider the matter; and on January 22, 1949, nineteen Asian nations announced for Indonesian independence. We did nothing as forthright as that. We were far less vocal than Russia in promoting the cause of Indonesian independence. Much of what we said and did about it in the Security Council of the United Nations was equivocal. When the Vietnamese were clamoring for their independence from the French, we were worse than equivocal. We actually threw our weight behind the French in trying to still the nationalist movement in Vietnam.

In each instance we subordinated our Asian foreign policy to our European policy and let European interests have their say. It was argued that we needed the French and Dutch support in Europe against the mounting threat of the Soviets, and that if we stood against them in the Pacific they would turn against us in the Atlantic. France was dangerously close to going Communist, it was said; and an American policy that was anti-French in Asia might tip the scales. Native leaders in other French colonies were also stirring uneasily, and it was thought that if the nationalist movement in Vietnam were given free reign, France's other colonies would erupt and demand independence. The Netherlands also had serious domestic problems. She too was struggling with Communism internally; and it was said that she badly needed all the wealth she could muster from Indonesia in order to rebuild her war-ravaged economy.

And so it was that we temporized with principles. Many times in the past a great power has had one policy at home, another abroad. England, meticulous to respect every minority at home, promoted repressive policies abroad. France, whose proudest boast was liberty, equality, and fraternity, squandered those ideals in her colonial policy. America, proud of her standards of freedom and justice at home, temporized with her principles in Indonesia and Vietnam. We threw our weight in diplomatic circles behind the Dutch and French. The Indonesian question was before the Security Council for about two years before the United States stood squarely for independence. It was not until mid-1949 that the United States began to put effective pressure on the Netherlands to withdraw. The name of Frank Graham, former senator from North Carolina and chairman of the Committee of Good Offices of the Security Council, is today revered in Indonesia for his efforts in the cause of Indonesian independence. Yet the independence, which was won late in 1949, is today thought by Indonesians to be due more to their own efforts than to anyone else's.

Our neglect in Indonesia has been compounded in Vietnam. Not one official American voice has been on the side of the Vietnamese against the French. Not one official American voice has proclaimed that the only government that can save Vietnam from Communism is an anti-French government. We dissipated much of our Asian prestige in dealing with Indonesia. We have squandered most of it in our attitude toward Vietnam.

All of Asia knows this. All of free Asia deplores it. Many Asians still look to America as a country that is just and fair, as well as one that is strong and rich. They admire the ideals of individual liberty that have been our proudest boast. That is why a shudder went through free Asia in 1950 when Dean Acheson and General George C. Marshall announced that we were coming to the aid of the French in Vietnam. I was in Asia in 1950 and felt the mounting indignation of the people against America for her alliance with the French. Military aid was necessary. But military aid, without a proclamation concerning Vietnamese independence, was a staggering blow. American prestige in Asia never suffered greater damage than it did that day. The hatred and suspicion which Asia has for the French in Vietnam is evidenced by the fact that only two Asian nations—Thailand and Korea—have recognized the Bao Dai regime.

If America had crossed the Pacific tendering support for Asia's independence movements, America's prestige would now be high. When we say, "You must be for us or against us," we alienate Asia. If we said, "We want to help you get your independence," we would be writing exciting history and making friendly alliances that would last through the years. The results in Asia would be profound. America, closely identified with the national ambitions of the Asian people, would be in a strategic position to help direct the counterrevolution again Communism. We would be welcome in every country; we would have laid a basis for political action that could easily save Asia from Communist domination. We cannot at this late date recapture all the ground we have lost. But we can yet salvage a good deal of it if we become the *real* champions of the Vietnamese and throw our weight behind an anti-French, non-Communist, truly independent regime in Vietnam.

Principles and Politics

If the price of French support in Europe is the underwriting of French policies in Vietnam, we must still adhere to our principles of freedom and justice and refuse to align ourselves with the repressive policies which the French have long imposed on the Vietnamese. If we trade our principles for this support or that support around the world, we become merely another great power engaged in exploiting one people for the benefit of another. That role leads only to political bankruptcy and bitterness. That role sacrifices our position of moral leadership. In that role we lose stature. Instead of showing the peoples of Asia an alternative to Communism, we in effect make Communism seem inevitable to them.

The so-called practical politicians may say that this course is daydreaming, that America must always stand fast to her allies, that the world of affairs is a hardheaded world where expediency must rule. *But as Jesus, Gandhi, and other great souls have shown, there is no more powerful voice in the world than the voice of conscience. The present-day struggle is for the balance of political power in the world. That struggle can be won only by ideas.* And there are no more potent ideas at work in all the world than America's standards of freedom, justice, and equality. The Communist creed is cheap and tawdry by comparison.

There is no other way for America to maintain her moral leadership than to be faithful abroad as well as at home to her principles. If the voice of America is always heard on the side of the weak and the oppressed, if America is against exploitation whoever the exploiter and the exploited are, then America becomes strong in the hearts of people the world around. Then Soviet Russia has powerful competition at the political level. Then Soviet Russia has competition so powerful that the purveyors of the Communist creed will go begging.

North from Malaya

The Politics of Self-Determination

Woodrow Wilson said in 1918 that self-determination was not "a mere phrase" but "an imperative principle of action, which statesmen will henceforth ignore at their peril." The independence of nations is still the fundamental principle in international affairs. Without it the world is doomed to eternal wars. Unless nations are independent in the Wilsonian sense, unless they are free to write their own constitutions and to choose the form of government they want, there can be no real world community, no true United Nations. Any world organization is strong only in so far as it is composed of representatives of the people. When the "grass roots" of each nation have their spokesmen in a world forum, that agency speaks with power and authority. When that forum voices only the interests of empire builders and feudal overlords, it breeds tensions and works against the cause of peace. The independence movement among peoples is the greatest assurance that any United Nations or any other form of world government will be strong and enduring.

A nation is like the individual. The individual, to be a happy, healthy member of a family or a society, must be a whole person —integrated and mature. He must stand on his own—independent and self-assured. Then he is able to give part of himself to others and become a responsible member of society. If he is not integrated and mature, he is subservient and dependent, unable either to lead or to contribute to the group.

Nations are the same. A Burma that had to speak through the lips of Englishmen would probably be a Communist Burma today. A Vietnam that could speak through its people would not be the sullen, rebellious Vietnam that today must speak through the French. A China that spoke for herself would not be the obstinate and vindictive China that today says largely what Russia suggests. A free and independent nation is ready for world citizenship. It is ready to sit in the councils of nations, to speak with authority, to stake the full measure of its devotion on the prin-

328

ciples that have made its people great. A nation that is a mere puppet of another nation becomes a pawn in international politics. It is powerless to reveal its soul or to consult its conscience. It serves a subservient role in a master plan. And history shows that the master plan is always some sinister, evil thing that has as its aim the exploitation of people. Many nations have succeeded in playing the imperial role. But none has played it more ruthlessly than Communist Russia plays it today.

The Tragedy of Red China

It was, of course, a tragedy that China went Communist. But a worse tragedy is that China came under the domination of the Soviets. Today no one can doubt that Red China (though not a satellite of Russia like Czechoslovakia, Poland, or Hungary) is subservient to Soviet influence, and a junior partner in Sino-Soviet affairs. Today Russia has 86,000 "technicians" in Red China —commissars, agents, engineers, officers, and the like. These men advise China what to do in times of crisis. And their weight is constantly on the side of influencing China against the West. Red China's campaign of hate against America is Soviet-inspired and Soviet-managed. Russia shapes China's policy in Korea. When Red China rejected India's truce plan for Korea in November 1952, she did so at Russia's insistence.

China has lost her independence as a result of the Communist revolution. No one knows it better than the Asians. They can now see at first hand how Russia builds her empire, how in practice Soviet Communism destroys the independence of a people. They see more clearly with each passing day that Red China's fate will be their fate should the Communists take over. Stalin's statement at the close of the Moscow Communist Party Congress on October 15, 1952, was one which no Asian leader missed. Stalin said that Moscow must assist Communist "shock brigades" in other countries. He called the Communist parties in other lands "fraternal parties" whom he promised to support in their struggle "for liberation" and "for the preservation of peace." He compared

329

their struggles with the Communist struggles under the Czar. Communist revolution is easier nowadays, he maintained, for in the days of czarist Russia "the smallest movement of progress was considered the heaviest crime." The success of the Russian Communists, he said, would be the inspiration for the "fraternal parties" the world around. In this speech Stalin made a threat which was more menacing to Asian governments than we in far-off America can know. The nature of Soviet imperialism becomes more and more apparent to Asians with each passing year.

There is in this development both hope and despair for the free world. There is hope because what the Soviets did to Red China has made independence more precious than ever to each Asian country. Because of Soviet policy, it is easier for America and Asia to become sturdy allies. Once America stops asking Asia to take sides and starts telling Asia that America stands ready to champion and defend her independence, the tide will begin to turn against Soviet imperialism.

That is, indeed, the reason why our intervention in Korea was sound by Asian standards. The issue in Korea is the independence of nations. That issue dominates Asian thinking today. No country is better qualified to exploit it than America. We fought one war to get our own independence. We never built an empire, in spite of our Philippine experience. It was Woodrow Wilson and his principles of self-determination of people that loosed ideas of freedom that are still powerful in Asia. Soviet Russia competes with America at the political level under a great handicap. While America's tradition is largely on the side of independence for nations, Russia is as hungry for empire today as it was under the czars.

Russia's control of Red China casts an ominous shadow over Asia. With Russian support Red China could break through the feeble French dykes in Vietnam and overrun all of Southeast Asia. In that event Red China would get the rice bowl of Asia—the food-surplus area—and have perhaps even Japan at her mercy. But whether or not Red China turns south for adventure, her alliance with Russia will cause trouble for its duration. Red China, aligned with Russia, will continue to be obstinate and perverse and fill the role the Soviets have designed for her. That role can cause endless trouble and confusion in Asia. For Red China is not merely a block of 500,000,000 people in one country. She also has an important segment of her nationals scattered throughout Southeast Asia. They have usually looked to a strong China for their inspiration and protection. Many of them now look to Mao Tse-tung as their leader. The majority are probably fence-sitters, waiting to flock to the side of the winner. Soviet control or influence of Red China will thus have repercussions far from Peking. It will be used to foster insecurity, promote unrest, encourage guerrilla warfare, and inspire underground activities in every Asian country. The Soviets would do the same without China. With China they have increased leverage.

Red China vs. the Soviets

The long-range strategy must be to pry China loose from the Soviets. It is a strategy with promise of success. For the two have old rivalries that make their present partnership vulnerable. Sinkiang, Outer Mongolia, and Manchuria bristle with difficulties for them. The potential friction is so great that no Sino-Soviet alliance is durable in the stretch of time measured by decades. For it must be remembered that China is no small nation that can be easily overwhelmed by force. And China, proud and 500,000,-000 strong, is not a nation that can be cowed, dictated to, or overwhelmed. She rivals Russia in some respects and is superior to her in others.

A strong China is Russia's great menace. A strong China, like a strong United States, makes Russia's dream of world conquest uneasy. If we had taken that view in 1950, Red China by now might have gone the way of Yugoslavia or at least be much freer of Soviet influence. In September 1950, before we crossed the 38th parallel in Korea, Red China seemed anxious to talk peace with the West. There were anti-Soviet elements in her councils

331

who were eager for it. That opportunity was missed. Red China, inspired by Russia to believe that Korea was a spear aimed at her heart, entered the conflict and promoted a "hate America" campaign. That move drove her into an evil alliance with Russia. She is there today. And there seems to be no immediate prospect for separating her from the Soviets. She is presently tied tight to the Soviet bloc, not only by the Sino-Soviet Treaty of Friendship and Alliance of August 14, 1945, but also by a program of military action and economic planning. Imports and exports have in fact laced the two countries closely together. She now receives about 70 per cent of her imports from the Soviet bloc and sends in return 77 per cent of her exports.

Pacific Union

There is no quick and easy panacea for the political disturbances of Asia. Statesmen will be plagued for years with crises, ultimatums, and uprisings. There are many forces of disequilibrium at work, including a mounting cost of living as rice reaches a higher price in Asia than it commands in the United States. No one can look ahead to the myriad *ad hoc* decisions that will have to be made. All we can hope to do is to shape a long-term policy toward Asia and to announce and maintain it.

That policy should encourage the development of a Pacific Union (or Asian League) among the nations of South Asia and Southeast Asia. It would operate within the framework of the United Nations and be a genuine Third Force for the promotion of democratic influences in the region. It would be free of the domination of any great power. It would give expression to the ideas of nationalism that sweep Asia; it would help foster and protect the independence of the countries of South Asia and Southeast Asia. It would be a force to neutralize the Communist influences and designs in the region and to curb any imperialistic tendencies of the regime of Red China.

The idea of a Pacific Union (or an Asian League), operating within the structure of the United Nations, is not new. Numerous

Asians have suggested it. Elpidio Quirino and Carlos Romulo of the Philippines have proposed it. The meeting of the nineteen Asian countries at New Delhi which Nehru summoned in January 1949 for consideration of the Indonesian question is a manifestation of the same forces at work. The Asian Socialist Conference in Rangoon in January 1953 was another. Throughout Asia the idea of federation is growing.

Some have visualized a Pacific Union as the counterpart of the North Atlantic Treaty Organization (NATO)—a military organization of Asian countries to defend themselves against Communism. Any effort to form such an organization would at present go for naught. Asia will not make a military alliance of that character. Such a federation would be aimed at either Red China or Russia. Asia at present will not rally against Red China. To Asians Communist China is not so much Communist as Chinese—the revolt of an Asian power against feudal overlords and foreigners. Suspicions of Russia's intent are now quite widespread. Yet those who denounce Russia defend Red China.

One has to see the depths of the misery and poverty of Asia to realize how heroic any escape can seem. Even an escape through Communism is an achievement in many Asian eyes. To most Asians the Communist revolution in China was an achievement for the peasants. Asians have known for centuries only governments which left no opportunity of escape for the man at the bottom. Though China's new government seems to the West more oppressive than the old, to many Asians it offers hope and promise of justice for the common man. This may be nonsense to us; but it is an article of faith that will prevent South Asia and Southeast Asia from uniting against Red China at this point in history.

It is also idle to conceive of a Pacific Union as a military alliance against the Soviets. Asia wants peace—and wants it desperately. Asia has been long exploited, long underdeveloped, long underfed. The new governments that came to power after the exodus of the foreign rulers have had staggering problems

333

on their hands. They had to learn the technology of the West and apply it. They had to go through the trials and tribulations of governing themselves. They still have health, educational, agricultural, and industrial problems so vast, so complicated as to be beyond our comprehension. Their capital is limited, their skilled personnel is few in number, their people are hungry, their problems are perplexing. They want to get on with solutions that provide political and economic answers and prevent crises. They want, in other words, progress, stability, and the other conditions under which Communist propaganda can be rendered ineffective.

This means that the Asian countries must devote the bulk of their budgets to peace, not to armament. Even an American offer to supply arms to a Pacific Union for defense would in Asian eyes make them choose sides *if any strings were attached.* Like Indonesia, the Asian Socialist Conference of 1953 that met in Rangoon stood solidly against choosing sides. The delegates spoke the mind of free Asia in urging a program that would work against a polarization toward one of the two great power blocs. They rejected "ideological neutralism." They voted "to defend democracy against all threats, internal as well as external." They condemned the Soviet type of Communism as the "complete subjugation of the individual and group to a centralized power." They announced in favor of the basic freedoms offered by the democracies. There is no doubt that free Asia is against Soviet Communism and Soviet imperialism. Yet there is also no doubt that most of free Asia today will avoid all military alliances with the West.

Nevertheless, as I have suggested, a Pacific Union of the countries of South Asia and Southeast Asia would serve important functions.

Closer relations among the countries of Asia are important to the welfare of each of them. More specifically, the countries of South Asia and Southeast Asia have long been dependent upon some great power. Since the middle of the nineteenth century each of these nations was oriented, not to one another, but to the metropole of some Western power. This orientation was so complete that Asians became strangers to each other. I was surprised to learn that the Filipinos knew more about America, the Vietnamese more about France, the Malays, Burmese, and Indians more about England, the Indonesians more about the Netherlands than any of them knew about each other. Now that the rule of European colonial powers is nearing the end, a new cohesive force must be found to hold this region together lest it become easy prey to the Soviets.

The nations of South Asia and Southeast Asia can do much to help each other. They can co-ordinate their efforts in the counter-revolution against Communism. They can prevent the Communists from playing one nation against the other. They can unite against any imperialistic designs of any nation. China historically has always been expansionist. She may move once more, this time under Red auspices. Red China, like the China of old, may consider her neighbors inferior and therefore subject to domination by her. Red China may even make a bid for world conquest. A Pacific Union could consolidate South Asia and Southeast Asia against that contingency, as well as against Soviet Communism. A Pacific Union could give free Asia a voice with which to answer the Asian Cominform which the Communists formed in 1952. A Pacific Union could give South Asia and Southeast Asia a new solidarity in peace and in war.

A Pacific Union can do much to help the countries of South Asia and Southeast Asia on their common problems. Those nations have mostly identical problems whether they be mass education, agricultural credit, rehabilitation of guerrillas, or public health. Regional co-operative efforts toward their solution would give impetus and inspiration to each of the countries and hasten the day when the blight of feudalism would be removed from the area.

In that connection Asia should have one or more international centers, such as Dr. James Yen has proposed establishing in the Philippines, where research can be undertaken, teachers trained, and studies in international problems made. Comparative studies of practical politics, political theory, religion, philosophy, socialism, capitalism, and Communism are necessary. Rural rehabilitation projects and public health programs must be developed. There must be centers where the politicians, business groups, philosophers, social workers, and farmers of Asia can meet and study and discuss their problems. An international institution for Asia could help dispel the isolation of the Asians and their ignorance of their neighbors and of the world. An institution of that character could be the instrument for making a Pacific Union politically alert and progressive.

India vs. Russia

The next great, cold war will be between India and Russia. The stakes in that war will be Red China. China belongs to Asia, not to Moscow. China's cultural ties run to India, Burma, Vietnam. China has millions of her sons and daughters in Southeast Asia. China is too big, too powerful, too proud to remain long in a subordinate position to the Soviets. India, I think, stands fair to win that cold war.

That war has started. One episode was India's resolution respecting the disposition of the Korean War prisoners which was presented to the General Assembly of the United Nations on November 17, 1952. There is indication that Red China encouraged the resolution. China, indeed, did not denounce it until Vishinsky of Russia had done so. Vishinsky charged India with trying to perpetuate the war. He charged V. K. Krishna Menon, who represents India in Moscow and who has been a sponsor of Indian-Soviet friendship, with being a stooge of Western imperialism. Mr. Menon, in the tradition of Gandhi, did not reply in kind. He said, "We speak to China." And his message in the main was that the Chinese are "a great and proud people, with an ancient civilization, with an immense capacity for reasoning and clear thinking. They are not daunted by fear. They have a great sense of justice and reason. . . . We have a common frontier over which there have been no wars. On both sides our invasions have been invasions of culture. . . . We shall in the future maintain this great empire of cultural relationships. . . . The Chinese Government, independent and powerful, and enjoying the backing of its people . . . no doubt makes its own decisions. . . . But that does not discharge us . . . from the responsibility of putting forward our point of view. . . . Our principal audience is to be found on the Chinese mainland."

Vishinsky knew that the threat to the Kremlin came not from Washington, D.C., but from New Delhi. Vishinsky knew that if the Soviet Ambassador to Peking had not reached Mao Tse-tung first, China might have accepted the resolution. And the Indians were sure that if the Indian Ambassador to Peking had been only a bit more alert, China could have been won over.

Following the Chinese rejection of the Indian resolution on Korea, Nehru did not give up hope. He still pleaded with China; he still defended China in public:

"For the first time, after forty years of civil war and domination by war lords, China has a strong centralized Government, and it is a great relief. There is a country now having a tremendous sense of power and national pride. The Chinese people—politics apart—have an astonishing capacity for hard work.

"It is a great power within its domain and likely to become much stronger.

"It is immaterial whether you like it or not. It has made a great difference in the world situation. Much of the trouble is due to the fact that we have tried to ignore certain patent facts which are too big to be ignored."

From this Korean war episode alone, the Kremlin knows that a free India will make Soviet influence in China uncertain.

India may fail to woo Red China from Russia. Russia is building up Peking as a new general staff for Southeast Asia. She is staking the conquest of Asia on an operation through China and planning to have Peking, with the appearance of independence, pull her

Asian chestnuts from the fire. Russia may succeed. Red China may turn south and try to subdue Southeast Asia by arms. She may even end up battling India for supremacy in Asia. No one can read the future well enough to know.

The West cannot by arms or by diplomacy pry China from Russia in the near future. But India has a good chance to do so. The violence of Vishinsky's language on the Indian resolution is a measure of the Soviet fear.

American Tolerance for New Ideas

The Asian Socialist Conference that met at Rangoon in January 1953 came out not only against Communism and colonialism but capitalism as well. Capitalism in Asia is mostly different from the capitalism we know. We identify capitalism with free enterprise, operating competitively in an economy of abundance. We identify with free enterprise dividends for stockholders, collective bargaining and good wages for labor, and a wide range for the individual initiative of management. Asia has different associations with capitalism. Capitalism in Asia was foreign capital that sucked a country dry and sent the profits abroad. To Asians capitalism is a system that pays labor a few cents a day. Capitalism in Asian eyes is one method the foreigner used to exploit the continent and to control it. Moreover, the Fabian philosophy from England and the Marxist literature from Moscow and Peking have greatly influenced Asian thinking. It was particularly the Marxist literature that had the appeal. The reason is that when the present generation of Asians started looking for ways and means of starting revolutions and throwing off their colonial yokes they found that the revolutionary literature readily available was Marxist. American literature on how to start a revolution was no longer extant. And Marxism taught socialism as one of its main tenets.

Those are the main reasons for the drift to socialism in Asia. Social justice is the talk in the villages, as well as in the capitals. The natural resources of the country must be developed for the benefit of all the people, not for a select few. Profits from enterprises must go into community projects, not into private pockets.

We must become accommodated to the idea that Asia will not be remade in the image of America. All the wealth we possess, all the bombs we command cannot force it. Asia starts from a different point of history with a different background from ours. She will borrow some ideas, but she will make her own political and social inventions. Asia today is seething with unorthodox ideas. That fact often makes Asia seem unreliable, dangerous, or even subversive to some. It is in that reaction to Asia that a great danger lies. If we are congenial only to the orthodox, we will be confused, if not alarmed, in Asia. Every Asian socialist, every unorthodox political leader will look like a dangerous undercover man for the Kremlin. If we have that attitude, we will miss opportunities for warm and enduring political alliances.

Our attitudes and practices have other important bearings on the future of Asia. When we practice discrimination against the colored races, our voice is not persuasive in Asia. There is quick tension in Asia when an American Negro is lynched. American prestige suffers whenever minorities here are denied equal protection of the laws. We must be strong in our faith of tolerance at home to be strong in Asia. The voice of leadership in Asia is the voice that champions equality of status irrespective of race, creed, or color.

The conflicts that are within each of us project themselves into all our relationships. The sense of guilt, the dark fear that lies deep in the subconscious, the unreasoning prejudice that fills the heart with emotion—these can build up to produce illnesses and accidents and become violent influences in family, community, and national affairs. They also can become powerful factors in international relations. Those who are too provincial, too frightened, too prejudiced to be tolerant of new ideas at home are almost certain to be intolerant of Asia. We begin and end each problem in human relations with the individual. We Americans will reflect abroad what we believe and do at home. Our policy abroad will be no more enlightened than what we profess at home and what we do at home. As the Secretary of State, John Foster Dulles, stated on January 28, 1953, ". . . the heart of a successful foreign policy is our national conduct and example, and that is a matter for every individual and not just the diplomats."

Our role in Asia must be as champion of the weak and the oppressed or it is not true to our character. We cannot fill that role unless we are faithful to our tradition of civil liberties. The decline of American prestige in Asia can be correlated to the decline in our respect for civil liberties at home. The renaissance of our foreign policy in Asia will be our rededication to the spirit and to the letter of the Bill of Rights. If we make it truly part of our lives, we need never fear that Soviet Russia can capture the political leadership of Asia, let alone the world. Freedom, justice, and equality will then easily become the fighting faith of millions whose dream of liberty is also the American dream.

The people of Asia are basically no different from us. They have the same weaknesses, the same strength. They know despair as well as hope. There are tears as well as laughter in Asia, love as well as hate, tenderness as well as cruelty. People pray in Mandalay as they do in Maine. There is also in Asia a deep longing for equality. People in India, Burma, Malaya, Indo-China remember when they were barred from clubs because they were colored. They know the sting of ostracism, the ache that comes from being called inferior. Jose Rizal, the national hero of the Philippines who was shot by the Spanish when he protested against tyranny, put the issue in simple terms when he cried, "We are *people!*" That cry expresses the gist of Asian aspirations. Asians want at long last to be respected as members of the human family.

Their pride is a beautiful, sensitive thing. I will always remember it from a fleeting moment of a night in Rangoon. I was discussing the Japanese occupation of Burma during World War II with an eminent Burmese jurist. He explained how the Japanese were at first welcomed as liberators, then gradually disliked, and finally hated. I asked him the reasons for the hatred. He flushed and his eyes flashed. And when he spoke he fairly shouted, "We hated them because they slapped us." The resentment that remained ten years after the event showed how deep this Japanese insult had cut.

Asia has above all else a lively sense of justice. Manu was a famous Hindu lawgiver. He promulgated the Manu Code and as a result of it his fame spread and his authority grew. In the eleventh century Burmese scholars studied the Code, but rejected it, because Buddhism, unlike Hinduism, knows no caste or class. Nevertheless, Manu was of such great stature the Burmese decided to make him a part of their mythology. So he was known in Burma as a cowherd who became King because of his proficiency in law.

One day two villagers came to Manu with a complaint. The plaintiff had a cucumber vine in his garden that spread into the yard of his neighbor and bore fruit there. Who owned the cucumbers, the plaintiff or the neighbor?

Manu decided in favor of the neighbor. For days Manu reflected on the decision, wondering if he had done justice. He finally decided he had erred. When he realized his error he took drastic action. He not only reversed himself; out of remorse, he resigned as King and became a hermit.

We of the West can never hope to save Asia from Communism or from any other form of tyranny. But if we have the sense of justice of Manu, and his humility, we can help Asia acquire the strength to win her own independence and to maintain and enjoy it.

INDEX

Agriculture: Burma, 232, 235, 241–43. Formosa, 267–69, 271, 273. Korea, 293–94. Malaya, 48–49, 80–90. Philippines, 125–26, 136–37

American Military Government, 294

American Survey Mission, 109

Annam (Central Vietnam), 152. *See also* Vietnam

Asia, feudal system in, 306; independence and, 322–24; India and, 336–38; isolationism of, 320–22; Pacific Union of, 332–36; Red China and, 329–31; Russia and, 331–32; self-determination in, 328–29; struggle in, 314–16; U.S. ignorance of, 317–19; U.S. policy in, 319–20; U.S. prestige in, 324–27; U.S. tolerance of, 338–41

Assembly in Korea, 294–99

Aung San, General, 221–22, 226–30, 255–56

Banga, hospitals of, 131; land surveys in, 132; location of, 129–30; resettlement in, 130; schools in, 131–32

Bangs, T. W. T., 22, 44, 88

Bank of Indo-China, 179–80

Bao Dai, Emperor, Vietnam, abdication of, 166; background

of, 194; French and, 204–5, 207; intellectuals and, 180; legislature granted by, 202–3; living quarters of, 184; Ngo Dinh Diem and, 180–81; recognition of, 195; rule of, 188–90, 196

Battery Workers Union, 57

Bell, Daniel W., 109

Borneo head-hunters, 21, 23, 25

Boy Scouts, Malaya, 80, 94–95

Brazier, John Alfred, 70–74

British: In Burma, 219–22, 239–41, 246, 255–56. In Malaya, Chinese and, 46, 91; future policy of, 99; guerrillas and, 39, 45; holdings of, 77; justice of, 55–63; labor policies of, 64–74; legislative power of, 91–92; plans for independence by, 96–99; Sakai and, 52–54; social reforms by, 94–95, 97–98; sovereignty of, 75; trade unionism and, 64–74; troops of, 22–23. In Vietnam, 170

Buddhism in Burma, 215–18; anti-Communism of, 218, 249–51; exploitation of, 221; philosophy of, 249–52

Buddhists in Vietnam, 188

Burma, 213–58; agriculture in, 232, 235, 241–43; anti-Communism in (*see* Sasana Council); Army of, 222–23; Chinese in, 239–41, 251; Chinese Na-

societies of, 28, 34, 44, 46; superstitions of, 30; trade unionism and, 57, 67–74, 95; University for, 93; wealth of, 76–80. In Philippines, 126, 130, 132; Communist activities of, 113–14; exploitation by, 126, 132; Huks and, 141; underground of, 113–14; visas for, 108. In Vietnam, 157–58, 179, 197

Chinese University, Malaya, 93

Civil liberties: In Burma, 238–39. In Formosa, 280–81, 283. In Korea, 297–98. In Vietnam, 162, 168–70

Civil Service in Korea, 292

Cochin China (South Vietnam), 148. See also Vietnam

Communist Conference in Calcutta, 39, 127, 222

Communists: In Burma, 213–58; Chinese, 251–52; co-operatives and, 235; Japanese occupation and, 221; labor and, 225–26, 244; land and, 242; MEO and, 235–37; political action of, 250–51; propaganda of, 240; PVO used by, 222; rehabilitation of, 226–30, 231–37; terrorism of, 219, 222–25, 235–36; Workers and Peasant Party of, 250–51. In Formosa, attitude toward, 288–89; Kuomintang vs., 288–89; land problems and, 274; political action against, 268; rural reforms and, 267–68, 274, 278. In Korea, 290–316; philosophy of, 307; Rhee supported by, 294. In Malaya (see Guerrillas in). In Philippines (see Huks in). In Vietnam (see Viet Minh)

Community organization in Burma, 231–37. In Formosa, 268

Constitution of Burma, 242–47. Of Korea, 297–99

Cowen, Myron, 109–10

De los Reyes, Andrea, 115–16, 119

Declaration of Independence, Vietnam, 167

Deserters in Vietnam, 184–85

Dong Khe, 175–79

Dorsey, Ronald, 114

Douglas, Helen Gahagan, 267

Dulles, John Foster, 313

Duque, General Calixto, 119

Eaton, Charles A., 267

Economic Cooperation Administration, 229, 248

Economic Development Corps, 128

Economy: Of Burma, 238–43. Of Formosa, 267, 270, 274–76. Of Korea, 291, 295–96. Of Malaya, 48–49, 79. Of Philippines, 108

Education: In Burma, 215, 219, 227, 229, 231–37, 244–46. See also Mass Education in. In Formosa, 266, 270–72, 282. In Korea, 292. In Malaya, 30, 47, 92–93, 95–99. In Philippines, 131–32, 135. In Vietnam, post-French, 159, 167–68; pre-French, 158

Eisenhower, President, 309

Elections: In Burma, 250. In Formosa, 281–82. In Korea, 297. In Philippines, 109, 139. In Vietnam, 167, 169, 198–99

Ethiopians in Korea, 303

Ex-Huks, 104–5, 120–21; rehabilitation of, 123

Famine, Vietnam 168
Federation Army of Malaya, 94–95
Federation of Malaya, 75, 91, 97; capital of, 28; population of, 76
Fifth Front, 261–89
Fiji Islanders, 23, 25
Fishing industry, Malaya, 31–33, 36–37, 43, 77
Food: In Formosa, 272–74. In Korea, 291, 295–96
Formosa, 134–36, 223, 232, 261–89, 314; agriculture in, 268–71; Chiang Kai-shek and, 276, 280–81, 287, 289; China given, 281; climate of, 262; Communists and, 267–68; co-operatives in, 267, 269, 271, 273; description of, 261–64; economy of, 267, 270, 274–76; education in, 266, 270–72; food problems of, 272–74; Goddess of Mercy Mountain in, 264–65; health in, 267, 270–72; industry in, 275–77; Japanese in, 264, 275–77, 282; labor in, 275–76; land problems in, 270–75, 283; law in, 279–80; police in, 279; political organization in, 276, 279, 281–82; population of, 272–73; Prime Minister of, 264–65; reconstruction in, 266–77; religion in, 278; revolution in, 266–77; U.N. and, 314; U.S. and, 265–67, 286–87, 289; women in, 282. See also Joint Commission on Rural Reconstruction
French in Vietnam, 147–210; civil liberties suppressed by, 162, 170; clergy of, 156; conquest by, 157; defensive tactics of, 152–55; distrust of, 177–78,

206–7; education by, 158–59; exploitation by, 160–63; Haiphong bombarded by, 173; Ho Chi Minh, negotiations with, 171–72; imperialism of, 156–63, 206; industrialization by, 159–60; Japanese compact with, 165; law of, 159; Nationalist China treaty with, 171; recontrol by, 169–73; self-government destroyed by, 158; troops of, 149–51; war costs of, 206
French Union, 204–7

Gaal Kampon, 44–45, 81
GAMO, 176–77
Genocide, 273
Goddess of Mercy Mountain, 264–65
Government Workers Union, 57
Grass Mountain, 263–64
Guerrillas: In Burma (see Communists in Burma). In Malaya, appeal of, 80; British and, 39, 45; camp protection of, 26; casualties among, 21; Chinese and, 23, 28–37, 46–47, 79–80, 92–94; education of, 47; hunting of, 25–27; income of, 43–45; Indians and, 78; informers on, 35–36; intelligence of, 26, 28, 35, 40; Japanese and, 38–39; jungle fighting of, 23–27, 39; Lee Meng with, 55–56; Malayan Racial Liberation Army, 47; Malays and, 44; nationality of, 23; number of, 22–23, 40; origins of, 38; procurement by, 28; propaganda by, 28, 45; regiments of, 35, 37; rest camps of, 47; Sakai as, 52–54; tactics of, 26–27, 38–47; terrorism by, 29, 39–44, 47, 58, 73–74, 80;

village aids to, 28–29. *See also* Chinese in Malaya, Malays, etc. In Philippines (*see* Huks). In Vietnam, 164. *See also* Viet Minh

Gurkhas, 23, 25, 35, 37, 47

Haiphong bombardment, 173
Ham Nghi, Emperor, 164
Hanoi, 150, 166, 192; hospitals of, 183–84; massacre at, 173
Hardie Report, 124, 140
Health: In Burma, death rate and, 245; education in, 229, 232–37, 246; improvement in, 244–46; Institute of, 246; malaria program and, 245; MEO and, 233–34; TCA and, 245–46; trained personnel in, 245–46; U.N. and, 245. *See also* Mass Education Officers. In Formosa, 267, 270–72. In Malaya, 95. In Philippines, 131, 135–37. In Vietnam, 177, 183–84.
Hobbs, General Leland, 119
Ho Chi Minh, 150–210; Allied co-operation with, 165; Army of Liberation of, 165; background of, 164–65; Buddhists and, 188; Catholics and, 186; coalition government of, 166–67; Communist tactics of, 169; domestic reform program of, 166–69; elections and, 167, 169; food programs of, 168; French negotiate with, 171–73; government headed by, 166–67; independence declared by, 167; meaning of name of, 166; military tactics of, 150–55, 190–93; propaganda methods of, 165–69; Red China and, 150–51, 169, 173; Russia and,

150; slave labor and, 151; troops of, 151; Viet Minh founded by, 165. *See also* Viet Minh
Home Guard, Malaya, 23
Housing in Burma, 236, 243–44
Hué, 152; description of, 199–200
Huklings, 116–17
Huks, 103–43; Americans in, 114–16; amnesty to, 121; Communist conversion of, 114, 139; government control by, 109–10; government seizure planned by, 103–4; land and, 127, 137; meaning of, 113; number of, 105; operations of, 108; organization of, 114; origins of, 113–14; Politburo of, 107, 109, 112; rehabilitation of, 123; resettlement of, 128–29; revenge motives of, 118–19; terrorism of, 107, 110, 123; women in, 115–17; World War II and, 113. *See also* Ex-Huks and Huklings

Independence for Malaya Party, 96
India, Asian influence of, 336–38
Indian National Congress, 68
Indians: In Burma, 239–41. In Malaya, 72–74, 76; Army and, 94; citizenship of, 95; Civil Service and, 95; Communists and, 78; draft and, 80; exploitation of, 78; labor and, 72; leadership of, 78; proportion of, 76, 78; schools for, 98
Indo-China. *See* Vietnam
Industrialization of Vietnam, 159–60
Industry: Of Burma, 239–41. Of Formosa, 275–77. Of Korea, 291. Of Philippines, 137

Informers, 34–36
International Mass Education Committee, 135
Iron Triangle, 290, 300–5
Irrawaddy River, 213–14, 222

Japanese: In Burma, attitude toward, 221–22; Buddhist exploitation of, 221; cruelty of, 256; occupation by, 215, 219, 221, 256. In Formosa, 264, 275–77, 282. In Korea, 291–92. In Malaya, 34–35. In Vietnam, Bao Dai and, 166–67; British use of, 170–71; French agreement with, 165; prisoners released by, 166
Johore, 22, 76
Joint Commission on Rural Reconstruction (JCRR), 267–77; agricultural improvements and, 268–70; Chinese origin of, 268; Communism and, 267–68; cooperatives and, 267, 269, 271, 273; founding of, 267; irrigation and, 267, 270; land reform and, 267; political aspects of, 268; program of, 268–77; Rural Health Division of, 270–72; village planning of, 268
Judd, Walter H., 267
Jungle in Malaya, 23–27, 39

Karens, 222–23
Korea, 290–316; agriculture in, 293–94; American Military Government in, 294; Army of, 300–5; Assembly of, 295–99; civil rights in, 297–98; Civil Service in, 292; Constitution of, 297; devastation in, 290–91; economy of, 295–96; education in, 292; elections in, 297; ex-

ploitation of, 291; food in, 291, 295–96; industry in, 291; Japanese and, 290–91; land problems in, 293–94; laws of, 296–97; organization of Republic in Exile of, 293; political decision on, 305–6; political organization of, 296–99; refugees in, 291; Republic of, 294; revolution in, 293; Russians in, 290; Supreme Court of, 298–99; survival of, 299; 38th parallel in, 290, 307–10; U.N. and, 299, 306; U.S. and, 306–16. See also Korean War, etc.
Korean War, 300–5; description of, 300–3; Ethiopians in, 303; Iron Triangle and, 290, 300–5; issues of, 315–16; morale in, 304–5; philosophy of, 306–16; Red China tactics in, 301, 309–10; U.S. soldiers in, 304–5
Kuala Kurau, 31–34
Kuala Lumpur, 20, 26, 28, 40–41, 64, 70, 72, 74, 80, 94
Kuantan, 34–36, 43, 45, 47
Kuomintang, Formosa, 278, 281–83, 288–89

Labor: In Burma, Communists in, 225, 244; laws of, 244; organization of, 244; strikes in, 226. In Formosa, 275–76. In Malaya, 39, 64–74; China Relief Fund and, 68–69; Communists in, 39, 67–74; exploitation of, 64–68; "pig business," 67; reforms in, 65, 67; strikes by, 68–70; wages of, 65–66, 72–73. See also Trade unions in. In Vietnam, 160, 196
Land problems: In Burma, 238; landlords and, 241–42; reforms in, 242–43. In Formosa, 270–

347

77, 283. In Korea, 293–94. In Philippines, 123–33; Chinese and, 126; corruption and, 128–32; Hardie Report and, 124, 140; Huks and, 127, 137; land ownership and, 124; Magsaysay and, 121–22, 128–33; outside influences on, 136; reforms of, 127–32, 136, 140; usury and, 132. In Vietnam, 197–98

Land Settlement and Development Corporation, 129–32

Landlords in Philippines, absenteeism of, 124–25, 132; Army action against, 121; Army support of, 119; evictions by, 121; Huks and, 140; incomes of, 125; power of, 140

Laos, 157, 206

Laurel, Jose P., 109, 138–42

Lava, Jose, 112

Law: In Burma, 248–49. In Formosa, 279–80, 283. In Korea, 296–97. In Malaya, 56–63. In Philippines, 120, 139. In Vietnam, 159, 169, 189

Lee Meng (Lee Ten Tai), 55–56

Legislative Yuan, Formosa, 281

Legislature in Vietnam, 202–3

Liberal Party in Philippines, 109–10

Lumber industry, Malaya, 43

MacArthur, General Douglas, 136, 138, 306, 309

Magsaysay, Ramon, 103–43; Army reorganized by, 118; Army training by, 120; assassination attempts on, 103–4, 110–11; constabulary reorganized by, 118; guerrilla work of, 113, 119–20; habeas corpus and, 120, 139; Huk rehabilitation by, 111, 123; propaganda campaign of, 121; Quirino and, 139, 141; Secretary of National Defense, 103, 110

Malacca, 75

Malaya, 19–99; aborigines of, 48–54; agricultural aid in, 48–49, 80–81, 88–90; British troops in, 22–23; Chinese University of, 93; citizenship in, 95–96; Civil Service of, 22, 35, 61, 75, 95; climate of, 48–49; culture of, 34, 76, 82; draft in, 80; economy of, 78–79; education in, 30, 90, 92–93, 95–99; Federation Army of, 94–95; Federation of, 75, 91, 97; fishing in, 31–33, 36–37, 43, 77; geography of, 75; guerrillas in, 20–99; High Commissioner of (see Templer, Sir Gerald); independence of, 96–99; Japanese in, 34–35, 38; jungle of, 23–27; labor in, 39, 64–75; law of, 56–63; lumber in, 43; medical care in, 95; melting pot of, 96–99; police in, 23, 26–27; political organization of, 91–92, 95–96; proto-Malays in, 48; Pygmies in, 48; racial problems of, 71, 76–78, 81, 94–95; Red Cross in, 30; religion of, 75–76, 79, 81, 84–85; resettlement of villages in, 29–30; rubber (see Rubber plantations); Rural and Industrial Development Authority, 44–45, 88–90; Sakai in, 48–54; small business in, 90; sterling contribution of, 98; terrorism in, 29, 39–44, 47, 58; tin (see Tin mines); trade unions, 39, 57, 64–74; University of, 92–93; U.S. trade with, 78–79; village councils in, 95;

women in, 65. *See also* Chinese in Malaya etc.

Malayan Chinese Association, 95

Malayan Civil Service, 22, 35, 61, 75, 95

Malayan Home Guard, 23

Malayan Mining Employers Association, 72

Malayan Racial Liberation Army, 47

Malays, Army and, 94; characteristics of, 76, 81; Chinese and, 38, 45, 76–78, 81, 91, 94–95; co-operatives for, 88–90; culture of, 34, 76, 82; draft of, 80; guerrillas and, 44–45; pawangs of, 35, 82–84; proportion of, 76; religion of, 75–76, 81–82, 84–85; schools for, 98; Shadow Play of, 84–88; superstitions of, 35; trade unions for, 95

Mandalay, 213–18, 223

Manila Boy, 103–6, 116, 122

Mao Tse-tung, 46, 134, 152, 240, 251–53, 288, 308–9, 312

Mass Education Council in Burma, 231–37, 246. *See also* Mass Education Officers

Mass Education Officers, 232–37; agriculture and, 235; centers of, 232, 235; Communists and, 235–37; community organization and, 231–37; health and, 233–34; liaison duties of, 234; methods of, 232–35; schools and, 234; training of, 232

Military Intelligence Service, Philippines, 112

Min Yuen, secret society of, 28, 44

Mirasol, Major Ciriaco V., 128

Mutual Security Agency, Formosa and, 272, 275, 277; Philippines and, 124; Vietnam and, 181–83

Narayanan, P. P., 72–74

National Assembly, Vietnam, 168

National Catholic Federation, 186

Nationalist China. *See* China, Nationalist

Nationalista Party, Philippines, 109

Nationalization in Burma, 240, 254–58

Nehru, Jawaharlal, 65, 98, 307–8

Ngo Dinh Diem, background of, 180; Bao Dai and, 180–81, 204; Presidency refused by, 181; reform platform of, 181

Nguyen Van Tam. *See* Tam

Pacific Union in Asia, 332–36

Pagodas, 215–21

Pan Malayan Federation of Trade Unions, 70–71

Pan Malayan Labor Party, 96

Pandit, Mme. Vijaya L., 141

Pawang (wise man), 36, 82–85

Penang, 57, 75

People's Liberation Army, 114

People's Voluntary Organization, 222

Perez, Mrs. Asuncion, 141–43

Phan Dinh Phung, 164

Philippine Army, corruption in, 108, 118–19; elections and, 139; ex-Huks in, 105; guerrilla training of, 120; landlords and, 119; Military Intelligence Service of, 112; reorganization of, 118–19; resettlement and, 128–29, 132; tenant aid by, 121–22

Philippine Constabulary, 104, 118–19

Philippine Land Tenure Reform, Analysis and Recommendations (Hardie Report), 124, 140

Philippine Rural Reconstruction Movement, 135

Philippines, 103–43; agriculture in, 125–26; Army of, 105, 108, 118–19; Chinese in, 108, 113–14; Constabulary of, 104, 118–19; co-operatives in, 132, 136; education in, 131–32, 135; elections in, 109, 139; farm modernization in, 136; government of, 108–9; Huks of (*see* Huks); industrialization of, 137; inflation in, 108; landlords in, 119; land problems of, 123–33, 136; Land Settlement and Development Corporation of, 129–31; law in, 120, 139; legal corruption in, 121; Military Intelligence Service of, 112; per capita income in, 137; political parties in, 109; population of, 137; public health in, 135–37; religion in, 105; road conditions in, 126; social discontent in, 135; taxation in, 108; underground in, 113–14

Philosophy of Burma, 247–48, 252, 254–58

Point Four Program, 248

Police in Malaya, 23, 26–27

Politburo: In Philippines, 107, 109, 112. In Vietnam, 169, 185

Political organization: In Formosa, 268, 276, 279, 281–82. In Korea, 295–99. In Malaya, 91–92, 95–96. In Philippines, 109. In Vietnam, 157–59, 195–96

Pomeroy, William J., 114–16

Population in Formosa, 272–74

Potsdam Conference, 169–70

Press censorship, Vietnam, 188–90

Proto-Malays, 48

Provincial Teachers College, Formosa, 271

Provisional Provincial Council, Formosa, 282

Pygmies, 48

Queen Mother, Vietnam, 200–2

Quezon, Manuel L., 110, 138

Quirino, Elpidio, 109–43; election of, 109; habeas corpus suspended by, 120, 139; land reforms and, 137–38; Magsaysay and, 139, 141; Taruc and, 127; weakness of, 110

Rangoon, 213–15, 223, 243, 248

Recognition of Red China, 311–14

Red China. *See* China, Red

Red Cross in Malaya, 30, 53

Refugees: In Burma, 243. In Korea, 291. In Vietnam, 181–84

Rehabilitation in Burma, 226–37

Religion: In Burma, 222. *See also* Buddhism. In Formosa, 278. In Malaya, 75–76, 81–82, 84–85. In Philippines, 105. In Vietnam, 156, 185–88

Republic of Korea Army, 300–5

Republic of Korea in Exile, 293

Resettlement: In Burma, 243. In Malaya, 29–30, 44, 52–54. In Philippines, 128–32. In Vietnam, 181–84

Revolution in Formosa, 266–77

Revolutionary Youth of Vietnam, 165

Rhee, Syngman, 292–99

Rizal, Jose, 110–12, 116

Roosevelt, Eleanor, 141

Roosevelt, Franklin D., 66

Roosevelt, Theodore, 313

Roxas, Manuel, 127, 138, 141

Rubber plantations, Malaya, employees of, 65–66, 72–74, 76;

exploitation in, 64–77; guerrilla damages to, 44; protection of, 67; trade unions in, 64–74
Rubber Tappers Union, 72
Rural and Industrial Development Authority, 44–45, 88–90
Rural reconstruction, Formosa, 266–67. *See also* Agriculture in Formosa, Land problems, etc.
Russia, India vs., 336–38; Korean policies of, 290, 309; Red China vs., 331–32; the enemy is, 315–16; Vietnam and, 150

Saigon, 157
Sakai, 48–54
Santiago, Tomas. *See* Manila Boy
Sasana Council, 249–50
Semar, 86–88
Senegalese, 149
Shadow Play, Malaya, 84–88
Singapore, 22, 75
Soekarno, 307
Spruance, Admiral Raymond A., 140–41
Stalin University, 114–15
Straits Settlements, 75
Summary, 317–41
Sun Yat-sen, 68, 266, 273–74

Taipei, 263–64, 274
Taiwan. *See* Formosa
Taiwan Federation of Labor, 276
Tam, Nguyen Van, President, 176, 196, 207; franchise and, 198–99; labor unions and, 196; land problems and, 197–98; six-point program of, 196
Tamil Indians, 64–65
Tanjong Malim, 28–29
Taruc, Luis, 103–4, 113–14, 116, 120, 127, 142
Technical Cooperation Administration, 245–46, 248

Templer, Lady, 20, 22, 40, 53
Templer, Sir Gerald, Boy Scouts and, 94–95; Civil Service and, 95; criminal law code and, 56–57; education and, 95–99; guerrillas and, 52–53; labor movement and, 71; reform programs of, 21, 93–96; resettlements by, 30, 44, 52–54; security measures of, 40–41
Terrorism: By Burmese Communists, 219, 222–25, 235–36. By Huks, 107, 110, 123. By Malayan guerrillas, 29, 39–44, 47, 58, 73–74, 80. By Viet Minh, 190–94.
Thirty-eighth parallel, 290, 307–10
Tiga Bintang (Three Stars), 38
Tin mines, Malaya, employees of, 76; exploitation in, 66–67; guerrillas and, 42–43; trade unions and, 64–74
Tonkin (North Vietnam). *See* Vietnam
Trade unions: In Burma, 244. In Formosa, 275–76. In Malaya, 57, 68, 70–74, 95–96. In Vietnam, 196
Truman, Harry S., 306, 309

U Myint Thein, 252
United Malay National Organization, 95
United Nations: Burma and, 223, 245, 248. Formosa and, 314
United States: Asia and, 317–41; Asian policies of, 319–20. Burma and, 248, 257–58; China Aid Act of, 266–67; ignorance of Asia in, 317–19. Korea and, 299; Korean policy of, 310–16. Malaya and, 78–79. Nationalist China and, 266, 278, 286–87.

351

Philippines and, 109; political action on Korea by, 306; prestige in Asia of, 324–27; support of Chiang Kai-shek by, 286–87; technical aid to Formosa by, 265, 287; tolerance of Asia by, 338–41; value of Formosa to, 289

University College, Burma, 215, 217

University of Malaya, 92–93

U Nu, Prime Minister, 218, 225, 247, 249, 307

Van Fleet, General James A., 300–1, 303–4

Viet Minh, 147–210; Catholics and, 186–87; Communist cells of, 189–93; deserters from, 184–85; founding of, 165; Hanoi massacre by, 173; land distributions by, 185; location of, 148; Mao Tse-tung and, 152; military tactics of, 150–55, 190–93; Politburo of, 169, 185; political action of, 155; radio of, 173; Red China and, 147, 208; terrorism by, 190–94; troops of, 151. *See also* Ho Chi Minh

Vietnam, 147–210; Army of, 149; Bank of Indo-China and, 179–80; British in, 170; Chinese and, 157–58, 179, 197; civil liberties in, 162, 168–70; civil war in, 150; colonization returns to, 169–73; consolidation of Indo-China into, 157–58; constitution of, 168–69; culture of, 161, 163; education in, 158–59, 167–68; elections in, 167, 169, 198–99; famine in, 168; French conquest of, 157; French exploitation of, 160–63;

French Union, membership of, 204–7; health in, 177, 183–84; Ho Chi Minh, President of, 166–73; hospitals in, 183–84; independence declared in, 167; intellectuals in, 180–81; labor in, 160, 196; land problems in, 197–98; law in, 159, 169, 189; middle class in, 162; population of, 162; pre-French political organization in, 157–58; press censorship in, 188–90; Queen Mother of, 200–2; reforms needed in, 208–9; refugees in, 181–84; religion in, 156, 185–88; resettlement in, 181–84; resistance movement in, 162; revolution in, 164–74; rice export by, 162–63, 208; standard of living in, 162; trade unions in, 196; women of, 182–83, 190–91, 199–200. *See also* French in Vietnam, Ho Chi Minh, Vietnamese, etc.

Vietnam Independence League. *See* Viet Minh

Vietnamese, 147–210; distrust of French by, 154, 177–78, 206–7; troops of, 149, 175, 187, 207

Wachis, 113–14

Welfare State in Burma, 238–43, 248–49, 253

Women: In Burma, 217, 239. In Formosa, 282. In Malaya, 65–66. In Vietnam, 182–83, 190–91, 199–200.

World Health Organization, 245

Yen, Dr. James, 135; China Aid Act and, 266–67; JCRR and, 267; mass education and, 266, 308; rural reconstruction and, 266–68

Young, Colonel Arthur E., 26–27

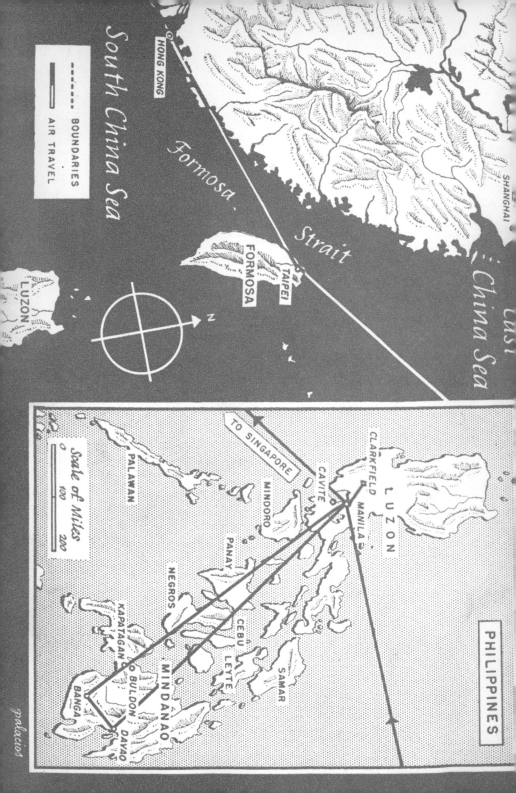